P12

Democracy and the Arts

DEMOCRACY AND THE ARTS

The Role of Participation

Terri Lynn Cornwell

Foreword by Mary Rose Oakar

New York
Westport, Connecticut
London

Copyright Acknowledgments

Quotations in Chapters 1 and 2 are taken from Carole Pateman, Participation and Democratic Theory (New York: Cambridge University Press, 1979), pp. 7, 14, 53, 54, 66, 105, 108, 110. Reprinted by permission.

Quotations in Chapter 2 are taken from Robert A. Dahl, A Preface to Democratic Theory (Chicago: University Press, 1962), pp. 4, 12, 32. Reprinted by permission.

Quotations in Chapters 3 and 6: Reprinted from Democracy in America by Richard D. Heffner. Copyright © 1956 by Richard D. Heffner. Reprinted by arrangement with New American Library, a Division of Penguin Books Inc., New York, N.Y.

Library of Congress Cataloging-in-Publication Data

Cornwell, Terri Lynn.
    Democracy and the arts: the role of participation / Terri Lynn
Cornwell; foreword by Mary Rose Oakar.
        p.   cm.
    Includes bibliographical references.
    ISBN 0-275-93070-X (alk. paper)
    1. Arts and society—United States. 2. Arts—United States—
Decision making. 3. Art and state—United States. I. Title.
NX180.S6C66 1990
700'.1'03—dc20   90-30004

British Library Cataloguing-in-Publication Data is available.

Copyright © 1990 by Terri Lynn Cornwell

Library of Congress Catalog Card Number: 90-30004
ISBN: 0-275-93070-X

First published in 1990

Praeger Publishers, One Madison Avenue, New York, NY 10010
An imprint of Greenwood Publishing Group, Inc.

Printed in the United States of America

The paper used in this book complies with the
Permanent Paper Standard issued by the National
Information Standards Organization (Z39.48-1984).

10 9 8 7 6 5 4 3 2 1

Contents

Figures

Foreword

As a former fine arts student and college professor, I have experienced the tremendous impact that artistic ventures have on society. Children gain self-esteem by participating in classroom activities that stress individual expression; they learn socialization skills by cooperating in theatre endeavors; and they learn to appreciate other cultures through museum exhibits. Adults, too, find participation in the arts gratifying to their everyday lives. The arts exist for art's sake—not only are the arts a means of self-expression, but they entertain and teach as well.

History teaches us that enhancement of the arts mirrors a truly civilized, cultivated society. The arts and humanities are essential for preserving the "human" elements of our society, for enriching the quality of human life. They reflect the freedom and creativity of what is truly American. Through performances and exhibitions, the arts preserve and interpret our cultural heritage, emphasizing the diverse traits that symbolize our nation's citizens.

Ideally, all segments of our society should have the opportunity and the access to the experience of artistic expression and creativity.

As the U.S. Representative of the 20th District of Ohio—located in the Cleveland metropolitan area, with its world-class orchestra and art museum, its outstanding ballet and numerous theatres—I am particularly interested in ensuring the continued vitality of America's cultural community.

During my tenure in office, I have introduced legislation that would enhance the arts in this country, because I believe that the federal government has an important responsibility to ensure the protection of our cultural heritage. In the 101st Congress, I introduced H.R. 219 to establish a Department of the Arts and Humanities in the Executive Branch. It is my conviction that the arts and humanities must be accessible to all people. As I work with my colleagues in Congress to find the best ways to enhance America's cultural heritage, I am always intrigued to discover new research which explores other opportunities that will guarantee that the arts prosper and flourish in our country for generations to come.

Democracy and the Arts: The Role of Participation looks at the arts/society relationship in a new way. The research presented here asks us to see the value of the arts as a participatory activity that helps to enhance our American brand of democracy. By looking at the arts from this new angle, we may be able to establish a clearer path to renewed partnerships that would ensure that all citizens are able to enjoy, learn, and benefit from the arts.

The Honorable Mary Rose Oakar
Democratic Representative, 20th District, Ohio
U.S. Congress

Preface

As I complete final editing of this book, the National Endowment for the Arts (NEA)—the largest cultural agency of our federal government—is embroiled in a controversy over funding of so-called "obscene art." Although this conflict relates to the discussion of First Amendment issues, censorship, and definitions of pornography, which are not dealt with in this book, it does bring arts advocacy to the forefront—for better or for worse—and lends itself to the broader discussion of democracy and the arts.

Some critics simply dismiss this current conflict: "Most people are too sensible to take the art lobby seriously," said columnist Jack Germond of "The McLaughlin Group" (NBC television, July 30, 1989). Others reiterate their disdain for all government arts funding: "[It's] porkbarrel for the intelligentsia. Abolish the NEA," said commentator George Will on "This Week with David Brinkley" (ABC television, October 1, 1989). Yet, so far the controversy has had a beneficial effect on the arts advocacy groups, in spite of the criticism: It has forced them to reexamine the role of government support, to look more critically at their strongest congressional allies and opponents, and to begin to understand the complex relationships they have with each other.

This book is a product of research started a decade before the current funding controversy, when the arts lobby was still quite young and while I was searching for a Ph.D. dissertation topic. As my research unfolded in the 1980s, I also became an active participant in the arts advocacy field, first with the American Arts Alliance and then with the fledgling Congressional Arts Caucus, during the Reagan administration. In short, my perspective of the arts lobby has been from distinct angles: I've been a part of the lobby as it confronted Congress, and I've also watched it from my perspective on an advocacy group within Congress itself. And now from the vantage point of a university in a midwestern city rich in the arts, I have the luxury of independently observing the interaction between the arts lobbyist and the politician.

My professional background, as well as my research, has shaped the scope of this book; my aim is to provide an introduction to the general topic of democracy and the arts, an initial look at the relationship between political participation and arts participation—all in the hope of stimulating additional research and discussion on a topic that deserves more attention.

By the time this book is published, the legislative process reauthorizing NEA will be well underway or even complete, and issues other than those highlighted here no doubt will have emerged. However, I have attempted to keep the facts and figures as current as possible. Certainly, the basic concepts underlying the formation of the NEA and the research presented here remain the same. What's more, the book is not a comprehensive examination of democratic theory or a complete history of arts education, arts advocacy, or arts legislation. And it is by no means a substitute for becoming an active participant in the arts.

Reading about art and its relationship to politics, or becoming an arts advocate, is simply a backdrop for active involvement in the art world itself. As philosopher George Steiner wrote in *Real Presences* (Chicago: University of Chicago Press, 1989), reading about art is no substitute for directly experiencing art: "Literate humanity is solicited daily by millions of words, printed, broadcast, screened, about books it will never open, music it will never hear, works of art it will never set eyes on" (p. 24). Yet, to many, the aesthetic encounter is the most "transformative summons available to human experiencing" (Steiner, p. 143).

The ideas expressed in *Democracy and the Arts: The Role of Participation* are built on this fundamental premise. An understanding of the power of art, from direct experience in as many arts activities as possible, enhances the work of the researcher, the writer, and the reader.

It is to those who share this belief that this book is dedicated.

Acknowledgments

The list of individuals who helped make this book possible includes numerous colleagues and friends, several of whom I would like to mention by name. First, I must thank my dissertation committee at the University of Maryland (Professors Thomas J. Aylward, Jackson Bryer, Ronald J. Terchek, Andrew D. Wolvin, and Roger L. Meersman, Chairman), who encouraged me to seek a publisher for my research. A Washington, DC, colleague, Margaret Wyzomirski, gave me guidance at various points during my early research. Others who were most helpful included Jerry Tubbs and Janet McKimmy from the Maxine Goodman Levin College of Urban Affairs, Cleveland State University; Ann Fleischman, aide to Hon. Mary Rose Oakar, Democratic Representative, 20th District, Ohio, U.S. Congress; and Linda Keegan, also from the Levin College, who provided expert editorial assistance.

Finally, I would like to thank Dean David C. Sweet of the Levin College and Cleveland State University for continued support during the final stages of publication.

Democracy and the Arts

Democracy and the Arts: An American Perspective

Growing up in a democracy as rich as the United States, I was privileged to have the opportunity to participate in a variety of the arts. From a first lesson on my grandfather's alto saxophone to the summer I studied piano at an idyllic chamber music camp, from my thrilling experiences as part of a university marching band to the semesters I sang in the concert choir, from my time as a church organist to my years directing children's theatre and amateur water ballets, all manner of arts have been a fulfilling part of my life. So much so, that I began to take an active part in the field of arts advocacy early in my professional career.

My first experience making an impassioned plea for more arts funding—the first and foremost task of an arts advocate—came when I attended a local school board meeting to request $25 for costumes and makeup for the students in my drama club. I must have been effective. The school board gave us $50! Never again would I see a doubling of an arts funding request.

Years later, I often remembered that incident as I wrote testimony for members of Congress who advocated increases in the more than $150 million budget of the National Endowment for the Arts (NEA)—a figure that is often considered so small that it is rounded to zero and virtually disappears in the context of dealing with the more than $1 trillion federal budget. Obviously, my background in both arts participation and advocacy creates a definite bias in the way I view cultural activities in a democracy. In writing this book, I attempted to look at the relationship between the arts and our political system in a fresh way to add to the cultural policy debate.

The idea for this book is an outgrowth of one of the first major studies examining American cultural policy in the twentieth century. The 1965 Rockefeller Panel Report called *The Performing Arts: Problems and Prospects*, asked the following question: If the United States was preoccupied with attaining a political democracy in the eighteenth century and an economic democracy in the nineteenth century, has the quest come to include, in the twentieth century, an attempt to establish a cultural democracy?[1] The report also noted that many Americans believed that democracy is incompatible with the attainment of high artistic standards.

The question of establishing a cultural democracy spurred the research that follows. In addition, this book supports the idea that a democracy is not only capable of fostering works of artistic excellence, but that it is also capable of creating broad-based audiences for such works.

Having begun with the idea that the United States in the twentieth century has been exploring ways to make cultural activities more democratic and that this premise had been cited by arts advocates as one of the reasons for government support, I began to examine the relationship between the arts and the political system known as democracy. A first critical task was to clarify the term "arts"—a word that became particularly prominent with the establishment of NEA in 1965.

In "Art vs. the Arts," Ronald Berman—a former chairman of the National Endowment for the Humanities (NEH) and a proponent of the elitist theory of art—noted that the term "arts" has become "an essential part of the vocabulary of policy." He also claimed that the term implied "creativity ... and the subsidy of associations, bureaucracies, and institutions. It means the distribution of funds for purposes *felt* to be artistic."[2] With the continued use of the term in the literature of cultural policy throughout the past several decades, the word "arts" has become an essential part of the political vocabulary. To some individuals, particularly those ideologically aligned with the conservative Berman, the term might carry negative connotations, but it is also symptomatic of how our society has come to view art in a democracy. In this study I use the term to encompass a wide variety of cultural activities. It is intended to have neither a positive nor a negative connotation.

In a brief commentary called "Art vs. Arts," Edwin Newman reminded us that "language will evolve and change. Definitions cannot be locked in forever, least of all in the realm of the artistic."[3] Newman emphasized that the term "arts" encompasses painting, sculpture, architecture, music, literature, ceramics, drama, film, dance, and more, and he quoted the poet Milton as giving us an early indication of what the term meant by describing Athens as "the mother of arts and eloquence."

By the mid–twentieth century, as more constituencies became involved with the creation of the first national cultural agency, the "arts" became aligned with the "humanities," which included the influential and venerable bloc of public and private colleges and universities across the country. This study, however, is limited to the "arts" as opposed to the "arts and humanities," although most of the discussion could apply to both. The two terms have been defined by the National Foundation on the Arts and Humanities Act of 1965, as amended December 20, 1985:

> (a) The term "humanities" includes, but is not limited to, the study and interpretation of the following: language, both modern and classical; linguistics; literature; history; jurisprudence; philosophy; archeology; comparative religion; ethics; the history, criticism, and theory of the arts; those aspects of the social sciences which have humanistic content and employ humanistic methods; and the study and application of the humanities to the human environment with particular attention to reflecting our diverse heritage, traditions, and history and to the relevance of the humanities to the current conditions of national life.
>
> (b) The term "the arts" includes, but is not limited to, music (instrumental and vocal), dance, drama, folk art, creative writing, architecture and allied fields, painting, sculpture, photography, graphic and craft arts, industrial design, costume and fashion design, motion pictures, television, radio, tape and sound recording, the arts related to the presentation, performance, execution, and exhibition of such major art forms, and the study and application of the arts to the human environment.

Phyllis Zagano succinctly defined the two terms when advising prospective grant seekers: "If you do it, make it, perform it, you go to NEA; if you study it, translate it, or dig it up, you go to NEH."[4]

Using the above definitions of the "arts," this book looks at these activities by relating them to political systems and, more specifically, by analyzing the interaction between arts activities and participatory democracy. A variety of works have analyzed the value of cultural activities to most major political systems—from the use of art as propaganda to the importance of cultural exchange. The value of art to democracy, in particular, has been examined more widely during the past twenty years.

Carl Cohen is one of the many theorists who have examined democratic political systems and the societal conditions necessary for them to exist. In his study, *Democracy*, he stated that democracy is a "system of community government in which, by and large, the members of a community participate, directly or indirectly, in the making of decisions which affect them all."[5] Furthermore, this form of government, according to Cohen, requires the existence of a community of rational persons who each possess: (1) the faculty of forming a plan or grasping a rule for a judgment of action; (2) the faculty for using that rule; and (3) the faculty for intellectual communication, reasoning with others.[6] This community of rational persons, with the use of majority rule and representation, also requires certain conditions:

Material conditions (a minimum level of well-being)
Constitutional conditions (principles embodied in a constitution)
Intellectual conditions (achieved through education of citizens)
Psychological conditions (willingness of citizens to compromise)
Protective conditions (the capacity to protect itself against external onslaught)

Intellectual conditions are most directly related to an examination of how the arts affect democracy, although arts participation can reinforce certain psychological conditions, as well. (See Chapter 4.)

Cohen said citizens of a democracy must receive four areas of education: a practical education that prepares them for the everyday problems of human life; a basic education to acquire fundamental intellectual tools; a technical education that leads to specialization in a particular field of endeavor; and a humane education, "the least common and least well appreciated."[7] The arts fall into the area of humane education as described by Cohen: "The study of history, the appreciation of great literature, the practice and criticism of the arts, the understanding of philosophical inquiry—these are the intellectual requirements of a people who would wisely govern themselves."[8] Thus, as Cohen concluded, education in the arts is a necessary part of the training of "rational" citizens, who are necessary for the proper functioning of a democracy.

Other political theorists have added to Cohen's argument that the arts benefit a democracy, but what about the reverse relationship? How is a political system beneficial or detrimental to the arts? In *Twigs for an Eagle's Nest: Government and the Arts 1965–1978*,[9] Michael Straight, former deputy chairman of the National Endowment for the Arts, described a three-part model of a society in which the arts flourished: In it, (1) the society forms a true community; (2) art is an integral part of social planning and city design; and (3) art is a central event bringing people together. He noted that all three existed in ancient Greek society, where the city-state was the political unit and the political system was beneficial to the arts: "There is no reason to believe that a democratic system of government, so-called, is any more favorable to the prevalence of art than the systems we call aristocratic, oligarchic, or totalitarian."[10] Although art in itself has little concern

with democracy, communism, or any other political system, a government can emphasize various aspects of cultural activities to enhance
that very system; art as propaganda, for example, has been an exceptionally useful tool in totalitarian governments throughout history.
The compelling fact remains, however, that the process of art is indif-
ferent, merely "an unpolitical manifestation of the human spirit, and,
though politicians may use it or abuse it for their ends, they can neither
create it nor control it nor destroy it."[11] However, if a society *chooses* a
democratic form of government and *chooses* to have a thriving culture,
how do the two interrelate? This question was the key to finding a
narrower, clearer focus for this book examining the arts and
democracy.

One way of looking at the interrelationship of democracy and the
arts is to explore specific theories of democracy, particularly theories
of participatory democracy. For the purposes of this book, the theories
of Carole Pateman proved most appropriate. In *Participation and
Democratic Theory*, Pateman provided a thorough discussion of participation in industry and the carryover effects that help to create a
"participatory society":

> We have considered the possibility of establishing a participatory
> society with respect to one area only, that of industry, but because
> industry occupies a vitally important place in the theory of par-
> ticipatory democracy, that is sufficient to establish the validity, or
> otherwise the notion, of a participatory society. The analysis of
> the concept of participation presented here can be applied to
> other spheres. . . .[12]

This key concept, referring to other spheres where experience with
participation helps reinforce the idea of a participatory society, became the basis for this book.

My research began at the close of an era of expanding governmental
cultural programs prior to the Reagan administration. However, largely
because of economic constraints, the period of the 1980s saw a change
in the direction of American cultural policy, from encouraging expanded programs to slowing their growth and even eliminating some.
Still, a number of theorists continued to highlight the usefulness of the
arts in a democracy during the Reagan years. In a paper presented to
the 1984 Annual Meeting of the American Political Science Association
in Washington, DC, W. D. Kay discussed arts policy in a democracy
and stressed that "not only is a nationwide interest in the arts compatible with democracy, it is a necessary condition for its attainment."[13] Kay concluded by encouraging further study: "Hopefully the
realization that democracy is a social system will begin to catch on in

political science, leading to a more thorough investigation of areas which, in the past, have been considered 'extra-political.'"[14] This book acknowledges Kay's encouragement and specifically applies the participatory theories of Pateman to the arts.

The research relied on historical-critical methodologies. Historical research covering the arts and democracy in three periods (Greece in the fifth century B.C., the Jacksonian era, and twentieth-century America) forms the foundation for the book, which provides critical observations of the arts/political system relationship during those periods. The emphasis, however, is on a critical examination of mid-twentieth-century democracy and the arts.

Extended arguments for or against government support of the arts in ancient Greece and the Jacksonian period are not examined, but major arguments for and against government's involvement with the arts during the twentieth century are enumerated. Because this research is based on the hypothesis that the arts are "good" for society, an extensive examination of the importance of art to society is not provided. Much has already been written justifying the value of cultural pursuits; furthermore, the benefits of participation in the arts—the major focus of this study—may not be a sufficient argument to convince the reader who does not already believe that the arts are important to society. Baumol and Bowen, in their landmark study of the economics of the performing arts, noted the same limitation: "We provide no inspirational message proclaiming the virtues of the live performing arts and their crucial role in the enrichment of human existence. The reader who is not already convinced would surely not be swayed by any report whose focus is the economics of performance."[15] However, a brief description of the "societal good argument" used by twentieth-century arts advocates in their justification of government's responsibility toward the arts is provided. In addition, a variety of early economic impact studies of the arts are examined, and survey research provides a profile of individuals whose work involves participation in both the arts and politics.

Chapter 2 begins with a discussion of pertinent terms and definitions and provides a brief overview of theories of democracy, from those of the ancient Greeks to the contemporary ideas of twentieth-century theorists. Pateman's *Participation and Democratic Theory* also serves as the foundation for an overview of contemporary theories of democracy that highlight the development of participatory theory. Based on the concepts of Rousseau, Mill, and Cole, Pateman's theory of participatory democracy is then outlined with emphasis on her discussion of participation in industry. Her concept that participation in areas other than politics develops "participatory skills" beneficial to a democracy provides the transition to the major focus of the study: participation in the arts.

An overview of arts participation from a historical perspective, in Chapter 3, establishes the framework for the extension of Pateman's theory. The literature from the field of sociology and the arts, as well as major general social theory sources, were part of the research for this chapter. As a background in social theory, the writings of Kenneth Burke (*Permanence and Change, A Grammar of Motives, A Rhetoric of Motives, Rhetoric of Religion*) and Talcott Parsons (*The Social System* and *The Structure of Social Action*) provide a foundation of general theory of human interaction. Parsons' theory in particular, with its systems approach, flows smoothly into the arts/sociology literature that uses systems diagrams.

Chapter 4 provides a continuation of the political theory background established in Chapter 2 in light of the historical perspective of participation provided in Chapter 3. In short, Chapter 4 takes Pateman's theory of participatory democracy and applies it to participation in the arts. A discussion of the concepts of active and passive participation concludes the chapter and provides the theoretical foundation for the arts participation discussions of subsequent chapters.

An examination of the interrelationship of the arts and politics in specific historical periods within the framework of the discussion on participation is contained in the next four chapters (5, 6, 7, and 8). Three periods were chosen to examine the democracy/arts/participation relationship: ancient Greece, because Greek democracy is considered a "pure" example of a democratic political system and because the arts flourished there; the Jacksonian era, because that period is considered to be the "purest" American example of democracy and the performing arts did not flourish then; and twentieth-century America, because as legislative director for the Congressional Arts Caucus, I had first-hand experience with government and the arts during this period.

Chapter 5 is introduced with a discussion of Robert Dahl's "three great historical movements toward democratizing the state": the democracy of ancient Greece and Rome, beginning about the end of the sixth century B.C.; the democracy of the city-states of northern Italy, around the tenth and eleventh centuries; and the movement commencing with the American and French revolutions.[16] Fifth-century Greek society and that of northern Italy both chose to foster democracy and the arts. These two democratic movements were unique, in part, because they involved small city-states and not gigantic nation-states, like those existing today; however, comparison of a democratic model, like that found in ancient Greece, with models of democracy in nineteenth- and twentieth-century America, can be useful in formulating workable models of the interaction between democracy and the arts. Chapter 5 continues with a discussion of participation in both politics and the arts in ancient Greece.

Chapter 6 examines Jacksonian democracy and the arts of that era in a manner similar to the discussion in Chapter 3. An overview of nineteenth-century American society, the theories of Tocqueville, and Dahl's model of Populist Democracy provide the foundation for the discussion on participation.

Dahl described twentieth-century American democracy as a hybrid model. Daniel Boorstin discussed the successes and failures of this model in *Democracy and its Discontents*. Boorstin's analysis serves as a background for Chapter 7, which examines the role of participation.

Chapter 8 begins with a background on America's unique system of support for the arts, including a historical overview of changes. A theoretical discussion of politics, economics, and the arts is followed by an examination of trends in both active and passive participation in the arts. A survey on politics/arts participation, designed specifically for this book, is analyzed at the conclusion of the chapter.

Chapter 9 provides a theoretical review of the book and general recommendations, including a discussion of the roles of the public and private sectors of the arts support network. It also includes suggestions for "fine-tuning" the support system to enhance participation. In essence, the final chapter provides material helpful for the creation of a model of American society in which the artistic community reinforces the skills of participation for the greatest number of citizens, thus helping to build a stronger participatory society. Such a society would conform to Pateman's model:

> The opportunity to participate in the alternative areas would mean that one piece of reality would have changed, namely the context within which all political activity was carried on. The argument of the participatory theory of democracy is that participation in the alternative areas would enable the individual better to appreciate the connection between the public and the private spheres. The ordinary man might still be more interested in things nearer home, but the existence of a participatory society would mean that he was better able to assess the performance of representatives at the national level, better equipped to take decisions of national scope when the opportunity arose to do so, and better able to weigh up the impact of decisions taken by national representatives on his own life and immediate surroundings.[17]

Increasingly, during the decade of the 1980s, scholars began to examine American cultural policies and noted the need for more analyses: "Of paramount importance in the establishment and maintenance of effective public cultural policy will be a significant improvement in the quality of information about the arts."[18] This book attempts to add a unique dimension to the body of historical-critical research integrating the arts with other aspects of society. The philosopher Kenneth Burke asserted that the arts are the highest form of communication, and I believe that much can be learned by illuminating various aspects of the relationship between this vital form of human communication and one of the world's predominant political systems.

Notes

1. Rockefeller Panel Report, *The Performing Arts: Problems and Prospects* (New York: McGraw-Hill, 1965), pp. 1–2.

2. Ronald Berman, "Art vs. the Arts," *Commentary*, Vol. 68, November 1979, p. 48.

3. Edwin Newman, "Art vs. Arts," *ARTS Review*, Summer 1984, p. 32.

4. Phyllis Zagano, "The Federalization of Culture," *Book Forum: Culture and Money*, Vol. VI, No. 1, p. 80.

5. Carl Cohen, *Democracy* (Athens, GA: University of Georgia Press, 1971), p. 7.

6. Ibid., p. 55.

7. Ibid., p. 164.

8. Ibid., p. 166.

9. Michael Straight, *Twigs for an Eagle's Nest: Government and the Arts 1965–1978* (New York: Devon Press, 1979).

10. Herbert Read, *To Hell with Culture* (New York: Schocken Books, 1964), p. xi.

11. Ibid.

12. Carole Pateman, *Participation and Democratic Theory* (New York: Cambridge University Press, 1970), p. 108.

13. W. D. Kay, "Arts Policy in a Democratic State," unpublished paper prepared for the Annual Meeting of the American Political Science Association, Washington, DC, 1984, p. 27.

14. Ibid.

15. William J. Baumol and William G. Bowen, *Performing Arts: The Economic Dilemma* (Cambridge, MA: The M.I.T. Press, 1966), p. 4.

16. Robert A. Dahl, *After the Revolution?* (New Haven: Yale University Press, 1978), p. 5.

17. Pateman, *Participation and Democratic Theory*, p. 110.

18. Anthony Keller, Introduction, "The Arts and Public Policy," *Journal of Arts Management and Law*, Vol, 13, No. 1, Spring 1983, p. 10.

Democratic Theory: General Considerations

Before a discussion of cultural matters, I must first set the scene by touching upon some basic definitions in political theory.

Chapter 1 introduced philosopher Kenneth Burke, who recognized the value of the arts; his theory of human action and language provides a background to explain why definitions of words, particularly political words, are so complicated. Basically, Burke outlined a theory describing the interaction of language and human action and man's continual attempt to more clearly define action through language. In *Rhetoric of Religion*, he provided this definition of man: (1) the symbol-using animal; (2) the inventor of the negative; (3) separated from his natural condition by instruments of his own making; and (4) goaded by the spirit of hierarchy.[1] (Because an appropriate, easily used symbol meaning both genders is not in common usage, terms of male gender in this book shall also apply to the female.)

According to Burke, the symbols man invents as he attempts to create a sense of order to the universe, in turn, define man's motives. The words used outline underlying motives for action; looking at language as motive provides a clearer perspective for analysis. Furthermore, as man moves along the hierarchy, he attempts to understand and to resolve conflicts by finding terms large enough to encompass both sides of the conflict. Burke called this "identification"—a more complicated form of motive ("motive in a perfected form").[2] In so doing, man is able to transcend the conflict and "pull himself up the hierarchical ladder."[3]

Burke's concept of symbols, the resolution of conflict, and "identification" help explain why political terms are difficult to define. Words like "democracy" and "democratic theory" attempt to encompass various conflicts to create clearer understanding in the realm of politics. Each step up the "hierarchical chain of substance is a symbolic resolution of the warring factions on the level beneath."[4] Robert A. Dahl described the conflict: "Democracy, it is frequently said, rests upon compromise. But democratic theory itself is full of compromises—compromises of clashing and antagonizing principles."[5]

The term "democracy" almost seems to encompass too many conflicts; "the thing democracy cannot be described properly by the word democracy."[6] Although "government by the people" has become a catchphrase for democracy (from the Greek words "demos," meaning the people, and "kratein," meaning rule),[7] the term is used for not only political democracy, but also economic and social democracy. Furthermore, conflicts occur in "microdemocracies" versus "macrodemocracies." Likewise, theorists use the term to describe a form of government that is, that can be, or that should be. This dilemma is expressed by Sartori: "In a somewhat paradoxical vein, democracy could be defined as a highflown name for something which does not exist."[8] But Sartori, like Burke, emphasized the importance of precise language in political theory. He has even eluded to an Orwellian world in which political chaos is connected with the decay of language.

At various times in this study the term "democracy" is used in each of the ways outlined above. Greek democracy is analyzed as a microdemocracy existing in Athens in the fifth century B.C. American democracy is discussed as a macrodemocracy as it existed mid–nineteenth century and as it exists today. Discussion of each period's political democracy is related to theoretical models for clarification. Reference to economic democracy focuses on the material conditions of all citizens, while social democracy emphasizes the nonmaterial conditions of equality. Of most importance to this study is reference to cultural democracy, which highlights access to all the arts for the greatest number. At the core of each analysis, however, is a discussion of the role of participation in each of the varying shades of democracy, along with a discussion of participation in concurrent cultural activities.

"Participation," a prominent theme in democratic theories emphasizing citizenship, can take many forms, including activities like voting, discussion of issues, working on a campaign, contributing money, or wearing a campaign button. James Leonard Danielson provided a seven-step hierarchy of political participation and noted that the higher the level of participation, the greater the cost to the participant and, consequently, the fewer the number of participants. His levels are: keeping informed and discussing political events, voting in community-wide elections, working in political organizations, indirectly contacting public policy makers, directly contacting public policy makers, competing for public office, and holding public office.[9] Pateman, however, has cautioned against "pseudo-participation" and stressed that participation must involve people influencing decisions affecting themselves (that is, eliminating cases where a person is merely present at a group activity or is only able to discuss a decision that already has been made).

J. R. Lucas has emphasized that the number of people involved in participation changes the activity. The more people involved, the more formal and less real a decision will be. Often, with more people participating, no information is overlooked and a better decision is reached; in addition, if one participates in a decision, one understands it more, will not regard it as alien, and will be more likely to support and defend it. In fact, Lucas argued that participation is both "a corollary and a cause of our speaking of communal decisions in the first-person plural rather than the third, and that a society in which this is the case is more united and cohesive than one in which most people regard themselves simply as subjects . . . ."[10]

With Lucas's general concepts of participation as background, Pateman developed her analysis of participation by emphasizing the workplace and adding additional refinements. In this context she clarified "partial participation"—when final decisions rest with management—and "lower/higher level participation"—referring to different management levels.

The analysis of participation in the arts in this book builds on Pateman's theories by including a discussion of various cultural activities involving a range of participation, from "active" (participation by artists, managers, board members) to "passive" (participation as audience members). This discussion of arts participation is then compared and contrasted to political participation in subsequent chapters.

EVOLUTION OF DEMOCRATIC THEORY

A clearer understanding of arts participation and its subsequent application to democracy can be gained by examining a brief outline of the evolution of democratic theory. Until the nineteenth century, the form of government known as democracy was "very unpopular" among theorists. (See Figure 2.1.) Rule by the masses was thought by Plato (c. 428 B.C.–348/347 B.C.) to lead logically to a surrender of power to a single tyrant. Although Aristotle (384 B.C.–322 B.C.) was more optimistic and believed the will of the masses could be wiser than the judgment of a few, he also thought democracy to be an unstable form of government. He preferred "aristocracy"—rule of the upper classes for the good of all the people. Thus, for the first 2,500 years of Western political theory, almost no one thought democracy

Figure 2.1

Time Line of Major Democratic Theorists

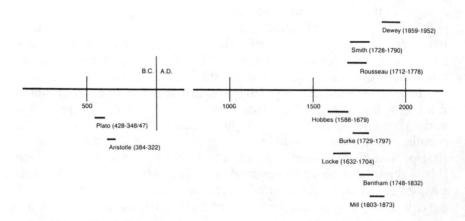

was a very good way of structuring political life.[11] Consequently, little encouragement was given to developing a theory of participatory democracy.

With the Protestant Reformation, democracy gradually reappeared in a more favorable light and "classical democratic theory" was born. Underlying the seventeenth-century political theories of Thomas Hobbes (1588–1679), John Locke (1632–1704), and Jean Jacques Rousseau (1712–1778) was the development of the idea of the social contract in early Calvinist writings. Here was formulated the concept of two contracts—that of man with God for spiritual order, and that of man with his king for civil order. Hobbes, writing to justify the Stuart restoration in England, saw man as basically self-serving. In *Leviathan* (1651), he described man in his natural state as living a violent life with no peace, industry, or culture. However, man, being rational, devised a social contract whereby, in order to be free, he surrenders his freedom to a king. Hobbes's classical studies include a translation of the work of the Greek historian Thucydides from which he learned of the perils of democracy, given the fate of ancient Athens. Participation for the common man in Hobbes's theories was, of course, very limited.

The classical liberal John Locke had a more optimistic view of man. In *Two Treatises on Government* (1690), he suggested limits on monarchs and outlined inalienable rights of "life, liberty, and property." His more extensive discussion of property included the ideas that property is essential; it allows people to provide for the basic necessities; and it gives people the opportunity to develop their characters. Locke was moving more in the direction of participation for a greater number of people.

With Jean Jacques Rousseau (1712–1778) came a more complex, but conservative, theory. He said, life in nature is peaceful but unfulfilled, that people form societies and surrender to the "general will," and that private property is a social right, but must not be accumulated in an unlimited quantity. Furthermore, the governmental entities must be small, like those of the ancient Greeks. Rousseau, whom Pateman called the "theorist par excellence of participation," placed more limits on participatory activity.

All three of these early democratic theorists believed men were essentially equal; had lived without government under a natural law; chose to organize government that served their interests; and should essentially be free. Hobbes, however, would have opted for democratic freedom under an absolute monarchy; Locke for a parliamentary republic; and Rousseau for carefully controlled democratic city-states.

During the eighteenth century, politics and economics began to emerge and "democratic capitalism" began to develop. Writing against a background of mercantilism and colonialism, Adam Smith (1728–1790) produced *Wealth of Nations* (1776), in which he advocated a free-market system fueled by the "invisible hand of supply and demand." According to Smith, the good of all is best served by each individual pursuing his own self-interest. Economic participation is essential to Smith's theory.

By the end of the eighteenth century, democratic theory had been through a classical period and a liberalizing era and was therefore ready for a fresh dose of "neoclassicism." Edmund Burke (1729–1797)—the founder of the modern neoconservative branch of democratic theory—followed the Hobbesian idea that governments are formed to maintain peace. Societal institutions are the product of the wisdom of centuries and often supersede the individual's desires—wide political participation is acceptable only from rational men dedicated to the common good. James Madison (1751–1836) likewise had little respect for pure democracy and warned against "powerful factions"; his theories are not particularly democratic to a proponent of participatory theory.

With Jeremy Bentham (1748–1832) came another era of liberal thinking. The father of contemporary liberalism, Bentham believed in the freedom of the individual to minimize pain and maximize pleasure. In *An Introduction to the Principles of Morals and Legislation*

(1789), he stressed that the object of all legislation is to find ways to provide the greatest happiness for the greatest number. With Bentham, the pendulum swung again to the positive side of participation, and with *On Liberty* (1854), by John Stuart Mill (1806–1873), the liberal tradition stressing individual freedom and an optimism about human nature continued. John Dewey (1859–1952), who believed in the intelligence and dignity of people and the power and wisdom of individual contributions to the collective good, brought these ideas into the twentieth century. With Dewey, liberalism reverted back to its central theme of equality, and participation was once again a positive element.

The mid–twentieth century has seen the two streams of democratic theory continue in strongly divergent paths. From the conservative stream flow theorists like Milton Friedman and William Buckley—champions of an elite government in which economic freedom is most important, yet participation is carefully controlled. Newspaper columnist George F. Will succinctly summarized this conservative view at a 1983 symposium on the problem of declining voter participation: "Problem? As more people are nagged to the polls, the caliber of the electorate declines. The reasonable assumption about electorates is: smaller is smarter."[12]

Moving in the opposite direction are men like Dahl and John Kenneth Galbraith—theorists describing government as the ally of individual freedom. Participatory democracy, a growing tributary of this liberal tradition, has even become noteworthy beyond academic circles. John Naisbitt's widely read book *Megatrends* (1982) outlines ten "critical restructurings" of American society. Listed as number seven is the change from a representative democracy to a participatory democracy.

Naisbitt has claimed that the "ethic of participation is spreading bottom up across America and radically altering the way we think people or institutions should be governed." Although he provided no extensive statistical research in his book, he did highlight various trends, including more widespread use of public referenda (for example, Proposition 13, a 1978 referendum in California where the voters chose to cut property taxes by 57 percent); the expansion of grassroots political activity; and various changes in corporate management allowing for more employee participation and more flexibility in response to consumers. Naisbitt has even considered the "thrust for participatory democracy" to be the "ideological backbone of the consumer movement." Consumer advocate Ralph Nader has agreed, describing the ultimate purpose of his organization as trying to expose "the greatest secret of a democracy—that it can work."[13]

CONTEMPORARY THEORIES OF DEMOCRACY

Contemporary theories of democracy follow two basic streams: those stressing the importance, yet limited use, of voting, and those supporting full participation in the political system by an increasing number of citizens. Although representative of the first stream, the theory of Joseph Schumpeter established the foundation upon which most major contemporary theories of democracy are based, including those of the participatory stream. Schumpeter revised classical democratic theory by asserting that democracy is not associated with any particular ideals or ends. In his framework, democracy is a method "for arriving at political decisions in which individuals acquire the power to decide by means of a competitive struggle for the people's vote."[14]

However, Schumpeter did not believe that universal suffrage was necessary, and furthermore, that participation has a central role. The only legitimate means of participation for citizens is voting for leaders and discussion (for example, citizens should not write their elected leaders in order to influence their votes). Dissatisfaction with leaders should be handled by a change at election time. Schumpeter is not a participatory theorist, but his ideas form the background for Pateman's movement into the second stream of contemporary democratic theory.

More recent theorists have provided Pateman with a stronger foundation for her theory—one being B. R. Berelson, who has stressed the opposite of earlier theories that assumed a politically homogeneous citizenry is necessary in a democracy. According to Berelson, heterogeneity is needed to keep a system stable while allowing it to perform contradictory functions. Pateman summarized Berelson's position: "In short, limited participation and apathy have a positive function for the whole system by cushioning the shock of disagreement, adjustment, and change."[15]

In contrast to Berelson, Dahl has considered the characteristics required for a political system to be called a democracy. His list of "institutional arrangements" centers on the electoral process, and he has stressed that in any form of social organization only a relatively small proportion of individuals will take advantage of decision-making opportunities. As Pateman noted, control by the people in a democracy, therefore, is exerted as they choose leaders who, in turn, make society's decisions.

Dahl described four general theories of democracy that have been a part of the American political experiment and that form the basis of the discussions in Chapters 6, 7, and 8. All of Dahl's theories have one common concern: "Preoccupation with the rights and wrongs of majority rule has run like a thread through American political thought since 1789."[16] A description of Dahl's models, as outlined in his book, *A Preface to Democratic Theory*, follows.

Madisonian Democracy is Dahl's first model and involves the following hypotheses:

If unrestrained by external checks, any given individual or group will tyrannize others.

The accumulation of all powers (legislative, executive, judicial) in the same hand implies the elimination of external checks.

If unrestrained by external checks, a minority will tyrannize the majority.

If unrestrained by external checks, a majority will tyrannize a minority.

Two conditions are necessary for the existence of a nontyrannical republic:

(1) There is no accumulation of power in the same hands.
(2) Factions must be controlled so that they do not act adversely to the rights of others or to the permanent rights of the community.

Frequent popular elections will not provide an external check sufficient to prevent tyranny.

If factions are to be controlled and tyranny is to be avoided, this must be attained by controlling the effects of faction.

If a faction is less than a majority, it can be controlled by the operation of "the republican principle."

The development of majority factions can be limited if the electorate is numerous, extended, and diverse in interests.

To the extent that the electorate is numerous, extended, and diverse in interests, a majority faction is less likely to exist, and if it does exist, it is less likely to act as a unity.

Democracy following the above model attempts to avoid majority rule, and Dahl therefore considered Madison's system almost outside the realm of democracy.

A second alternative, Populist Democracy, centers on the principle that political equality is, according to Dahl, an "end to be maximized, that is, to postulate that the goals of every adult citizen of a republic are to be accorded equal value in determining government policies."[17] Jacksonian Democracy conforms to this model, which maintains—to use Tocqueville's phrase—the "absolute sovereignty of the majority." Dahl provided two propositions for Populist Democracy:

The only rule compatible with decision making in a Populist Democracy is the majority principle (in choosing between alternatives, the alternative preferred by the greater number is selected).

Populist Democracy is desirable, at least for governmental decisions, as a final appeal when other specified processes have been exhausted, and among adult citizens.

Participation plays a major role in this form of democracy, which is analyzed in Chapter 6.

Dahl's third model, Polyarchy, requires the following conditions:

During the voting period:
1. Every member votes.
2. All votes carry equal weight.
3. The alternative with the greatest number of votes is chosen.

During the prevoting period:
4. Any member may insert a preferred alternative among those scheduled for voting.
5. All those individuals possess identical information about the alternatives.

During the postvoting period:
6. Alternatives (leaders or policies) with the greatest number of votes displace any alternatives with fewer votes.
7. The orders of elected officials are executed.

During the interelection stage:
8.1. Either all interelection decisions are subordinate or executory to those arrived at during the election state, that is, elections are controlling,
8.2. or new decisions during the interelection period are governed by the preceding seven conditions, operating, however, under rather different institutional circumstances,
8.3. or both.

Clearly, Polyarchy is an unworkable theoretical model in today's macrodemocracies having low voter turnout and lack of consistent information dissemination.

Dahl's final model, the American Hybrid, more closely resembles democracy as we experience it today:

On matters of specific policy, the majority rarely rules.
Not minority rule, but minorities rule.
In a sense, the majority rules (when minorities reflect consensus).
Majority tyranny is a myth.

If there is any protection for minorities, it is not in the U.S. Constitution, but in extra-constitutional factors (e.g., intensity of
minority feeling).

Constitutional rules determine which groups are given advantages
or handicaps.

All active and legitimate groups can make themselves heard at some
crucial stage in the decision process.

Madisonian Democracy, Populist Democracy, Polyarchy, and the
American Hybrid are all models of a form of community government,
the variety of which knows no practical limit. Cohen provided a
general definition encompassing Dahl's more specific models:
"Democracy is that system of community government in which, by
and large, the members of a community participate, directly or indirectly, in the making of decisions which affect them all."[18]

In one of his later works, Dahl concentrated on the idea of the
community and specific role of participation. In *Democracy in the
United States: Promise and Performance* (1976), he pointed out that man
has a need for other human fellowship, yet can not seem to live
without conflict. Therefore, he searches for ways to adjust the conflict
to make community life possible. This is the final stage making us
political animals. Also, in his later works, Dahl suggested redistribu-
tive policies—floors and ceilings on use of political resources and the
formation of organizations and coalitions—to adjust the conflicts arising because of social, economic, and educational inequalities. He is
particularly concerned with stability problems resulting from
economic inequality.

Dahl has also warned about the possible dangers of an increase in
participation. In *A Preface to Democratic Theory*, he suggests that expanded political activity from the lower socioeconomic groups, for
example, where "authoritarian" personalities are more frequently
found, could threaten the stability of the democratic system.[19]

Contemporary theorist Giovanni Sartori has extended Dahl's
theories with greater emphasis on the fear that increased participation
in the political process leads to totalitarianism. He notes that the
apathy of the majority should be accepted as fact; to try to change this
would threaten the maintenance of the democratic method.

Pateman also cited theorist Harry Eckstein, who has formulated the
conditions necessary for a democratic system to maintain itself stably
over time. His first proposition is that a government will tend to be
stable if its authority pattern is similar to the authority patterns of
other spheres of society. He concluded that for a democratic system to
be stable, the structure of authority in national government cannot be
"purely" democratic.

Pateman outlined a theory of contemporary democracy, drawing together ideas common to Berelson, Dahl, Sartori, and Eckstein—a theory that "focuses on the operation of the democratic political system as a whole and is grounded in the facts of present-day political attitudes and behavior as revealed by sociological investigation."[20] In her theory, democracy is defined as a political method characterized by the competition of leaders (elites) for the votes of the people at periodic, free elections, which are the major means by which the majority exercises control over leaders. "Participation" means: choices of decision makers exercised in order to protect private interests.

THEORIES OF PARTICIPATORY DEMOCRACY

In contrast to Pateman's outline of a contemporary theory of democracy are the theories in which participation has a greater function than merely a protective device. Calling participation "a prominent theme in citizenship democracy," Dennis Thompson provided a list of the functions of participation:

To help ensure that "sinister interests" of the rulers do not prevail (citizens need adequate opportunities to object by voting)

To see that excluded interests can be satisfied (the purpose of pressure groups)

To increase each citizen's political knowledge (participation fosters political knowledge rather than the reverse)

To increase the sense of legitimacy (participation gives citizens the sense that the acts of government are legitimate)

To increase each citizen's feeling of "self-realization" (participation gives citizens a sense of being in control of their destinies) [21]

Certain conditions are required to keep the system stable: The level of participation by the majority should not rise much above the minimum necessary to keep the democratic method (electoral machinery) working; that is, it should remain at about the level existing at present in the Anglo-American democracies. The suggestion, by Dahl and others, that nondemocratic attitudes are relatively more common among the inactive means that any increase in participation by the apathetic would weaken the consensus on the norms of the democratic method, which is a further necessary condition.[22] Although no "democratic character" is required of all citizens in this theory, social training in the democratic method can take place in a variety of nongovernmental authority structures.

Pateman bases her theory of participatory democracy on concepts initially drawn from Rousseau, who advocated a form of government existing in a society in which all citizens are educated to reach their full potential, are joined in a genuine community, and, through public education by participation in many spheres of society, perpetuate political democracy. Pateman highlighted the theories of Rousseau and John Stuart Mill as classical theories providing the basic postulates of participatory democracy. The work of G. D. H. Cole expands these postulates in the context of twentieth-century, large-scale, industrialized society. The following discussion highlights the contributions of Rousseau, Mill, and Cole to Pateman's theory.

In Rousseau's theory, each citizen participates in political decision making—a process having a psychological effect on the participants that is reflected in the interrelationships among all of society's institutions and individuals. This participation protects private interests and ensures good government. According to Rousseau, individuals should be forced through the participatory process into socially responsible action. Government functioning in this manner enables individuals to accept collective decisions more easily and to feel they belong to a community. This process, in turn, helps produce a "true" community in which individuals have similar ideas and beliefs. Pateman summarized Rousseau's importance by stating that his arguments form the basis of the theory of participatory democracy.

Participation for Mill also served an educative function: individuals absorbed in "private money-getting occupations" do not develop the capacity for responsible public action, but given the opportunity to participate in public affairs, they begin to take the public interest into account.[23] Mill stressed that responsible participation at the national level by citizens in large-scale societies requires preparation at the local level. Mill, however, differed from Rousseau in the realm of equality: He rejected Rousseau's belief in the necessity of political equality for effective participation and instead stressed the importance of education. "It is not useful, but hurtful, that the constitution of the country should declare ignorance to be entitled to as much political power as knowledge," Mill wrote.[24]

The most important aspect of Mill's theory for the present discussion is his expansion of the educative effect of participation to a new area of social life—industry. Like the individual's participatory experience in local affairs, experience in industry could also reinforce political participation, but the authority relationship in industry would have to be "democratized." The usual superiority-subordination system would have to be replaced with a system of cooperation, or equality, among workers and managers: They would be elected to positions of power in the manner that representatives at the local government level are chosen.

Cole's concepts provide the next step in the expansion of Pateman's theory of participatory democracy. Cole's theory stresses that industry is the primary arena for preparation of a truly democratic government in today's industrialized society. Building on Rousseau's argument that will, not force, should form the basis of social and political organization, Cole outlined a theory of associations in which society is defined as an array of associations held together by the wills of their members. In addition to participation at the local governmental level, individuals must be able to participate in the internal organization of local associations in order to "learn democracy," according to Cole. (Participation in a variety of arts advocacy organizations provides an excellent example of "learning democracy" through participation in the arts. See Chapter 4.) But, he said, participation in industry decision making is most important, because industry accounts for the majority of time that most individuals spend in superior/subordinate relationships.

With the foundation laid by the theories of Rousseau, Mill, and Cole, Pateman outlined her theory of participatory democracy. This theory contains the following major hypotheses:

Individuals and their institutions cannot be considered in isolation from one another.

The existence of representative institutions at the national level is not sufficient for democracy.

To maximize participation, social training for democracy must take place in spheres other than the political realm. (This point in Pateman's theory provides the crucial link to this book.)

The major function of participation is an educative one, including both the psychological aspect[25] and the gaining of practice in democratic skills and procedures.

Stability of the system presents no problem; the system is self-sustaining through the educative impact of the participatory process.

In addition, participation has an integrative effect in that it aids in the acceptance of collective decisions.

Under this theory, a participatory society is necessary for the existence of a truly democratic government, and the most important arena in which to learn participation is industry: "If individuals are to exercise the maximum amount of control over their own lives and environment, then authority structures in these areas must be so organized that they can participate in decision making."[26]

Participation in Industry

Various empirical studies researching political behavior and attitudes provide a background for the extension of Pateman's ideas involving participation in other spheres of society. These studies have shown a positive correlation between participation and the sense of political efficacy, the belief that an individual's act of participating can have an impact on the political process. Persons possessing a sense of political efficacy are more likely to participate in politics. In addition, they feel more effective in their everyday activities. According to Gabriel A. Almond and Sidney Verba, "the belief in one's competence is a key political attitude."[27]

Almond and Verba's *The Civic Culture* outlines their groundbreaking cross-cultural study of individual political attitudes and behavior. In all five countries studied (United States, Great Britain, Germany, Italy, and Mexico) a positive relationship held between the sense of political efficacy and political participation, with the sense of competence being greater at the local level. (See Figure 2.2.) In addition, a higher level of competence existed in the United States and Great Britain, where

Figure 2.2

Participation in Family, School, and Job

Remembered influence in family decisions

Precentage who remember they had	U.S.	U.K.	Germany	Italy	Mexico
Some influence	73	69	54	48	57
No influence	22	26	37	37	40
Don't know, don't remember, and other	5	5	9	15	3

Freedom to participate in school discussions and debates

Precentage who remember they	U.S.	U.K.	Germany	Italy	Mexico
Could and did participate	40	16	12	11	15
Could but did not participate	15	8	5	4	21
Could not participate	34	68	68	56	54
Don't know and other	11	8	15	29	10

Consulted about job decisions

Precentage saying they are consulted	U.S.	U.K.	Germany	Italy	Mexico
Sometimes or often	78	80	68	59	61
Rarely or never	21	19	29	36	38

Source: Gabriel A. Almond and Sidney Verba, *The Civic Culture* (Boston: Little, Brown & Co., 1965), pp. 275, 276, 281. Used with permission.

there are more opportunities for local political participation. These findings lend support to Mill's argument stressing the importance of local political institutions in which experience in democracy may be gained.

In the 1989 publication *The Civic Culture Revisited*,[28] Almond reiterated that the study highlighted the fact that political-cultural variables and the socialization processes which create and maintain them play an important part in the explanation of political structure and process.

The Civic Culture also highlighted the effects of participation in voluntary associations and found a correlation between the sense of political efficacy and association membership. Furthermore, this correlation was higher among active members, particularly those involved in political associations. Under this hypothesis, arts advocates would have a high sense of political efficacy. (See discussion of survey in Chapter 8.)

Almond and Verba indicated that significant socialization experiences affecting later political behavior take place early in life in addition to adulthood. The research of David Easton and Jack Dennis involving children's images of government also has shown how "political socialization" occurs.[29] They defined "political socialization" as the way in which a society transmits political orientation (knowledge, attitudes, values) from generation to generation, and produced a landmark survey of 12,000 American school children in second through eighth grade.

The survey found that young children are "politically primitive"; the first political image taught is that of the president; the supportive image of a government is widely and regularly reproduced; learning increases by gradually incorporating more and more images, including Congress, voting, and eventually the concept of democracy. According to Easton and Dennis, a child "learns to like the government before he really knows what it is. And as he learns what it is, he finds that it involves popular participation (voting) and that this is a valuable part of its countenance."[30] Their study asked respondents to remember whether they had been able to participate in family or school activities and whether they believed they were able to participate in politics. Although higher indication of participation in family and school was correlated with a greater sense of political efficacy, correlation was not as strong as the relationship between competence on the job and "subjective political competence" (that is, the belief in the ability to influence government). Almond and Verba unequivocally concluded that there is evidence that the impact of participation in nonpolitical decision making—at home, school, and job—is cumulative.[31]

Ronald Milton Mason's research also has indicated that empirical evidence supports the contention that "social participation operates on political participation through a psychological propensity to participate."[32] With a focus on the workplace, Mason found that participatory opportunities in business were likely to increase participation in government. Pateman closely reviewed the studies in industry, specifically research on differing work environments and workers' attitudes. In her search, she found that a participatory work environment included management teams elected by the workers, monthly policy meetings open to the workers, and use of referenda to allow all individuals to make some decisions. For example, R. Blauner studied the American printing, textile, automobile, and chemical industries and found that only certain work situations were conducive to the development of attitudes that underlie a sense of political efficacy. In both the automobile and textile industries, workers had very little opportunity to contribute their own ideas, often had no control over the pace of their work, and were unable to exercise any leadership qualities. They consequently failed to develop self-esteem or a feeling of self-worth, in contrast to their counterparts in the printing and chemical industries, where workers had a higher degree of control over their work.

Pateman also pointed to C. Argyris, who has argued that the contemporary work environment fails to help individuals develop self-esteem or self-confidence and that workers have little opportunity to use their abilities or to exercise their initiatives. Although Argyris does not directly investigate the relationship between attitudes developed at work and activity in politics, he does speculate that they may be linked: "It seems clear from this evidence that the argument of the participatory theory of democracy that an individual's [politically relevant] attitudes will depend to a large extent on the authority structure of his work environment is a well-founded one."[33] P. Blumberg has been even more emphatic in his assessment:

> There is hardly a study in the entire literature which fails to demonstrate that satisfaction in work is enhanced or that other generally acknowledged beneficial consequences accrue from a genuine increase in workers' decision making power. Such consistency of findings, I submit, is rare in social research.[34]

As cited earlier, these concepts have been highlighted in popular literature as well. Naisbitt's discussion of participatory democracy in *Megatrends* stressed the importance of extending the participatory environment into the corporation. In that work, he noted that greater participation brings the worker a greater feeling of control over his environment and therefore greater self-esteem. His examples include: the formation of employee rights organizations, such as the Honeywell Corporation's Quality of Work Life groups; the increase in the number of outside directors on corporate boards; and greater activism among shareholders. According to Naisbitt, all of these activities help to facilitate people's involvement in decision making. In short, the workplace can reinforce the participatory skills required in the political realm.

Tom Peters, who along with Bob Waterman wrote the popular book *In Search of Excellence* (1983), spent six years researching American corporations known for their excellence, in order to determine the management concepts they shared. Rather than a list of strict management principles, he discovered the importance of nontangible concepts: pride, love, enthusiasm, fun.[35] A participatory corporate environment nurtured these feelings in employees and managers alike. "Commitment, not authority," stressed Peters, produces results.

Participation in Other Spheres of Society

With her analysis of participatory democracy and the importance of participation in the work environment, Pateman concluded: "We do learn to participate by participating and that feelings of political efficacy are more likely to be developed in a participatory environment."[36] In addition, she described a "participatory society" in which experience in all areas helps to develop individuals' participatory skills. So often, we depend on a participatory environment in politics, but in home, school, and other areas we appeal to the authority of parents, teachers, and others. John Dewey stressed that these habits are "inconsistent with the democratic method."

"Democracy is a way of life," he explained. "The struggle for democracy has to be maintained on as many fronts as culture has aspects: political, economic, international, educational, scientific and artistic . . . ."[37] Pateman would agree. She specifically suggested beginning with the family and referred to theories of childrearing which have a more democratic flavor. The theories of Talcott Parsons, which are discussed in Chapter 3, support Pateman's ideas that social structure can reinforce political participation. In addition, so as not to nullify the effects of a "participatory" family structure, children should have more democratic educations, according to Pateman. Furthermore, young adults could gain additional participatory skills by making decisions in their communities. Looking at society in general, Pateman concluded:

The argument of the participatory theory of democracy is that participation in the alternative areas would enable the individual better to appreciate the connection between the public and the private spheres. The ordinary man might still be more interested in things nearer home, but the existence of a participatory society would mean that he was better able to assess the performance of representatives at the national level, better equipped to take decisions of national scope when the opportunity arose to do so, and better able to weight up the impact of decisions taken by national representatives on his own life and immediate surroundings. In the context of a participatory society the significance of his vote to the individual would have changed; as well as being a private individual he would have multiple opportunities to become an educated, public citizen.[38]

Indeed, "multiple opportunities" can be found in the arts.

Notes

1. Kenneth Burke, *Rhetoric of Religion* (Los Angeles: University of California Press, 1955), p. 40.

2. Kenneth Burke, *A Rhetoric of Motives* (Los Angeles: University of California Press, 1950), p. 19.

3. John W. Kirk, "Kenneth Burke's Dramatistic Criticism Applied to the Theatre," *Southern Speech Journal*, Spring 1968, p. 168.

4. Burke, *A Rhetoric of Motives*, p. 141.

5. Robert A. Dahl, *A Preface to Democratic Theory* (Chicago: University Press, 1962), p. 12.

6. Giovanni Sartori, *Democratic Theory* (Chicago: University Press, 1962), p. 12.

7. Cohen, *Democracy*, p. 3.

8. Sartori, *Democratic Theory*, p. 3.

9. James Leonard Danielson, "Democratic Patterns of Political Participation: The Ideal and the Real," Ph.D. dissertation, University of Minnesota, 1971, p. 18.

10. J. R. Lucas, *Democracy and Participation* (Harmondsworth, Middlesex, England: Penguin Books Ltd.,1976), p. 142.

11. Paul Corcoran, "The Limits of Democratic Theory,"*Democratic Theory and Practice*, Graeme Duncan, ed. (New York: Cambridge University Press, 1983), p. 18.

12. George F. Will, "In Defense of Nonvoting," *Newsweek*, October 10, 1983, p. 96.

13. Ralph Nader, *Sunday Morning*, CBS television, October 17, 1982.

14. Joseph Schumpeter, *Capitalism, Socialism and Democracy* (London: George Allen & Unwin, 1943), p. 269.

15. Pateman, *Participation and Democratic Theory*, p. 7.

16. Dahl, *A Preface to Democratic Theory*, p. 4.

17. Ibid., p. 32.

18. Cohen, *Democracy*, p. 7.

19. Dahl, *A Preface to Democratic Theory*, p. 89.

20. Pateman, *Participation and Democratic Theory*, p. 14.

21. Dennis F. Thompson, *The Democratic Citizen* (New York: Cambridge University Press, 1970), p. 53.

22. See Pateman, *Participation and Democratic Theory*, p. 100.

23. These ideas, however, run contrary to those of theorists like the 1986 Nobel Prize winner in economics, James McGill Buchanan, whose theory states that most political decisions are not made in the public interest but for private economic reasons. In *An Economic Theory of Democracy* (New York: Harper & Brothers, 1957), Anthony Downs has also supported the idea that political decisions are intricately tied to economic decisions: "Parties in democratic politics are analogous to entrepreneurs in a profit-seeking economy" (p. 295).

24. John Stuart Mill, *Considerations of Representative Government* (New York: Henry Holt and Company, n.d.), p. 188.

25. The psychological aspect of participation involves building the individual's feeling of self-esteem. As used in this study, "self-esteem" is the fourth in the hierarchy of human needs described by the psychologist Abraham Maslow. In Maslow's theory, needs are arranged in a hierarchy, with lower needs having to be satisfied before the upper needs.

26. Pateman, *Participation and Democratic Theory*, p. 54.

27. Gabriel A. Almond and Sidney Verba, *The Civic Culture* (Boston: Little, Brown & Co., 1965), pp. 206–207.

28. Gabriel A. Almond and Sidney Verba, ed., *The Civic Culture Revisited* (Newbury Park, CA: Sage Publications, 1989).

29. David Easton and Jack Dennis, "The Child's Image of Government," *The Learning of Political Behavior*, Norman Adler and Charles Harrington, ed. (Glenview, IL: Scott, Foresman & Co., 1970).

30. Ibid., p. 96.

31. Ibid., p. 297. (See survey results in Chapter 8. Some of their results are indicated in Figure 2.2.)

32. Ronald Milton Mason, "Participatory and Workplace Democracy," Ph.D. dissertation, The University of Iowa, 1976, p. 73.

33. Pateman, *Participation and Democratic Theory*, p. 53.

34. Pateman (p. 66) quotes Blumberg (P. Blumberg, *Industrial Democracy: The Sociology of Participation* [London: Constable, 1968], p. 123).

35. Tom Peters, lecture, "A Passion for Excellence: An Evening with Tom Peters," PBS, August 22, 1986.

36. Pateman, *Participation and Democratic Theory*, p. 105.

37. John Dewey, *Freedom and Culture* (New York: G. P. Putnam & Sons, 1939), p. 129.

38. Ibid., p. 110.

Participation in the Arts:
A Historical Perspective

This chapter provides two views of how the frequency and kind of individual participation in the arts have varied throughout history: a systems-approach "snapshot" of various societies and a longitudinal view of history by looking at cycles of participation. Both views can help us to begin an examination of changes in participatory patterns and how they relate to a society at a particular time.

The ideas of social theorist Talcott Parsons provide a stepping stone for the discussion of social systems and establish the foundation for a later discussion using the systems approach. Parsons looked at society from an action frame of reference where individuals interact "under such conditions that it is possible to treat such a process of interaction as a system in the scientific sense and subject it to the same order of theoretical analysis which has been successfully applied to other types of systems in other sciences."[1]

He defined three classes of objects: social, physical, and cultural. A social object is an actor who can respond or interact; a physical object is an empirical entity that cannot respond or interact; and a cultural object is a symbolic element of the society, of ideas, or of beliefs. When enough interaction has occurred to be able to differentiate to a cultural level, a social system has developed. This system

> consists in a plurality of individual actors interacting with each other in a situation which has at least a physical or environmental aspect, actors who are motivated in terms of a tendency to the "optimization of gratification" and whose relation to their situations, including each other, is defined and mediated in terms of a system of culturally structured and shared symbols.[2]

The stability of the system is maintained by a communications process that shares the symbolic system and forms a "cultural tradition." Parsons stressed that culture is *transmitted, learned,* and *shared.* The arts function as a symbol system through which culture is transmitted, learned, and shared; they also create our national identity. Through participation in the arts—either active or passive (see Chapter 4)—individuals learn society's beliefs and values. Thus, Pateman's contention that participation is learned by participating would be true under Parsons' theory in a society that values participation and transmits this belief through the arts.

A SOCIOLOGICAL VIEW OF THE ARTS

Reflected in the life of humanity are many natural cycles—the ebb and flow of the tides, the changing of the seasons, the regular movement of the earth that causes day to turn to night. These periodic changes parallel the organic cycles of humanity—the diastolic/systolic pumping of the heart, the inhale/exhale rhythm of the respiratory system, and the daily periods of rest required of the human body. History itself can be viewed from a similar perspective. The roots of the cycles in history are in the "natural life of humanity,"[3] noted Arthur M. Schlesinger, Jr., in *The Cycles of American History,* and, as civilization's recordkeeping skills have improved, the number of documented historical cycles has increased proportionately.

However, the more developed the level of culture, the more complicated are the cycles and network of relationships initiating them. Very simple cultures, on the other hand, can easily illustrate the effects of various changes. This principle was clearly demonstrated by Arnold Hauser in his landmark study, *The Social History of Art,* published in 1951. Intertwining sociology and history, Hauser highlighted art and its relationship to society from prehistoric times to what he designated "the film age." His overview shows how changes in the rhythm of life have been reflected in art, with changes more dramatically observed in the simpler cultures: "there is nothing in the whole history of art which illuminates so clearly the connection between a change in style and the simultaneous change in economic and social condition as the transition from the earlier to the late Stone Age."[4] For man during the Stone Age, art was in the realm of magic. But as man began to domesticate plants and animals and began his conquest of nature in the late Stone Age, leisure time became available and the style of art changed. Artist/magician specialists developed, and a "peasant art" evolved. (Hauser has noted that folk art has meaning only in contrast to the art of the ruling class.) This cycle of increased arts participation linked with an increase in leisure time and later with a rise in economic conditions can be seen throughout history.

Ancient Greece

By the time civilization was experimenting with formal political systems, societies had much experience with various economic and social hierarchies, and the term "art" was a concept that could be defined. However, because "any object dubbed to be a work of art necessarily acquires a selective meaning that depends on the distinct codes used by artists and audiences,"[5] this definition has been subject to change over time and in different societies.

While the ancient Greek society in which he lived experimented with democracy, Aristotle gave the Greek civilization its first thorough definition of "art." Writing in the fourth century B.C., Aristotle had before him the great theatrical tradition of Greece; consequently, his analysis of drama most clearly illustrates his general theory of art. According to Aristotle in *Poetics*, all artists (poets, painters, musicians, dancers) "imitate action," and the arts themselves are distinguished by the *object* imitated, the *medium* employed, and the *manner* or mode of imitation. Furthermore, the natural instincts of imitation and harmony and rhythm cause humans to experience pleasure in response to a work of art. Imitation causes pleasure because recognition of what is being imitated occurs, while harmony and rhythm cause pleasurable awareness of the form of the art. Both content and form were important to Aristotle.

In his analysis of art, Aristotle accepted the Greek idea that the fine arts have no end beyond that of providing pleasure derived through their use of imitation and harmony and rhythm. But in his discussion of tragedy, Aristotle more clearly defined a special quality of pleasure—the purgation or catharsis of the passions of fear and pity. Francis Fergusson stressed that these emotions highlight the universality of art:

> The passions of tragedy must spring from something of more than individual, more than momentary, significance. The masters of tragedy ... mingle pity and fear in the right proportions. Having given us fear enough, they melt us with pity, purging our emotions, and reconciling us to our fate, because we understand it as the universal human lot.[6]

Thus, tragedy to Aristotle was the highest form of art, "attaining its end more perfectly."[7]

Given the background of Aristotle's definition of art and the rigid structure of the ancient Greek society, a systems diagram[8] outlining arts participation is constructive. Providing a basis for sociological analysis, support systems (and their effects on the kinds of art produced, recognized as art, rewarded, and disseminated) have been documented by scholars working in a variety of disciplines[9] and have helped to clarify the culture/society relationship.

Figure 3.1 is a systems diagram of arts participation in ancient Greece, based on Robinson's systems diagram of contemporary arts participation (Figure 3.3).[10] As in the twentieth century, production in ancient Greece remained in the hands of the individual artist, but the distribution system was quite different. In ancient Greece, the state was the most important distributor of the most predominant art form, theatre. Robinson stressed that the exchange of money continues to be the lifeblood of the system, but, in general, more is obtained than merely art. With the flow of money, people also obtain prestige, access to the world of culture, identification with an upper social class, or simply the "good feeling" of interacting with a communications medium attempting to provide insight into the deeper meaning of human life.

Figure 3.1

Systems Diagram of Arts Participation: Ancient Greece

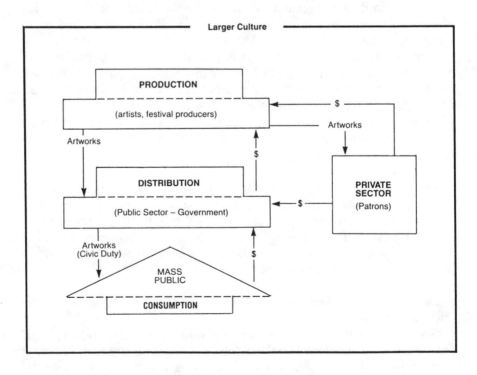

As Figure 3.1 shows, economics played an important role in the ancient Greek system of arts participation. In Athens, the wealthy helped pay the bills for the state-supported theatre. With such extensive financial assistance, low admission prices, and even subsidized tickets, audience participation was high for all classes. (See Chapter 5.) As Aristotle noted, theatre in Greek society performed the important function of providing a catharsis of strong emotions in which the Greek mass population could share. Because of this definition of art, increased participation as an audience was greatly encouraged.

Although the mass Greek population attended the theatre under the established political system, the life of the lower class lacked much exposure to the other fine arts. According to Hauser, Athens governed "in the name of the people, but in the spirit of the nobility."[11] Clearly, political democracy did not lead to economic democracy. The average citizen had little or no time for individual arts participation as a musician or a poet, and although he might work as a craftsman, painter, or sculptor, his handiwork adorned only the homes of the wealthy. (Handicrafts and work in the visual arts were in the category of "dirty, manual work" as opposed to the arts participation of the poet, who worked "cleanly," and was considered part of the aristocracy.) His arts participation was merely as an audience member at the state-sponsored play festivals where the performance was democratic (presented to the masses) but the content was aristocratic (heroic sagas).[12] With sculpture, painting, music, and poetry limited to the wealthy, and later with the demise of the ancient Greek experiments in democracy, the masses lost their state-sponsored access to the performing arts and widespread participation declined.

The Middle Ages to the Nineteenth Century

With the changes in society brought about by the Middle Ages in Western society, art once again became closely tied to religion and structured along rigid class lines. The Church, which revived rites and ceremony, used art as a unifying element. Furthermore, the Church was so conscious of the extra-aesthetic forces of art that it regulated all cultural elements which served religion.[13] During this period, the historical patterns of arts patronage became more clearly delineated and began to follow the overall pattern of the dominances of classes, elites, and other social and economic institutions over society.[14] Literature and visual art remained in the monasteries while peasants continued the tradition of folk art. With the rise of a commercial economy, money became the bridge between groups separated by birth. Society became more secularized and culture could be bought more easily.

Although literature began to seep into the lower classes, only the wealthy continued to be able to afford painting and sculpture.

Until the sixteenth century, the majority of artistic endeavor was dominated by religious preoccupation. The naturalism ushered in by the Renaissance brought an increased demand for works of art, and artists were elevated from mere artisans to "free intellectual workers."[15] Arts participation continued to parallel the amount of money and leisure time available to the various social classes.

Although the Elizabethan Age perpetuated the strict class structure, the dynamic quality of social life kept the boundaries between classes in a state of flux. This state of flux made possible the unique mix of classes evident in the audiences that flocked to Shakespeare's plays. These theatrical events "brought together the tavern public, representatives of the cultured upper classes, and the members of the middle class who were neither particularly cultured nor absolutely uncivilized."[16]

The growth of a new reading public during the next century continued cultural leveling to a small degree. The rise of the well-to-do middle class stimulated literary sales. But a strict artistic culture was still limited to the society of court aristocracy, where art could be bought and many of the puritanical constraints of the middle class were absent. By the beginning of the eighteenth century, changes in the structure of the cultural audiences "formed the beginning of the democratizing of art which reaches its culmination in mass attendance of cinemas."[17]

The Nineteenth Century

As the nineteenth century progressed, middle-class use of the arts to achieve prestige increased, and cultural activities were used "to celebrate the triumph of the bourgeoisie over society."[18] Correspondingly, with a democratizing era in the United States, this attention by the masses to art was described by the Frenchman Alexis de Tocqueville in his epic chronicle of society in nineteenth-century America:

> I do not believe that it is a necessary effect of a democratic social condition and of democratic institutions to diminish the number of those who cultivate the fine arts; but these causes exert a powerful influence on the manner in which these arts are cultivated. Many of those who had already contracted a taste for the fine arts are impoverished: on the other hand, many of those who are not yet rich begin to conceive that taste, at least by imitation; the number of consumers increases, but opulent and fastidious

consumers become more scarce . . . the productions of artists are more numerous, but the merit of each production is diminished.[19]

In other words, Tocqueville noticed much attention being paid to the arts by an increasing number of people, and as demand exceeded supply, the quantity of the artistic product increased while the quality decreased: "In aristocracies, a few great pictures are produced; in democratic countries, a vast number of insignificant ones."[20]

Tocqueville also found very little American poetry. The democratic mind, he believed, is less likely to produce poetic literature than the aristocratic mind:

Aristocracy naturally leads the human mind to the contemplation of the past, and fixes it there. Democracy, on the contrary, gives men a sort of instinctive distaste for what is ancient. In this respect, aristocracy is far more favorable to poetry; for things commonly grow larger and more obscure as they are more remote; and for this two-fold reason, they are better suited to the delineation of the ideal.[21]

The status of literature was also described by Tocqueville: "When a traveler goes into a bookseller's shop in the United States, and examines the American books upon the shelves, the number of works appears very great,"[22] but Americans "have then, at present, properly speaking, no literature."[23] He did, however, acknowledge journalists as authors and described the tremendous volume of newspapers and pamphlets circulated in the nineteenth-century United States.

American authors, in particular, succeeded in reaching large numbers of people. Historian Frank Luther Mott compiled a record of bestsellers reaching one percent of the population during the decade they were published.[24] Among nineteenth-century authors with four or more bestselling books were James Fenimore Cooper and Mark Twain. Because artists began to appeal to mass audiences, styles were simplified in order to be immediately accessible to an audience.

In general, the United States that Tocqueville observed seemed to be importing European art, as well as attempting to produce art of its own—all with the goal of increased mass audience participation. Private distributors, like P. T. Barnum, presented European artists such as singer Jenny Lind in tours across the country, while a variety of cities were in the process of forming orchestras, theatres, opera companies, and museums. In fact, many of America's largest orchestras were established during the nineteenth century. Founded during this century were the major orchestras of New York (1842), St. Louis (1880–1881), Chicago (1885), and Pittsburgh (1895).[25] The mid-nineteenth century also saw the beginnings of American opera and theatre companies, although European singers and actors continued to be the feature attractions in most major cities.

Figure 3.2 shows this system of cultural distribution (the rise of arts institutions concurrent with the promotion of European art and artists and increased arts participation). Once again, the role of economics is clear. Only individuals who could afford admission to museums, theatres, and opera houses could attend. Unlike ancient Greece, where the performing arts in particular were so integral to the state-sponsored festivals, most arts attendance in the nineteenth-century United States remained a matter for the wealthy: The United States in the last quarter of the nineteenth century, for all its protestations of egalitarian sentiments, was exceedingly class conscious, and nowhere was there a more public, and quite possibly more brilliant, display of this than at the opera and the symphony.[26]

Figure 3.2

Systems Diagram of Arts Participation:
Nineteenth-Century America

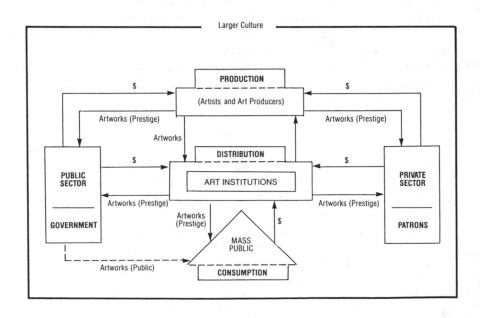

The Twentieth Century

As the United States entered the twentieth century, art still was defined socially as an activity of the elite, but aesthetically the definition began to change. For social philosophers like John Dewey, art became anything that would cause an aesthetic experience: "A follower of Dewey, for example, would encourage ordinary people to do ordinary things—and to perceive them when done by others—in an artistic manner."[27] This change in definition set the stage for the expansion of a new category of popular arts: "'Mass culture' was in the incubator waiting to be hatched."[28] A mass reading public was already being cultivated with "more dailies, weeklies, monthlies, and quarterlies published in America than in all the countries of Europe."[29] The print media clearly held the mass audience until the advent of television in the 1950s. Newspaper circulation in the United States gradually increased from an average of .21 daily papers per household

Figure 3.3

Robinson Systems Diagram of Arts Participation

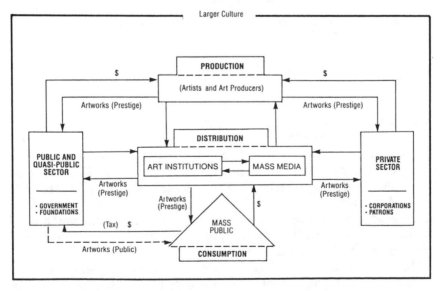

Source: John P. Robinson, ed., *Social Science and the Arts* (Lanham, MD: University Press of America, 1985). Used with permission.

Figure 3.4

DeFleur Systems Diagram of Mass Media

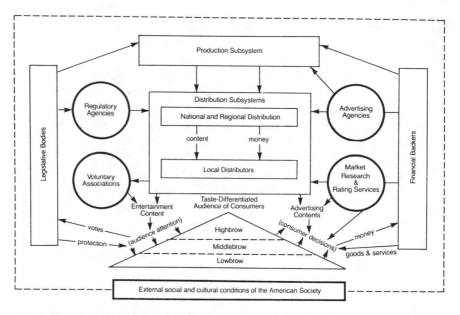

Source: Melvin L. DeFleur and Sandra J. Ball-Rokeach, *Theories of Mass Communication* (New York: Longman, 1982). Used with permission.

in 1850 to more than 1.3 in the 1920s, '30s, and '40s. During the 1950s, as television began to enter nearly every household, newspaper circulation began to decline.

Movie attendance increased during the 1920s, fluctuated during the Depression, when admissions dropped by more than 30 percent between 1930 and 1932, then began a steady increase when the late 1930s ushered in the golden age of the movies. But, "clearly, the rapid rise of television, beginning at the end of the 1940s and continuing through the next decade, had the deepest possible impact on the mass attendance of the motion picture."[30]

Melvin DeFleur's model of the mass media as a social system (see Figure 3.4) illustrates the interrelationships of all forms of media and society. The Robinson diagram (see Figure 3.3) provides a simplified version of DeFleur's diagram to show the arts participation system in the twentieth-century United States. Both Robinson and DeFleur stressed the importance of economics in maintaining the stability of the system. Changes in the flow of money cause corresponding changes in the entire system.

A key component the DeFleur diagram, however, has relevance to the discussion of arts participation: DeFleur indicated the "taste-differentiation" of the audience.[31] This concept of taste differentiation has become an important aspect for marketing almost every product in twentieth-century United States society. A variety of research systems have emerged to measure the values and attributes of consumers to increase sales of items as diverse as laundry detergent, breakfast cereal, and even the performing arts.

At the forefront of this research was the Values and Lifestyles (VALS) program of SRI International in Menlo Park, California. VALS and similar systems based on audience "taste" explain the dynamics of the audience portion of the systems diagrams in this chapter and provide a useful tool for predicting audience participation.

Originated by social scientist Arnold Mitchell, who began with the needs theory of Abraham Maslow, the VALS system provides a profile of nine different lifestyles. Figure 3.5 describes the hierarchy of these lifestyles and indicates the percentage of the United States population estimated to comprise each style.

A 1984 study by the Association of College, University, and Community Arts Administrators (ACUCAA)[32] focused on attendance at, and preference for, live professional performing arts (music, theatre, and dance) of the most affluent and generally sophisticated 40 percent of Americans. Four segments of the VALS program (Achievers, Experientials, Societally Conscious, and Integrateds), comprising 66 million adults, were analyzed. Some of the basic demographic results follow:

Women dominate attendance levels (two to one in the case of theatre).

Attenders are less likely to be married than single, divorced, or separated.

Musicgoers are the youngest; theatregoers the oldest.

Many more frequent theatregoers, as opposed to music- or dancegoers, consider themselves as upper or upper middle class.

More than half of the frequent theatregoers have household incomes exceeding $35,000, as opposed to 43 percent of frequent concertgoers and 32 percent of dancegoers.

In his overall summary, Mitchell noted that the data shows theatregoers as "markedly the most upscale, mature, and conservative of the three attendance groups." They appear to be the strong Achievers. Musicgoers are much younger and more liberal (Experien-

Figure 3.5

Value and Lifestyle Segments (VALS)

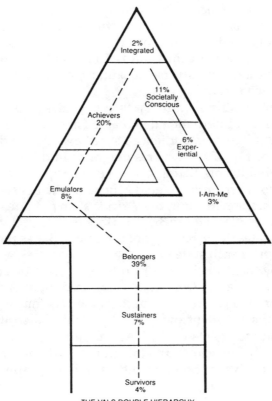

THE VALS DOUBLE HIERARCHY
OF PSYCHOLOGICAL MATURITY

INTEGRATED: Psychologically mature, large field of vision, tolerant, understanding, sense of fittingness.

SOCIETALLY CONSCIOUS: Mission-oriented, leaders of single-issue groups, mature, successful, some live lives of voluntary simplicity.

ACHIEVERS: Middle-aged, prosperous, able, leaders, self-assured, materialistic, builders of the " American dream."

EXPERIENTIAL: Youthful, seek, direct experience, person-centered, artistic, intensely oriented toward inner growth.

EMULATORS: Youthful, ambitious, macho, show-off, trying to break into the system.

I-AM-ME: Transition state, exhibitionistic, narcissistic, very young, impulsive, dramatic, experimental, active, inventive.

BELONGERS: Aging, traditional, conventional, contented, intensely patriotic, sentimental, deeply stable.

SUSTAINERS: Living on the edge of poverty, angry, resentful, street-wise, involved in the underground economy.

SURVIVORS:
Old, intensely poor, tearful, depressed, despairing, far removed from the cultural main-stream, misfits.

tials and Societally Conscious), while dance patrons are "downscale" relative to the other two forms, but they are "strongly upwardly mobile." A similar arts audience analysis based on "taste" has been described by Linda Fritschner and Miles Hoffman as the "consumer attribute hypothesis." They noted that taste, needs, or preferences may be the primary factor determining consumption, rather than education, occupation, or income.[33]

The VALS system and other audience analysis systems are also excellent examples of the emerging science of socioeconomics, which blends elements of psychology and political science with sociology and economics. Mainstream economics views people as "two-legged calculators—efficient, cold-blooded on their own," while socioeconomics "assumes people to be muddle-headed and internally conflicted, part selfish but part caring and morally dedicated, often—but not always—moving in herds."[34]

The above discussion of arts attendance as it relates to the VALS system is based on an elitist definition of the arts, which has permeated audience research since the landmark study by Baumol and Bowen in 1966.[35] This definition considers a limited number of activities to be in the realm of art. Baumol and Bowen, for example, limited their study to "professional performing arts" (live performances of music, opera, dance, and theatre).

Through extensive survey research, Baumol and Bowen concluded that the audience for the professional performing arts in the 1960s was quite unlike the general population of the United States. Arts audiences encompassed a small and elite segment of the general population. They were older, exceptionally well educated, and wealthier—an elite market.

Some studies since Baumol and Bowen, however, have indicated that arts participation has increased and that some audiences are now more representative of the general population, but, according to arts and economics researcher David Cwi, this is principally due to the fact that society has changed:

> Our research suggests that the growth in the arts is due principally to an expansion of the audience tree and the addition of some new professional branches and not due to an expansion of the reach of the "arts" as they are defined by Baumol, Bowen, and others. The historic sociological base has grown and now encompasses a larger share of the population.[36]

Herbert Gans also has noted a changing America: the long-term transformation of the U.S. economy, more people having more money and more leisure time, a rise in schooling, an increase in social mobility, and the declining power of high culture.[37]

But Cwi has suggested that society should change the definition of "art" so that it encompasses a wider range of activities, encompassing all those that people report when asked if they participate in the arts. A new definition, including not only the fine and performing arts, but also the media arts (radio, television, film), as well as some folk arts (fabric art, folk dancing, storytelling, and so on) would ensure a more democratic arts policy. United States society has begun to change its definition of the arts (see Chapter 4); this new definition could be a reflection of the increasing value of arts participation in our society.

THE CYCLES OF PARTICIPATION

The history of arts participation can be viewed as a pattern of cycles. That is, similar to the cycles of history Schlesinger described. When art is defined as an integral part of society and important for all classes, participation is high; when art becomes closely identified with the upper class and is defined as an elitist activity, mass participation is low. As the definition of art changes, participation across classes is modified accordingly.

Schlesinger would call these cycles periods of public purpose vs. private interest. Bursts of public activity and idealism are followed by the need to rest. Focusing on the United States in the twentieth century, he would see the opening decades of World War I and the Progressive movement as a time of public action, followed by the private interest period of the 1920s. With President Franklin D. Roosevelt, the New Deal, and World War II, the pendulum swung back to public interest. The Eisenhower presidency of the 1950s brought another cycle of private interest followed by another public commitment characterized by the Great Society programs in the 1960s. Each period of public interest had a "detonating issue."[38] In the 1930s the issue was the Depression, while in the 1960s it was racial justice and the Vietnam War.

Because the public sphere exhausts, people turn to private interests, and the explosion of individualism, first noticed in the United States by Tocqueville, when left unchecked, becomes a threat to democracy. In Schlesinger's view, the 1980s were an era of "enormous potentialities for disintegration in contemporary America—the widening disparities in income and opportunity; . . . the multiplication of the poor and underclass; . . . the deterioration of education."[39] He stressed that neither public purpose nor private interest will solve all of these problems, but because democratic values are more deeply rooted in the United States than capitalistic values, the public purpose may once again prevail.

Public purpose/private interest cycles are also reflected in American society's changing definition of art and the value it places on participation. Until the beginning of the Depression, art in the United States was defined as an activity of the wealthy and was supported by private patrons. With the "detonating issue" of the Depression came the first massive government arts programs of the 1930s (see Chapter 8) in the public interest. These programs disappeared during the next two decades of private interest, but government involvement—following public interest—reappeared again with the establishment of the National Endowment for the Arts in 1965.

Three key points should be highlighted from the discussion in this chapter:

The number of people participating in the arts depends on the particular society's definition of art and the value it places on art.

Opportunities to participate by all classes increase with the democratization of society and/or a change in the definition of art.

Economics has a key role in all societies to make the system function.

Regardless of society's definition of art, the value it places on art, or the number of persons involved in the arts, Pateman would say that given the appropriate environment, those who do become involved will reinforce their participatory skills. Participation itself changes the character of the participants, which, in turn, changes society.

The following chapters use the theory of participatory democracy as outlined in this chapter and the description of arts participation as provided in the next chapter to build a theory of arts participation to establish a model to use in the descriptions of three specific historical periods: Athens of fifth-century B.C., the United States during the Jacksonian era, and the late twentieth-century United States.

Notes

1. Talcott Parsons, *The Social System* (Glencoe, IL: The Free Press, 1951), p. 3.

2. Ibid., pp. 5–6.

3. Arthur M. Schlesinger, Jr., *The Cycles of American History* (Boston: Houghton Mifflin Company, 1986), p. 27.

4. Arnold Hauser, *The Social History of Art* (London: Routledge & Kegan Paul, 1951), p. 42.

5. Remi Clignet, *The Structure of Artistic Revolutions* (Philadelphia: University of Pennsylvania Press, 1985), p. 92.

6. Francis Fergusson, Introduction, *Aristotle's Poetics*, pp. 34–35.

7. Ibid., p. 118.

8. In *Social Science and the Arts* (John P. Robinson, ed. [Lanham, MD: University Press of America, 1985], p. 104), Robinson noted that systems diagrams are extremely useful in portraying social institutions and the actors involved: "A systems diagram is intended to be totally descriptive and value-free. It does not distinguish dependent and independent variables. That means that it can be compatible with a variety of theoretical approaches and assumptions, perhaps even those that appear totally contradictory to one another. The value of systems diagrams is that they can act as a road map to identify how organizations and actors fit into an overall art world . . . .Any change in the system will probably activate all actors in the system to take adaptive action to protect or expand their own turf in the process."

9. Vera L. Zolberg, "Changing Patterns of Patronage in the Arts," *Performers and Performances: The Social Organization of Artistic Work*, Jack B. Kamerman and Rosanne Martorella, ed. (New York: Praeger, 1983), p. 251.

10. Robinson, p. 107. Robinson's chart is, in turn, based on Melvin DeFleur's representation of the mass media as a social system. (See page 40.)

11. Hauser, *The Social History of Art*, p. 97.

12. Ibid.

13. John Dewey, *Art as Experience* (New York: G. P. Putnam's Sons, 1934), p. 329.

14. Jack B. Kamerman and Rosanne Martorella, *Performers and Performances: The Social Organization of Artistic Work* (New York: Praeger, 1983), p. 25. Kamerman and Martorella characterized the historical pattern of patronage as moving from church to secular aristocrats and their courts, to the emerging national states, and finally, to the bourgeoisie (ticket purchasers, private patrons, universities, and local, state, and national arts agencies).

15. Hauser, *The Social History of Art*, p. 311.

16. Ibid., p. 413.

17. Ibid., p. 950.

18. Kamerman and Martorella, *Performers and Performances*, p. 26.

19. Alexis de Tocqueville, *Democracy in America*, Richard D. Heffner, ed. (New York: New American Library, 1956), p. 172.

20. Ibid.

21. Ibid., p. 179.

22. Ibid.

23. Ibid., p. 174.

24. Barbara Tuchman, lecture, "The Book," sponsored by the Center for the Book (Washington, D.C.: Library of Congress, 1980), p. 24.

25. Russell Lynes, *The Lively Audience: A Social History of the Visual and Performing Arts in America, 1890–1950* (New York: Harper & Row, Pub., 1985), p. 20.

26. Russell Lynes, *The Emerging Audience* (New York: Harper & Row, 1985), p. 20.

27. Edward C. Banfield, *The Democratic Muse* (New York: Basic Books, 1984), p. 27. Will Morrisey ("Culture in the Commercial Republic," *Book Forum: Culture and Money*, Vol. VI, No. 1, p. 124) has compared the democratic ideas of Walt Whitman with those of John Dewey: "Bureaucratize Whitman and you have John Dewey."

28. Lynes, *The Lively Audience*, p. 27.

29. Ibid., p. 7.

30. Melvin L. DeFleur and Sandra J. Ball-Rokeach, *Theories of Mass Communication* (New York: Longman, 1982), p. 62.

31. Herbert Gans also said that a similar designation of the audience into "cultural strata" is more accurate than an "elite vs. popular culture" (Herbert Gans, "American Popular Culture and High Culture in a Changing Class Structure," *Arts, Ideology, and Politics*, Margaret Jane Wyszomirski and Judith H. Balfe, ed. [New York; Praeger, 1985], p. 40).

32. Arnold Mitchell, *The Professional Performing Arts: Attendance Patterns, Preferences, and Motives* (Madison, WI: ACUCCA, 1984).

33. Linda Fritchner and Miles Hoffman, "The Community and the Local Arts Center," *Art, Ideology, and Politics*, Margaret Wyzomirski and Judith H. Bolfe, ed. (New York: Praeger, 1985), p. 104.

34. Amitai Etzioni, "Socio-Economics," *Washington Post*, January 1, 1987, p. C3.

35. William J. Baumol and William G. Bowen, *Performing Arts: The Economic Dilemma* (New York: The Twentieth Century Fund, 1966).

36. David Cwi, "Changes in the U.S. Audience for the Arts," proceedings from the Fourth Annual Conference on Cultural Economics and Planning, Avignon, France, 1987, p. 32.

37. Gans, "American Popular Culture and High Culture in a Changing Class Structure," pp. 46–49.

38. Schlesinger, *The Cycles of American History*, p. 33.

39. Ibid., p. 46.

4

Participatory Democracy and the Arts

A key concept of this study is that participatory democracy is enhanced by creating participatory experiences for individuals in as many spheres of society as possible. This chapter looks at the sphere of the arts through the lens of participation to see how artistic activities can help develop both the individual's feelings of personal effectiveness and self-confidence in everyday interactions, as well as specific skills transferable to participation in the political arena.

Before looking at specific participatory activities and discussing how to increase them, a major concern of all participatory theories should be discussed. That is the question of stability. Pateman has asserted that stability presents no problem in her theory; through the educative impact of the participatory process the system is self-sustaining and stability is not threatened. The stability question has also been raised in connection with cultural activities and usually falls under the "elite theory of art" that assumes "popular art" belongs to the masses who, given the chance, dilute and destroy "high art," which only the elite can understand and appreciate.

Political scientists today are showing greater interest in this comparison of cultural and political theories. In a paper presented to the 1984 Annual Meeting of the American Political Science Association in Washington, DC, W. D. Kay noted:

Even a superficial comparison between the democratic theory literature and that of popular culture reveals that the two have much in common: the arguments employed in empirical or elitist democratic theory are identical to those used to justify elitism in art, while the optimism expressed in the participatory democratic theory literature is echoed by those who would see participation in the arts enhanced.[1]

Kay outlined the elite theory of democracy, which claims that most people are apathetic and do not wish to learn the skills required to participate more fully in the political system: "The widespread popularity of this mass culture is proof for many that the public is unwilling to accept the challenges of high art, preferring instead the less 'strenuous' versions."[2]

In "A Critique of the Elitist Theory of Democracy," Jack L. Walker described society in terms of the "elite" and the "citizens at large." According to Walker, the elite possess the commitment and skill to make the direct political decisions and require "enough" people to participate so that they may compete for the support of large and cross sections of the population. However, Walker warned: "If the uninformed masses participate in large numbers, democratic self-restraint will break down and peaceful competition among the elites, the central element in the elitist theory, will become impossible."[3]

Peter Bachrach's explanation of the elite theory is consistent with Walker's. Bachrach stated that all elite theories consider the masses "at best pliable, inert stuff or at worst aroused, unruly creatures."[4] Bachrach and Walker have both noted that elite theories are formulated in an attempt to bring democratic theory closer to empirical reality and, in the process, have changed the goal of democracy from broad participation to stability and efficiency. Providing an alternative outlook, Bachrach has stressed that the theory of democracy should be based on the assumption that the majority of individuals gain in self-esteem by participation in meaningful community decisions. The opponents of elitism in art believe the same is true for participation in cultural activities.

Margaret Wyszomirski has provided a more detailed comparison of various "participatory behavior." She compared various forms of political participation with attendance at various cultural activities:

The most "passive" forms of voting and arts consumption (voting in presidential elections and reading literature/broadcast cultural programming) occur in virtually equal proportions: approximately 55 percent voting turnout vs. 56 percent literature and 58 percent cultural programming. At the next level, voting in state/local, off-year elections vs. attendance at any art event/museums at least once during a year, the figures are approximately 44 percent vs. 39 percent. Finally, at the level of high participation, personal involvement (e.g., contribute money, run for office, etc.) or primary turnout vs. attendance at "high" arts events (opera, symphony, theatre, dance, museums), the figures are 2–10 percent/25 percent for political activity while "high" arts activity ranges from 3 percent (opera) to 23 percent (museums). In other words, the arts are no more elitist than is political participation.[5]

Another aspect of participation relevant to both polictics and the arts involves acceptance of collective decisions. An important hypothesis of Pateman's theory is that through participation, whether by discussion or voting, individuals are more willing to accept and support group decisions. Continued practice in the decision making process builds skills transferable from one sphere to another: "There is evidence that the impact of nonpolitical decision making—at home, school, and job—is cumulative."[6]

The concept of decision making in the arts ranges from the freedom to choose a specific art form in which to participate, thereby reinforcing the psychological feeling of self-confidence, to actual voting as a board member of a cultural organization or contributing money as part of the complex decision making chain involving tax policy. (This ultimate means of decision making has been carefully analyzed in *Patrons Despite Themselves: Taxpayers and Arts Policy* by Feld and is discussed in Chapter 8.)

In extending Pateman's theory to the arts, a few limitations must be noted. In most discussions of political theory the concept of the "citizen" is generally clarified—not so in studies relating to the arts. Participation in our democratic political system, by definition, is open to virtually any adult born in this country or qualified by naturalization. These are the citizens profiled in the various political studies mentioned in this book. All other cultural studies, surveys, and other similar research involve adults without reference to their citizenship status. Since children are not eligible for active political participation, emphasis has been on adults, although the importance of arts education for children has been noted, too.

In the various studies, both political and cultural, parallels with other demographic data have been noted. For example, amount of education tends to be positively correlated with increased participation in the arts and with increased sensitivity to democratic principles. In their study of people's attitudes toward democratic principles (majority rule, minority rights, etc.), James Prothro and Charles Grigg found that neither age, sex, nor party affiliation caused much variance in attitudes. Attitudes did vary somewhat with education, community, and income; however, the greatest difference on every statement was between high and low education.[7] Similarly, a 1977 study, produced for the National Endowment for the Arts, analyzed 270 audience studies completed after 1970 and clearly indicated: "Educational attainment is the single most important variable in the social profile of attenders."[8]

In *Democracy in the U.S.: Promise and Performance*, Dahl noted that participation levels vary with socioeconomic status. Fifty-seven percent of the individuals in the highest category of political participation were from the upper status group, while 59 percent of individuals in the lowest category of political participation were from the low status group.[9] Dahl also noted that the effect social and economic status has on political participation is greater in the United States than in other democracies.

PARTICIPATION IN THE ARTS

A basic hypothesis of this study is that participation in the arts helps individuals become, as Pateman has described, "educated, public citizens" and hones their participatory skills. Arts participation can be classified as either "active" or "passive," ranging from the artist whose entire life is his art to the individual who merely happens upon a cultural program while turning the dial of the television set. (See Figure 4.1 for a depiction of the wide range of these activities.) Obviously, these activities could be listed on a continuum from more active to less active (that is, patrons are not entirely "passive" participants, as Figure 4.1 indicates); however, the purpose is not to catalog all behaviors, but to provide an overview.

Active Participation: The Individual

Again, Figure 4.1 shows active participation in the arts may take one of many forms, ranging from total involvement as an artist—amateur or professional—to the lesser involvement of persons serving as board members of arts organizations. All individuals can participate with varying degrees of decision-making power. In general, the more renowned the professional artist, the more decision-making power he can exert within his chosen art. (Japan's designation of certain artists as "National Treasures" is a prominent example. In many cases, however, an artist is not recognized in such a way until after his death.)

Another area of participation open to prominent artists is that of simply attracting attention to a political cause or candidate. Hardly a week goes by when a major artist is not testifying before a congressional committee or making an appearance at a fundraiser. The Congressional Arts Caucus, an advocacy organization within Congress, has been particularly adept at bringing artists to Capitol Hill to focus attention on various arts issues. (See Chapter 8.)

Figure 4.1

Participation in the Arts

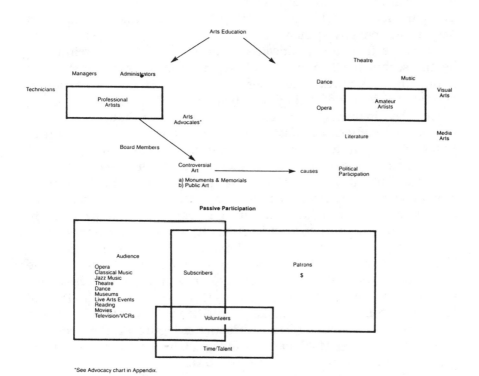

*See Advocacy chart in Appendix.

Although an autocratic director, for example, can put great limits on a theatrical production, the other creative artists potentially can exercise their decision making within the realm of their arts (for example, lighting design, set design, and so on). Amateurs, of course, have a large amount of decision-making power simply by choosing their arts activities and having no restrictions on their creativity. That an artist—whether amateur or professional—knows he has decision-making power contributes to his self-esteem, thereby reinforcing the psychological foundations needed for a participatory society.

Although this study focuses on participatory behavior of adults, a brief discussion of the children's arts participation would be instructive at this point. Figure 4.1 indicates that most amateur and professional artists have had, as children, an arts education background. Whether natural talent or rigorous education or a combination of the rigorous education or a combination of the two directs a child to become a professional artist will not be discussed here; however, several parallels between arts education and political education will be examined.

As noted in Chapter 2, children are taught to like government even before they know what it is. Their first concept is of the president, and learning gradually expands to include more complex political ideas.[10] The participatory behavior of voting is stressed, and the idea of a benign national government permeates the educational system. More extensive participatory political skills, however, may not be reinforced by the school itself or by the children's family environments. As adults, the only participatory behavior evident in a large portion of U.S. citizens is that of voting in a presidential election.

The scenario involving arts education is similar, although even more negative in many cases. Most schools have some form of arts education beginning in the early grades. As in the case of gaining political knowledge, children are taught to like the arts before they know what they are, but all too often the arts are not intertwined with the remainder of the curriculum: they do not permeate the curriculum as does the concept of a benign national government; and arts education is not rigorously structured to gradually teach more complex concepts. Clearly, this is not entirely the fault of arts educators, but is a symptom of the educational priorities of our society, which, on the whole, has given the arts a low priority. For example, many Americans still do not agree with proponents of the Suzuki method, with its goal "not to teach music, but to make good citizens," as noted during the July 5, 1981, CBS *Sunday Morning* broadcast. Figure 4.2, derived from a 1984 study called *Music and Music Education: Data and Information*, gives statistical evidence of these attitudes.[11]

In 1977, a landmark study analyzing arts education was published: *Coming to Our Senses: The Significance of the Arts for American Education* was the culmination of research by a distinguished panel of arts education experts, chaired by David Rockefeller, Jr. The panel affirmed the importance of the arts to a complete education:

> The arts are a function of life itself, and the process of making art—both creative and recreative—can give insight to all other areas of learning. The arts help people understand themselves in historical, cultural, and aesthetic terms; they provide people with broader choices about their environment and influence the way they do their work and live their lives. Since artistic expression is also truly basic to the individual's intellectual development, it must be included as a component of all education.[12]

The panel then outlined fifteen recommendations based on the following three principles:

Figure 4.2

U.S. Student Ratings of Course Importance
(grades 7-12, 1983)

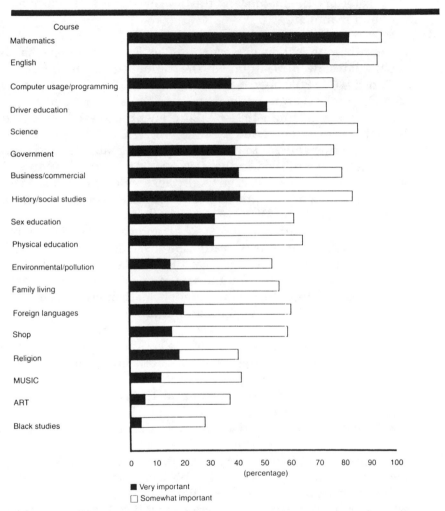

Source: Music and Music Education: *Data and Information* (Washington, D.C.: Music Educators National Conference, 1984), p. 63.

(1) The fundamental goals of American education can be realized only when the arts become central to the individual's learning experience, in or out of school and at every stage of life.
(2) Educators at all levels must adopt the arts as a basic component of the curriculum deserving parity with all other elements.
(3) School programs in the arts should draw heavily upon all available resources in the community: the artists, the materials, the media, and the total environment—both natural and manmade.

Since the publication of *Coming to Our Senses*, progress has been positive but slow. A 1984 study by the National Council for Educational Statistics (NCES) showed that from 1972 to 1973, 74 percent of U.S. secondary schools offered instruction in the arts; the percentage increased to 90 percent in 1981–82. Enrollment increased from 18 to 24 percent during that period of time, yet while "the percentage of schools offering courses in music increased, the number and percentage of students enrolled in these courses declined."[13] Another 1984 study by NCES stated: "It is generally acknowledged that students in the secondary schools of the United States are exposed to very little instruction in the arts."[14]

With the release of *A Nation At Risk*[15] and the subsequent renewed interest in education, arts educators enthusiastically joined the public debate. Backed by the College Board Report called *Academic Preparation for College*,[16] which listed the arts as one of the six basic areas of required study (the others being English, mathematics, science, social studies, and foreign language), arts education advocates began to state their case to local school boards, state departments of education, and even the U.S. Congress. In 1984, a congressional resolution was passed to recognize the importance of the arts to a complete education. Although it did not appropriate any money or establish a program, the resolution was a positive signal from the national government. At the same time, the chairman of the National Endowment for the Arts, Frank Hodsoll, announced major arts education initiatives for his agency.

The private sector also began to take interest. In 1984, the Getty Center for Education in the Arts published *Beyond Creating: The Place for Art in America's Schools*. This report profiled seven school districts with exceptional visual arts programs and listed three critical factors in changing art education:

(1) A Change in Perspective: the need to alter the assumptions about the value of art, its place in the curriculum, and how it should be taught.

(2) Advocacy and Support: the need for politically skilled advocates to gain community support to develop and maintain successful programs.
(3) Academic Rigor: the need for art programs to be conceived and maintained just as other academic subjects are.[17] Of particular note is this study's mention of "politically skilled advocates."

Although it is a latecomer to the world of advocacy, the arts education community has the potential to learn quickly the participatory skills so effective in politics; most importantly, it has begun to take the need for political participation seriously. (See discussion of advocacy groups below.) Yet even by the late 1980s, enhancing arts education was still quite difficult. For example, in 1989, only one-third of New York City's 600 elementary schools had arts programs.[18]

The 1987 survey *Americans and the Arts* noted that "a majority of American adults (55 percent) believe that school children have not had enough exposure to the arts."[19] Furthermore, the 1988 report *Toward Civilization* from the National Endowment for the Arts indicated that because cultural education is not viewed as serious and because schools cannot agree on appropriate curricula, the arts themselves are in jeopardy. Similarly, a 1988 survey from Ohio State University (OSU) indicated that 80 percent of adult citizens in Ohio agreed there should be more emphasis on the arts in public schools.[20]

Of course, arts education can be reinforced or expanded at home or in private study, and professional artists may emerge. But, in general, adult participation—at least as attendees of arts events—seems to be related to early arts education. In fact, the OSU survey found a direct correlation between school arts participation and later attendance at arts events.

Although arts education for the creation of future audiences could be much improved, opportunities for active participation in an art form are available for many children outside school. This is one of the areas in which arts participation helps reinforce a participatory society by building the self-esteem of its citizens. From community musical and theatrical groups to the private dance studios and figure skating arenas, many children have the opportunity for creative expression. Ironically, the overlying authority structure of learning an artistic skill often must initially be autocratic—at least until the child assumes the self-discipline required. Clearly, the essence of art seems to be the democracy of free creative expression within the rigorous autocracy of perfecting the skill. Wilson Carey McWilliams connects this thought directly with democracy: "In common with democracy, art teaches that the pain of self-rule is preferable to the comfort of being ruled by others."[21]

Many adults must decide whether to continue the life of a professional artist or merely to dabble in an art form and move on to the most passive forms of participation, which are discussed later in this chapter. The choice of becoming a professional artist encompasses participation as a single creative individual or as part of collaborative efforts in the performing arts. In general, the individual writer, musician, or visual artist has virtually total control over the initial creation of his art, except when guidelines are dictated by a patron. Having total control and working alone a large portion of the time, the artist may develop the tendency to withdraw from society and shun participation in other spheres. Some artists, however, participate to a greater degree than the average citizen, particularly if a public issue develops around a particular work of art. (See discussion on public art below.)

Performing artists, on the other hand, must learn to subjugate their creative decisions and cooperate with the choices of a director or conductor. Robert R. Faulkner has studied the sociological organization of orchestras and noted: "This special world of concerted action that emerges between performances and conductors reveals many problematic features relevant to the sociological study of authority."[22] Faulkner described conductors not by their musical communication, but by the varying roles they play in organizational communication: the orchestra can be seen as a social system where members exercise varying degrees of decision-making, depending on the conductor's style. A musically competent conductor, who is also adept at organizational communication, can bring forth the best individual and collective musical decisions and create a positive participatory atmosphere.

In a professional artist's world are numerous support personnel, including designers, administrators, and board members. As already discussed, decision-making power can vary and, as in the case of other industries, can cause varying degrees of discontent, leading to the formation of trade unions. Clearly, participatory skills are reinforced in labor unions, and many political scientists agree with the general proposition: "Trade unions help sustain political democracy in the larger body politic."[23]

The numerous artists' unions that have multiplied over the past quarter century provide one of the most outstanding arenas in the arts for acquiring participatory skills. From Ronald Reagan, who obviously learned much as president of the Screen Actors Guild before winning the U.S. presidency, to the numerous artists rapidly taking part in grassroots political activity, the artistic community is becoming much more sophisticated politically.[24]

The boards governing most nonprofit arts institutions also provide a setting for exercising participatory skills. Although generally more politically active than the majority of the population, board members often add arts advocacy to their agendas. Panels of witnesses who testify at local, state, or national levels often include influential board members of prominent arts institutions.

The types of individuals mentioned thus far often find their roles overlapping. When this occurs, both decision-making power and participation increase. For example, artists are now being included as board members of a wide range of arts institutions, while some cultural organizations are completely run by artists. These groups have formed an advocacy organization for themselves known as the National Association of Artists Organizations (NAAO), one of the younger arts advocacy organizations. Although small, this group is quite active politically and is beginning to generate grass-roots activity. (See Figure 4.3 for an example of advocacy material prepared by NAAO.)

A brief overview of the older advocacy groups shows an interesting participatory trend. All of the advocacy organizations discussed in this section, with the exception of the American Arts Alliance (AAA), are classified by the Internal Revenue Service as nonprofit, tax-exempt educational organizations under IRS Code Sec. 501(c)(3). This classification benefits each organization by providing tax-exempt status and by encouraging individuals to voluntarily contribute money to the organization. These individuals can then claim a charitable contributions deduction on their tax returns. However, 501(c)(3) organizations, because of their favorable tax treatment, are then restricted on the amount of so-called "lobbying" they can do. (See Appendix A for a chart illustrating the roles of these organizations.)

The longer a particular arts discipline has been honing the participatory skills of its members, the more active it becomes politically. (See Chapter 8.) America's museum community was the first in the arts to establish an information clearinghouse (in this case, to serve all kinds of museums) and eventual advocate at the national level. The American Association of Museums (AAM) was formed in 1906, and today it has approximately 10,000 members (2,000 institutions and 8,000 individuals), which form a national network capable of substantial grassroots political activity. Since the establishment of the National Endowments for the Arts and Humanities (NEA and NEH) in 1965, AAM has been a major participant in the national arts lobby, which testifies annually on behalf of these federal agencies. In addition, as the arts lobby has become more sophisticated, AAM has been able to broaden its advocacy to include tax changes, copyright concerns, and other legislative issues affecting specific segments of its members. AAM is instrumental in arranging for prominent museum directors, board members, scientists, and professors to testify before congres-

Figure 4.3

NAAO Action Memo

RE: March 6, 1986
President's proposed cuts to cultural
funding 000 postal subsidies elimination
Write NOW......Write NOW....Write NOW...

National
Association
of Artists'
Organizations

There's trouble ahead if we do not start writing to Congress now. Why?

- the President's proposed budget for cultural institutions
  - elimination of IMS (and Historic Preservation Fund)
  - decrease in NEA and NEH budgets
  - Increase in Smithsonian and National Galery budgets
- Elimination of postal subsidies for non-profits

Yes, we have an enormous Federal deficit that must be addressed. But, if cuts are to be
made they must be made by Congress in a fair and educated manner. Congress will
probably reject the President's budget ontheir own but they still need to know where
artists' organizations stand while they formulate their own budgets. The increase in
budget for the Sminthsonian and National Gallery must not carry over to our detriment
into their budgets. Both are extremely waelthy and pleasing to the funder's eye.

Figures follow giving an overview of recent cultural budget history.

	FY '86 Approp.	FY '86 level under G-R-H *	FY '87 Pres. proposal
National Endowment for the Arts **	165.661	158.538	144.900
National Endowment for the Humanities	138.641	132.679	126.440
Insitute of Museum Services	21.394	20.474	.330
Historic Preservation Fund	24.795	23.729	-0-
Smithsonian	199.983	191.384	215.240
National Gallery of Art	36.831	35.247	37.007

* G-R-H is for Gramm-Rudman-Hollings first phase of cuts. We haven't discussed G-R-H
  here because of the possibility it may either be found entirely or partly unconstitutional
  by the Supreme Court. More about that later.

** Also its important to bear in mind that NEA is operating until FY 88 under
   Congressionally imposed funding levels. So, unless something very radical were to happen,
   no matter what, NEA's funding level can not be raised above:
   For FY 87.......... FY 86 + 4%

   For FY 88.......... FY 87 + 4%

   As you can see, without Gramm-Rudman-Hollings, without the Federal deficit crisis, we

   are already working under severe budget restrictions.

Write now and write alot. Certainly you can find time, or a volunteer, or a staff member
to put out letters to your legislators.

Here are some suggestions:

For NEA and IMS funding tell them specifically:
- about one of your IMS or NEA funded projects
- the number of people from theirstate and/or community that benefited
- make it clear every penny counts - tell them how much you do with how little
  you have...try to find an incisive comparison for this.
- site positive effects NEA funding has on receiving additional funding

sional committees, to visit or call members of Congress directly on specific legislation, or to have the entire AAM membership write letters as part of an overall grassroots political effort.

Professional symphony orchestras in the United States also formed a service organization, called the American Symphony Orchestra League (ASOL), to serve as an information clearinghouse and arts advocate for its members. Similarly, OPERA America represents professional opera companies, while the Theatre Communications Group (TCG) serves the needs of the several hundred regional theatres across the country.

The American Council for the Arts (ACA), representing all aspects of the arts, including artists, institutions, and arts supporters, accomplishes its advocacy function mainly through education. ACA publishes numerous arts-related materials, hosts a variety of seminars, and maintains a paid lobbyist in Washington, DC.

With the growth and creation of the state arts agencies, following the establishment of the NEA in 1965, came the formation of the National Assembly of State Arts Agencies (NASAA), which was incorporated in 1974 as a service organization for the 56 state and jurisdictional agencies. As part of its advocacy network, NASAA presents testimony to Congress during the appropriations hearings for NEA and provides other necessary information. And, in 1978, the National Assembly of Community Arts Agencies was born. Now called the National Assembly of Local Arts Agencies (NALAA), this organization, like its older sister NASAA, gives testimony at appropriations hearings and monitors other legislative issues for its members.

Because of the various regulations preventing the aforementioned organizations from extensive lobbying and in order to speak with a more unified voice, representatives from these so-called "service organizations" established yet another arts advocacy organization. In 1977, with the establishment of the American Arts Alliance (AAA),[25] active lobbying efforts were initiated. The only legally sanctioned national arts lobby in the United States, the AAA is a coalition of nonprofit, professional performing and exhibiting arts institutions representing dance, opera and theatre companies, symphony orchestras, and art museums. Unlike the other advocacy groups, AAA is not classified as a "501(c)(3)" organization (that is, money contributed to AAA cannot be deducted by the contributor on his tax return) and therefore is able to actively engage in lobbying activities. The organization's objectives upon formation were: (1) to establish in Washington, DC, a fully professional legislative monitoring, analysis, and lobbying office; (2) to become involved with federal agencies and their arts programs and regulations; (3) to begin a public action network, and (4) to create a strong coalition for the arts.

AAA's initial lobbying efforts centered around the annual appropriations process for the NEA, NEH, and the museum agency established in 1976, the Institute of Museum Services (IMS). As the organization grew, other issues were added: tax changes, the postal subsidy for reduced-rate mailing for nonprofit organizations, copyright regulations, and a variety of miscellaneous legislation.

Often, however, the position of the AAA on certain issues conflicts with that of other advocacy groups. AAA speaks for the nation's professional arts *institutions*, whose agendas may differ somewhat from the agendas of individual artists, the state and local arts agencies, or the smaller community cultural organizations. Despite the differences, arts advocates have shown a surprising degree of unity, particularly during the appropriations process. When asking for a "larger pie" for the federal cultural agencies, they have become quite convincing as the discussion below illustrates.

A major reason for this unity in the arts advocacy network was the release of President Reagan's first budget in 1980, which proposed to cut funding for NEA and NEH by 50 percent and to eliminate IMS. The grassroots lobbying campaign during the first few months following news of the budget indicated that arts supporters had learned effective participatory political skills. In addition, this occured when a unique arts advocacy group was forming within Congress. Organized informally at the end of 1980, the Congressional Arts Caucus became an official Legislative Service Organization of the U.S. House of Representatives and, in conjunction with the intense advocacy for maintaining strong federal arts and humanities programs, grew to be one of the largest caucuses on Capitol Hill.

The tremendous growth in the number and activity of arts advocacy groups would not have occurred without a major reorientation for the arts in American society. Writing about arts advocacy for *American Arts*, an ACA publication, Joseph Wesley Zeigler attributed two factors as responsible for that reorientation: (1) the acceptance of the centrality of the arts to society; and (2) the reality of public ownership of the arts.[26] Whether or not today's society really believes that the arts are central is debatable, but the fact that public funding for the arts has increased so rapidly over the past several decades does indicate that more and more people believe that the arts belong on the public agenda. Certainly, political participation to influence the public agenda has become a legitimate activity for patrons, volunteers, and artists alike.

In short, arts supporters have "come to grips . . . with the 'care and feeding' of politicians."[27] Like other sophisticated lobbies, the arts lobby now knows that its organizations are numerous and organized, that its members are educated voters, and that in general the lobby has the support of significant people of means whom politicians should want to impress.[28] Active participation in this tangential, yet vital, arts activity most definitely lends positive reinforcement to the creation of a participatory society.

Active Participation: The Art

A second category of active participation occurs when a work of art is so controversial that artists and others are pushed into political participation. Two recent cases provide examples of two subcategories: (1) monuments and memorials; and (2) public art. Another major subcategory would be works of art that are so controversial they become candidates for censorship. A complete discussion of works in this subcategory and the political participation they cause is not included in this book.

Monuments and Memorials: The Vietnam Veterans Memorial. No other memorial in the history of our country has created more controversy than that in honor of our Vietnam veterans. An examination of the evolution of this monument from design to dedication provides an outstanding example of an artwork that generated perhaps more political participation than many wanted to see, but the entire process and final resolution helped mend a long-frayed corner of the fabric of American society.

Initiated by Vietnam veteran Jan Scruggs,[29] the Vietnam Veterans Memorial Fund, Inc., was formed in April 1979 to establish a national memorial in honor of all Americans who served in the Vietnam War. On July 1, 1980, Congress passed a resolution dedicating a two-acre site in Constitution Gardens for the memorial, to be built with private funds.

A design competition—the largest in the history of this country, with 1,420 entries—was held in 1981. The winning design, created by a twenty-one-year-old undergraduate architecture student from Yale University, began to draw criticism and created immediate repercussions. Less than two weeks after the competition, U.S. Army Colonel James Revels, the supervisor of publications for the U.S. Army's *Pentagram News*, was fired for allowing publication of a "scathing attack" on the proposed memorial.[30] A lively debate began in letters to the editors of the District of Columbia's major newspapers, and the artist, Maya Lin, found herself at the beginning of a long period during which her art would be the focus of much participatory behavior, ranging from mild public discussions to intense public demonstrations.

The minimal design of Lin's art (see Figure 4.4)—a V-shaped, polished black granite wedge, ten feet high at the center with 200–foot sides gradually receding to ground level and engraved with the names of the nearly 58,000 Americans who died in the war—was called "a direct evocation of an emotional experience, which, one way or another, is what art is all about."[31] In the design description of her entry, Lin wrote: "Walking into the grassy site, we can barely make out the carved names upon the memorial wall. The names, seemingly infinite in number, convey the sense of overwhelming numbers, while unifying the individual with the whole."[32]

By 1982, Lin's design had been approved by the Commission of Fine Arts, a committee of seven members selected by the president, which was formed in 1910 to advise the federal government on all architectural developments undertaken in Washington, DC. Her design had also been praised by many art critics and had received accolades from the American Institute of Architects. And the powerful design continued to generate controversy. Then–Secretary of the Interior James Watt threatened to delay the groundbreaking until a more traditional memorial was selected, and twenty-seven Republican congressmen called the design "a political statement of shame and dishonor" in a letter to President Reagan. Texas millionaire H. Ross

Figure 4.4

Vietnam Veterans Memorial

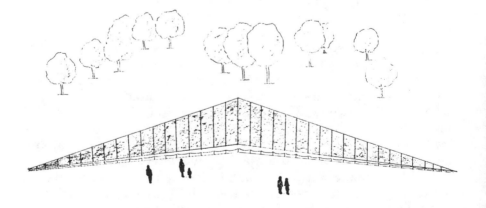

Perot called the design a "trench" and indicated that the project should be changed.[33]

Responding to the criticism, the Fine Arts Commission approved changes to the design that would allow an additional, more traditional monument to be included at the site. This change met with Watt's approval, as well as that of many congressmen. Republican Congressman Henry Hyde of Illinois noted the change in the Congressional Record:

Some wise person once suggested that politics is too important to leave to the politicians. I would presume to assert that war memorials may be too important to leave simply to artists and architects. After all, the memorial is going to speak for me and my constituents, and keep expressing a message of honor, pride, and a debt of unpayable gratitude for many, many decades to come.[34]

March 26, 1982, was the official groundbreaking for the memorial, and most protestors had been appeased with the addition of a traditional design. But placement of this second network continued to wrap people in controversy, and the original artist herself began to speak publicly. "This farce has gone on too long," stated Lin. "I have to clear my own conscience."[35] She was not consulted on the new design elements, and feared they would change the way her work would be viewed.

As a counter to Lin's comments, the second artist chosen to create the more traditional monument, Frederick Hart, noted that no one had seen his sculpture and that he had not even decided on its scale or placement. But by September 1982, Hart had unveiled his design of three Vietnam soldiers, which was approved by the Fine Arts Commission in October and hailed as a suitable "compromise"—a political solution "to the complex problem of designing a public monument or memorial that is both aesthetically satisfying and symbolically appropriate."[36]

At the nation's capital, Veterans' Day 1982 marked a week dedicated to Vietnam veterans, with ceremonies at the memorial, a parade to honor the veterans, and a candlelight vigil at the National Cathedral, where the names of the Americans killed in the war were read over three days. The week seemed to symbolize a national healing of the serious wounds left by Vietnam. But it was not until 1983, when the National Capitol Planning Commission approved final placement of Hart's statue and Watt concurred, that the controversy began to recede.

The next year, Veteran's Day 1983, Hart's statue was placed and dedicated in a grove of trees far enough away from the original monument so both could be viewed as separate works of art. Although each work attempts to communicate the complex national emotions involved in our perception of the Vietnam War, they are entirely different: aesthetically, Hart's and Lin's concepts are like oil and water. Not only do they represent the opposing stylistic poles of realism and abstraction, but they also embody dramatically different ways of dealing with the symbolism of public memorial art.[37] The two works seem to typify the extremes of the elitist/populist theory of art, the conservative juxtaposed with the liberal: "If Lin's memorial is a tribute to Jane Fonda, then Hart's is a tribute to John Wayne."[38]

But despite the two extremes, the two memorials now exist together as one symbol of our collective memory of a most turbulent period[39] in our country's history:

> So, in the end, we have a political pastiche of heroism and loss, a trio of warriors larger than life, and a list of the dead. Instead of a resolution, we have an artistic collision of ideas, an uncomfortable collage of our Vietnam legacy. Maybe, just maybe, that's fitting.[40]

Public Art: Tilted Arc. The second subcategory of art that can stir active participation is public art—art to be integrated with spaces open to the public. In the United States, many cities and states, as well as the federal government, have programs known as "percent for art." In general, from one-half of one percent to one percent of the cost of a new public building is allocated for art to be included in the design of the building.

The federal government's policy emanates from the General Services Administration (GSA) and is called the Art-in-Architecture Program. Established by the GSA as a policy in 1963,[41] the program allows one-half of one percent of the estimated cost of construction of new buildings for the incorporation of works of art. Since the program's inception, the "public art" incorporated into new buildings has met resistance on many occasions.[42] For the first fifteen years of the program, approximately 20 percent of the nearly 200 projects commissioned drew criticism.[43] But, in most cases, public dislike gradually disappeared. One particular work, which has seemed to generate more than its share of controversy, is used here as an example of public art "that has the power to provoke public controversy."[44]

In the summer of 1981, a 120–foot-long, 12–foot-high, 73–ton steel sculpture resembling a free-standing curved wall was installed at 26 Federal Plaza in New York City. (See Figure 4.5.) The monumental work of art, *Tilted Arc*, by minimalist artist Richard Serra, was commissioned under the GSA's Art-in-Architecture Program at a cost of $175,000.

Figure 4.5

The Tilted Arc

Almost immediately, the sculpture, which "does force a confrontation with the viewer,"[45] enraged groups of employees in the surrounding office buildings. Nearly one thousand federal workers signed a petition calling for its removal and stating that the sculpture casts "an ominous shadow not only on we [sic] who work here but on the public as well."[46]

The workers felt the open space of the plaza was now obstructed by a large steel wall, forcing them to alter their traffic patterns. Serra, however, defended his work: "I was trying to redefine the space and I think that's what bothered people. It offends people to have their preconceptions of reality changed."[47] Serra had carefully studied the site and spent two years creating the work, which "divides the plaza into discrete sculptural volumes, changing the 'content'—the scheme—of the plaza from one of decoration to one of sculpture."[48]

For several years following the initial protests, the furor seemed to subside, but by the end of 1984 the protests started again. In November, Edward Re, chief judge of the U.S. Court of International Trade, sent a letter to to Ray Kline, Acting Administrator of GSA, saying:

Three and one-half years have passed since the erection of the Tilted Arc . . . . The reaction of those who work in the area, who must look at this "work" on a daily basis, is uniformly negative. The Chief Judges of the United States Courts, the United States Attorney for the Southern District, and many other federal and state judges and public officials have repeatedly expressed their strong desire to me and to others that this steel wall be removed. ...Time has not mellowed this slab of iron, and the natural elements, assisted by would-be graffiti artists, have further desecrated the plaza to the point where it has become intolerable.[49]

Re also emphasized that, had the GSA decision makers discussed the sculpture with responsible community representatives, it probably would not have been erected. (GSA has since changed its system to include representatives from the area where the art is to be located.)

With this new wave of criticism, the regional director of GSA, William Diamond, scheduled a public hearing to consider removing Tilted Arc (Figure 4.6). As a testament to the ability of public sculpture to generate political participation, the hearing audience was "standing room only." Local politicians, government officials, leading artists, and arts professionals testified before a five-member panel. Fifty-six witnesses spoke in favor of removing the art, while those against its removal totaled 118.[50] A most eloquent statement in the work's defense was in a letter from former Senator Jacob K. Javits, read by his wife:

Art requires freedom for the artist to make his statement about the life and times in which the artist lives. It is an expression of the deepest values of our society. The purpose of the program, as I understood it when I voted as a member of the United States Senate to authorize it, was essentially to express the commitment of our country to artistic expression as a vital element of our culture. Let us never forget, that the enslavement of Soviet art for political purposes is condemned by us, not because it may not be pretty or pleasing but because it is false.[51]

During the months after the hearing, the public debate continued. Ted Weiss, the U.S. representative from the district in which the sculpture was located, hosted a meeting of several other members of Congress who were visiting New York City as part of a Congressional Arts Caucus cultural trip. Weiss, although one of the strongest arts supporters in Congress, sided with his many vocal constituents who wanted the art removed. Other congressmen on the trip, however, disagreed, and, following the regional director's decision to recommend removal, wrote to the new GSA Acting Administrator Dwight Ink:

Figure 4.6

Announcement Describing GSA Hearing

SPEAK OUT!

GSA WILL HOLD A PUBLIC HEARING ON
WAYS TO MORE FULLY UTILIZE THE
PLAZA ON THE LAFAYETTE STREET
SIDE OF THIS BUILDING.
THIS COULD INCLUDE THE RELOCATION
OF THE LARGE METAL SCULPTURE
KNOWN AS THE "TILTED ARC". THE
PUBLIC HEARING WILL BE HELD ON
WEDNESDAY, MARCH 6, 1985 AT 10:00 AM
AT THE COURT OF INTERNATIONAL TRADE,
1 FEDERAL PLAZA (ADJACENT TO THE
FEDERAL BUILDING).
WE WOULD LIKE TO HEAR FROM YOU.
CALL 264-4068 TO GET MORE DETAILS
AND SCHEDULE A TIME TO
"SPEAK OUT"

We were deeply concerned to learn of action taken by the New York Regional Office of the General Services Administration which may compromise the intent and interests of the Art-in-Architecture program. . . . A decision to remove the sculpture would undermine government commitment to the program—one that was recently commended for a design excellence award by President Reagan for its courage in supporting stimulating and often controversial works of art.[52]

As did members of Congress, *The New York Times* offered opinions on both sides of the issue. Its editorial of May 31, 1985, urged removal: "The public has to live with *Tilted Arc*; therefore the public has a right to say no, not here."[53] But the *Times* also printed a strong support of the sculpture by art critic Michael Brenson: "It is now emphatically clear that removing the sculpture from the site for which it was commissioned and conceived would be a serious mistake."[54]

On May 31, 1985, Ink, the acting administrator, issued his decision to request the National Endowment for the Arts to appoint a panel to attempt to find an appropriate site for relocating the *Tilted Arc*. He also asked NEA to join GSA in developing model procedures for strengthening the Art-in-Architecture Program, and he concluded that regardless of whether a suitable location for the Arc would be found, several low-cost options were needed to improve the environmental character of the Federal Plaza, making it more acceptable to employees. Protests continued, however, and opponents involved the courts. Early in 1988, after several previous decisions, the 2nd U.S. Circuit Court of Appeals ruled the sculpture could be removed, and in March 1989, in the middle of the night, *Tilted Arc* was disassembled and taken to a government motor pool in Brooklyn, to occupy eight parking spaces. According to Diamond, a new art form now occupied the plaza, "open space." Benches and planters were installed "so that the public can enjoy the plaza again."[55]

Clearly, Tilted Arc has provided one of the most fascinating examples of art generating political participation. The artist, Richard Serra, may or may not have been active politically prior to the controversy, but he certainly was following public display of his work. He wrote numerous letters to local, state, and federal officials, including President Reagan; he circulated his own petitions; he testified before the New York hearing panel; and he even met with the congressmen at the art site during their brief visit in April 1985.

As noted earlier, the art also caused more than one thousand persons to sign petitions, more than one hundred to appear at the public hearing, and dozens to write letters for or against the sculpture.

Michael Brenson described the power of the work to provoke such reaction:

> It can seem to thump its chest, raise its fist and pound its way head down across the pavement . . . . *Tilted Arc* is confrontational. But it is also gentle, silent and private. It is an intimidating block of steel, but it is also a line, a bolt through space. It does seem to be breathing down on us, but it also lies down and shuts up and offers us a refuge. Almost always, it seems to be gesturing, reaching out—speaking—asking us to consider where we are and what we think.[56]

Tilted Arc seemed to do more than ask. It pushed the individual, at the very least, to declare his like or dislike and made participation inevitable. In its own way, "it has pushed the whole notion of public art—what it is, what it could or should be—into clearer focus for a great many people."[57]

Passive Participation in the Arts

The above discussion has shown the wide range of active participation in the arts and how that activity can reinforce the concept of a participatory society. Arts participation in a less active way can also be helpful. Ranging from merely participating as an audience member to a small degree of decision-making as a patron of the arts, passive participation involves an increasing number of Americans.

Passive Participation: The Audience. The arts seem to be holding their own in the ever diminishing number of free hours available to Americans, according to the 1988 survey *Americans and the Arts*.[58] For the first time since 1973, however, arts attendance began to fall. The 1988 survey was the fifth in a series, conducted by the Harris organization since 1973, in which 1,504 adult Americans were interviewed by telephone.[59] The table on page 72 shows the percentage of respondents who said they attended an arts event at least once during 1987, 1984, 1980, and 1975.

With the exception of museum attendance, which plateaued in 1980 at 60 percent, attendance at arts presentations continued to rise between 1975 and 1984, but by 1987 almost all categories noted a decline (except dance attendance, which held steady). Harris noted that while the arts have held their own, they have had to fight harder for a share of Americans' free time. If the amount of leisure time continues to fall,

	1987	1984	1980	1975
Movies	74%	78%	75%	70%
Theatre	65%	67%	65%	63%
Popular Music	57%	60%	53%	46%
Opera/Musical Theatre	27%	35%	25%	(Not surveyed in '75)
Classical Music	31%	34%	26%	25%
Dance	34%	34%	25%	23%
Museums	55%	58%	60%	56%

greater participation in the arts may have to occur in new ways—possibly through videocassettes.

Sociologist Judith Balfe has explained the participation decline by looking to members of the "baby boom" generation, many of whom she considers "consumers" of the arts. Compared to their elders, this generation would rather attend museums and jazz concerts and listen to classical radio (often tuning in National Public Radio) than participate as an audience member of a theatre, opera, or orchestra event.[60] As noted in Chapter 3, it is instructive to compare the percentages of the population attending various arts events with participation in various political activities—the lesser degree of political participation corresponding with the more easily accessible arts events. This comparison indicates that arts participation permeates the general population no more or less than political participation and can therefore be analyzed in a similar manner, while theories espousing the beneficial effects of more participation can apply to both politics and the arts.

As an attender, an individual participates in a very minimal manner with very little direct decision-making power other than the choice of which event to attend. One means of increasing audience participation is to offer individual theatregoers, for example, a ballot on which to choose possible plays for inclusion in future seasons. Another unique way is to allow the audience to vote for a particular ending of a theatrical production, as did the 1985 Broadway show *The Mystery of Edwin Drood*, where the audience decided who committed the crime and the ending was adjusted accordingly.

Another key to greater attendance, as most arts administrators have come to realize, is to persuade attenders to become subscribers. Once an arts organization has made the decision to court the "saintly, season subscriber," as opposed to depending on the "slothful, fickle single-ticket buyer,"[61] attendance virtually increases automatically. Of course, because purchasing a subscription requires a greater initial commitment of funds, subscribers tend to push the audience profile more toward the upper classes (see VALS discussion in Chapter 3). Arts manager Danny Newman has emphasized the importance of subscribers for an increase in participation:

> The subscriber is our ideal. He arrives at our auditorium with a positive attitude. He wants us to succeed, and he's thrilled when we do. . . . His awareness of everything connected with the art form heightens. He begins to develop and articulate his own opinions about performance values. Now, should a critic, in his estimation, attack us unfairly, he may write a denunciatory letter to the editor. He also begins to write us letters—16–page ones— advising us on casting and repertoire selection.[62]

The subscriber clearly is a prime target for administrators trying to boost attendance and active participation in the art world in general.

Levels of participation as an audience member were defined as part of a unique audience development program undertaken in the 1960s during the initial stages of the organization of the Tyrone Guthrie Theatre in Minneapolis. Finding no research at the time regarding the psychological analysis of arts attenders, the "audience developers" went on to describe three types of people:

Type #1: People who know they like classical theatre and culture for its own sake or because their attendance at such events gives them intellectual and/or social status.
Type #2: People who are uncertain about whether they like or would like classical theatre or things on a so-called "cultural level" and are not driven by the social-status urge.
Type #3: People who are quite positive that they do not and will not like classical theatre or anything having to do with culture or art.

The identification of these "Yeses, Maybes, and Noes," as they have come to be called, served as the basis for the Guthrie Theatre's promotional strategy.

Although, in general, the groups could be identified by socioeconomic and educational-occupational characteristics, similar to the VALS categories mentioned earlier, their complete profile is more complex. The Guthrie researchers noted that "the only thing that can be stated unequivocally is that a person with a college education earning a relatively high income in the professional or business world is more likely to be a Yes or a Maybe than a No."[63] In 1987, the Guthrie audience profile was reexamined. Attendance curves flattened in the 1980s, but the socioeconomic profile of the audience remained the same—the same kinds of people attended and the same kinds stayed away.[64]

By reinforcing the participation of the Yeses, encouraging more participation of the Maybes, and periodically trying a unique promotional ploy to lure the participation of the Noes, almost any kind of an arts audience can be built. This passive, yet well-cared-for audience then quite possibly becomes ready to move to a higher level of participation. With each step upward on the participatory scale, decision-making power increases and additional participatory skills are reinforced.

Passive Participation: The Volunteer. A special category of arts participation has been reserved for the volunteer. Although board members—and even some administrators—of arts institutions often serve in a voluntary capacity, they are not placed in the category of "volunteer." For the purpose of this book, the volunteer most generally offers his time and skills to the arts institution without solicitation. Board members, on the other hand, are most often sought after by the institution itself because of their social status or large financial resources.

According to a 1985 study by Yankelovich, Skelly and White, Inc., an overwhelming majority of Americans believe they should volunteer.[65] Of those respondents who believed they should volunteer, 49 percent did not volunteer in 1984. A person in this group would probably be one of the "Maybes" and, under the right circumstances, could be persuaded to participate as a volunteer.

A true volunteer, however, asks to participate simply for the satisfaction of assisting an organization whose art pleases him, but recent trends indicate that volunteers want more responsibility and the chance to participate in the decision-making process.[66] Organizations wishing to keep a large, stable volunteer staff are beginning to accept these attitudes and change their management style accordingly.

The Smithsonian Institution, in utilizing nearly 4,000 volunteers, has successfully incorporated them into the management structure and does not fail to praise them in its many publications:

> By definition, the volunteer is motivated by his own will. Not driven by external compulsion or the hope for measurable reward, he works because he wants to, much as Smithson did. If a volunteer finds priceless premiums—as many do here—the rewards derive from the work itself, which intangibly enriches the worker.[67]

This "intangible enrichment" adds to the individual's self-esteem—once again, weaving another thread in the psychological quilt underlying a participatory democracy.

Passive Participation: The Patron. When an arts participant—whether an attender or a volunteer—makes the decision to more actively support a cultural activity by contributing money, he moves to another level of passive participation: he becomes a patron.

Although the Yankelovich survey did not focus specifically on arts attenders, the general conclusions provide insight into charitable behavior that is relevant to giving in the arts. For example, the study demonstrated a relationship between attenders, volunteers, and patrons, that is, regular attendance can be an excellent predictor of patronage. (A particularly strong relationship exists between regular attendance at religious services and giving to religious charities.)

In addition, the survey showed a relationship between contributed time and giving: "The average contribution of those who volunteered was $830, compared to $530 for those who did not volunteer."

Also, because the study showed that an overwhelming majority of individuals believe they should give financial support and volunteer their time, much potential for increasing the number of as patrons exists. During the last two decades, energetic arts managers have made much progress in increasing private patronage. In 1970, giving to the arts and humanities totaled $663 million, while in 1988 contributions reached $6.82 billion. (See Chapter 8.) Although these figures include gifts from corporations, bequests, foundations, and individuals, individual giving continues to play a dominant role.[68]

As individual giving has increased, patrons are becoming more aware of their roles as decision makers; they have the relatively minor choice of which arts organization to give to and some can even decide to make a dollar contribution to build art museums named after themselves.[69] In fact, "cultural barons and patrons have enormous influence over what is performed or seen."[70]

There is a caveat involved in this discussion of patronage, however: many researchers believe that tax deductions for charitable contributions are the incentive for a large portion of giving by individuals in the United States. These researchers study "income elasticity"[71] of giving, measuring the extent to which people give more as their income increases, and "price elasticity," the extent to which people give more as giving becomes cheaper.[72] Studies have shown that as income increases by one percent, people increase giving by less than one percent, but as price decreases by one percent, people increase giving by more than one percent. In other words, these relationships indicate that as income increases, giving increases, but by a lesser percentage, and as an individual's tax bracket increases, giving also increases, but by a larger percentage. With higher income coupled with the tax-law incentive, a larger percentage of contributed money flows from members of a small segment of the population. The giving decisions of this segment therefore control a large portion of public funds. In short, the charitable contributions deduction "places control of public funds in the hands of a group of people that is not only small in number compared with the population that pays for government aid, but is also demographically distinct—especially as regards income and education—from most of those who pay the bill."[73]

To debate the merits of subsidy by indirect tax incentives is not the purpose of this book; however, the pattern of decision-making within the arts system is important here. Proponents of the elite theory of art would maintain that the current indirect system works fine as long as an economic class structure remains and major decision-making resides in the upper levels. Those who prefer a more democratic system should examine incentives more carefully to determine what changes would induce greater participation and decision-making on the part of patrons and volunteers.[74]

Increased arts participation should lead, as Pateman has suggested, to a participatory society. Brian O'Connell, president of Independent Sector, an umbrella group of nonprofit organizations from across the country, would agree: "The degree and pervasiveness of giving and volunteering in America are certainly major factors in our uniqueness as a country. Perhaps they help explain the very preservation of our democracy."[75]

Notes

1. Kay, "Arts Policy," p. 12.
2. Ibid., p. 14.
3. Jack L. Walker, "A Critique of the Elitist Theory of Democracy," *American Political Science Review*, 1966, 60:2 (June), p. 286.
4. Peter Bachrach, *The Theory of Democratic Elitism: A Critique* (Lanham, Md.: University Press of America, 1967), p. 2.
5. Margaret Jane Wyszomirski, "Philanthropy, the Arts and Public Policy," *Journal of Arts Management and Law*, Vol. 16, No. 4, Winter 1987, pp. 21–22.
6. Almond and Verba, *Civic Culture*, p. 297.
7. James W. Prothro and Charles M. Grigg, "Fundamental Principles of Democracy: Bases of Agreement," *Empirical Democratic Theory*, Charles F. Cnudde and Deane E. Newubauer, ed. (Chicago: Markham Publishing Company, 1969), p. 248.

8. Paul DeMaggio, Michael Useem, and Paula Brown, *Audience Studies of the Performing Arts and Museums* (Washington, DC: National Endowment for the Arts, 1978), p. 2.

9. Robert A. Dahl, *Democracy in the U.S.: Promise and Performance* (Chicago: Rand McNally, 1976). On p. 450, Dahl cited the studies of Sidney Verba and Norman H. Nie (*Participation in America: Political Democracy and Social Equality* [New York: Harper & Row, 1972], p. 131). Dahl's discussion is similar to my discussion of the VALS program and arts participation in Chapter 3.

10. Norman Adler and Charles Harrington, *The Learning of Political Behavior* (Glenville, IL: Scott, Foresman and Company, 1970), p. 95.

11. *Music and Music Education: Data and Information* (Washington, DC: Music Educators National Conference, 1984). The charts show the low rating of importance for art courses.

12. American Council for Art in Education, *Coming to Our Senses* (New York: McGraw-Hill Book Company, 1977), p. 248.

13. *A Trend in High School Offerings and Enrollments: 1972–73 and 1981–82* (Washington, DC: National Council for Education Statistics, 1984), p. 20.

14. *Course Offerings and Enrollments in the Arts and the Humanities at the Secondary School Level* (Washington, DC: National Council for Educational Statistics, 1984), p. x.

15. *A Nation At Risk* (Washington, DC: National Committee on Excellence in Education, 1983).

16. *Academic Preparation for College* (New York: The College Board, 1983).

17. *Beyond Creating: The Place for Art in America's Schools* (Santa Monica, CA: The Rand Corporation, 1985), p. 6.

18. Lee Daniels, "Long Seen As Frill, Arts Education Gains Support," *New York Times*, July 19, 1989.

19. National Center for Research in the Arts, *Americans and the Arts V: Highlights from a Nationwide Survey of Public Opinion*, American Council for the Arts, 1988, p. 24.

20. "Opinions of Ohio Citizens About Education for the Arts," Ohio Alliance for Arts Education, 1988.

21. Wilson Carey McWilliams, "The Arts and the American Political Tradition," in *Art, Ideology and Politics*, p. 30.

22. Robert R. Faulkner, "Orchestra Interaction: Some Features of Communication and Authority in an Artistic Organization," *The Sociological Quarterly*, Spring 1973, p. 148.

23. Seymour Martin Lipset, *Political Man: The Social Bases of Politics* (Garden City, NY: Doubleday & Co., 1960), pp. 375–395.

24. As legislative director for the Congressional Arts Caucus, I worked with all the major arts advocacy groups. Several, in particular,

were adept at political skills. One excellent example is provided by the successful lobbying efforts of a coalition of unions: Actors Equity Association, Screen Actors Guild, American Federation of Television and Radio Artists, International Alliance of Theater and State Employees, and American Federation of Musicians. This coalition was responsible for the insertion of very specific language in the Tax Reform Act of 1986—the most major overhaul of the Tax Code since 1954. The language cited "certain performing artists" and allowed them, under certain conditions, to take business deductions not allowable to other taxpayers.

25. The nation's humanities community has become organized politically in a manner similar to the arts. For example, the National Federation of State Humanities Councils recently opened a Washington, DC, office, and an organization similar to the AAA, the National Humanities Alliance, was established to coordinate lobbying efforts.

26. Joseph Wesley Zeigler, "Passionate Citizenship," *American Arts*, May 1983, pp. 22–23.

27. William Blair, quoted by Zeigler, ibid., p. 23.

28. Ibid.

29. Ironically, another work of art—a powerful film about Vietnam veterans, *The Deerhunter* (1978)—gave Scruggs the idea for a memorial. The 1987 Vietnam film *Platoon* also stirred much public discussion and was compared to the Vietnam Veterans Memorial by one conservative critic: "It is the same message conveyed by the Vietnam Memorial, which critics are right to see as an insult to that war—and to war in general . . . ." (Michael Kinsey, "From *Rambo* to *Platoon*," *Washington Post*, February 18, 1987).

30. Charles McCollum, "Colonel Is Fired over Article Criticizing Vietnam Memorial," *Washington Star*, May 16, 1981, p. A1.

31. Wolf Von Eckard, "Of Heart and Mind," *Washington Post*, March 18, 1981, p. B1.

32. Quoted by Carl Schoettler, "War Memorial Still a Year Away," *Baltimore Sun*, July 11, 1981, p. A4.

33. "Watt May Delay Viet Memorial," *Baltimore Sun*, January 12, 1982, p. A2.

34. Henry J. Hyde, *Congressional Record*, March 25, 1982, p. E1276.

35. Quoted by Rick Horwitz, "Maya Lin's Angry Objections," *Washington Post*, July 7, 1982, p. B1.

36. Benjamin Forgey, "All in a Century's Work," *Washington Post*, July 17, 1982, p. C1.

37. Benjamin Forgey, "The Statue and the Wall," *Washington Post*, November 10, 1984, p. B8.

38. Elizabeth Hess, "A Tale of Two Memorials," *Art in America*, April 1983, p. 126.

39. Because Lin's art stands in the nation's capital in a prominent place and comments on the turbulent Vietnam period, it elicited much reaction. Other art, however, has made the same comments about the "waste of war." Robert Frost's comments in his poem "November"—a mere whisper hidden from daily public view—are every bit as powerful: "November" likens the autumn's cycle from glorious color to fallen leaves to a nation and laments "the waste of nations warring."

40. Ellen Goodman, "A Monument to Our Discomfort," *Washington Post*, September 25, 1986.

41. Because the program is not legislated, as it is in several states, it can be modified or eliminated by GSA as policy changes. In 1966 the program was suspended, in part because of a major controversy over Robert Motherwell's large abstract expressionist mural for the new Boston City Hall, *The Kennedy Assassination*, and because of unprecedented cost increases in construction (Jo Ann Lewis, "'Don't Laugh—It's Your Money,'" *Washington Post*, October 28, 1979, p. G8).

42. The federal government's public art program is not alone in causing controversy. As corporations have taken a larger role as patrons of the arts, they have also encountered problems. For example, an outdoor sculpture for the front of its new building in Cleveland, Ohio, was commissioned in 1985 by the Standard Oil Company. In 1986, however, the new chairman, Robert B. Horton, found the sculpture, *Free Stamp* by artist Claes Oldenburg, to be "inappropriate" and offered to place it elsewhere in Cleveland. Oldenburg, claiming the piece is "site specific," refused (Daniel Grant, "Oldenburg Rejected," *Art & Artists*, November/December 1986, p. 16).

43. Jo Ann Lewis, "Don't Laugh," p. G1.

44. "Atilt over *Tilted Arc*," *ARTnews*, December, 1981.

45. Don Thalacker, quoted in *ARTnews*, ibid.

46. Ibid.

47. Quoted by Don Hawthorne, "Does the Public Want Public Sculpture?" *ARTnews*, May 1982, p. 56.

48. Harriet Senie, "The Right Stuff," *ARTnews*, March 1984, p. 52.

49. Edward D. Re, letter to Ray Kline, November 5, 1984.

50. Calvin Tomkins, "Tilted Arc," *The New Yorker*, May 20, 1985.

51. Quoted by Douglas C. McGill, "Artists and Officials Argue Over Removing Sculpture," *New York Times*, March 7, 1985, p. B6.

52. Letter from Sens. Howard Metzenbaum and EdwardKennedy and Reps. Tom Downey, Frank Horton, Hamilton Fish, Jr., and James Jeffords to Dwight Ink, May 6, 1985.

53. "Intrusive Arc," *New York Times*, May 31, 1985.

54. Michael Brenson, "The Case in Favor of a Controversial Sculpture," *New York Times*, May 9, 1985, p. B1.

55. William Diamond, quoted in *New York Times*, June 15, 1989, p. 16.

56. Brenson, "The Case in Favor of a Controversial Sculpture," p. B35.

57. Ibid. Margaret Jane Wyszomirski and Judith H. Balfe, after reviewing the GSA and NEA records on *Tilted Arc,* concluded: "Public sculpture of a particular medium (corten steel), style (minimalist), and scale (monumental), when installed in certain settings (old urban with high structural and population densities), is likely to provoke an intensely negative public response. Change any one of these conditions and controversy is likely to be reduced" ("Philanthropy, the Arts, and Public Policy," *Journal of Arts Management and Law,* Vol. 16, No. 4, Winter, 1987, p. 9.).

58. National Research Center for the Arts, Inc., an affiliate of Louis Harris and Associates, Inc., *Americans and the Arts V: Highlights From a Nationwide Survey of Public Opinion,* American Council for the Arts, (New York: 1988), p. 6.

59. Statistics from surveys in which persons "self report" activity often differ from surveys in which activity is carefully defined, watched, and recorded by outside observers. In the case of the Harris poll, differences are caused by the varied definitions of arts events.

60. Judith Huggins Balfe, "Baby-Boom Generation: Lost Patrons, Lost Audience?" *The Cost of Culture: Patterns and Prospects of Private Arts Patronage,* M. J. Wyszomirski and Pat Clubb, ed. (New York: American Council for the Arts, 1989), p. 15.

61. Danny Newman, *Subscribe Now!* (New York: Theatre Communications Group, 1977), p. 15.

62. Ibid.

63. Bradley G. Morison and Kay Fliehr, *In Search of an Audience* (New York: Pitman Publishing Corporation, 1968), p. 51.

64. Bradley G. Morrison and Julie Gordon Dalgleish, *Waiting in the Wings* (New York: Pitman Publishing Corporation, 1968), p. 51.

65. *The Charitable Behavior of Americans,* A National Survey Conducted by Yankelovich, Skelly and White, Inc. (Washington, DC: Independent Sector, 1986), p. 53.

66. Shirley Keller, "The New Volunteer," *American Arts,* July 1981, p. 11.

67. Philip Kopper, *Volunteer! Oh, Volunteer!: A Salute to the Smithsonian's Unpaid Legions* (Washington DC: Smithsonian Institution Press, n.d.), p. 9.

68. *Giving USA: The Annual Report on Philanthropy for the Year 1988,* (New York: AAFRC Trust for Philanthropy, 1989).

69. An extremely large bequest ($1.3 billion) to the Getty Museum in California skewed the 1982 national philanthropy figures to indicate a much larger increase than was actually the case.

70. Faye Levine, *The Culture Barons* (New York: Thomas Y. Crowell Company, 1976), p. 11.

71. Economists often investigate "elasticity"—proportional changes in behavior in response to changes in economic incentives.

72. Alan L. Feld, Michael O'Hare, J. Mark Davidson Schuster, *Patrons Despite Themselves: Taxpayers and Arts Policy* (New York: New York University Press, 1983).

73. Ibid.

74. Ibid., for example, recommended that the charitable contributions deduction be replaced by a tax credit of approximately 30 percent to provide more "equity, effectiveness, pluralism, and rationality within the system" (pp. 219–220). (See Chapter 9.)

75. Brian O'Connell, testimony before Senate Subcommittee on Intergovernmental Relations, October 20, 1980.

5

Democracy and the Arts in Ancient Greece

Having set forth my theory of particpation in the arts, I chose to test my ideas by examining various historical periods most appropriate to an analysis involving democracy and the arts. For example, in his book *After the Revolution?* Robert Dahl described three great historical movements toward democratization involving ancient Greece and Rome, beginning about the end of the sixth century B.C.; the city-states of northern Italy in the tenth and eleventh centuries; and the United States and France in the eighteenth century.

The democracies of Greece and northern Italy fostered works of artistic excellence, particularly in the architecture of public places, and showed that "democracy is not inconsistent with beauty and magnificence in the public sector."[1] These two democratic movements were successful in part because they involved small city-states, not gigantic nation-states like those existing today. In particular, a discussion of the democratic model, like that found in ancient Greece, is most appropriate to help clarify the various principles of participation outlined in previous chapters.

GREEK DEMOCRACY: AN OVERVIEW

The first great historical movement toward democratizing the state corresponded with the first great theatrical age in the history of Western civilization: Athens in the fifth century B.C. had chosen to cultivate democracy as well as the arts.

The fate of the political system in Athens, one of history's best examples of a microdemocracy, may have been influenced, however, by factors beyond man's control. Dahl and Tufte speculated that the mountains of Greece may have kept families in isolated pockets, contributing to the formation of small political units: "Geography, then, may have exerted a more profound and arbitrary influence on Western political thought than philosophers like to admit."[2] No matter why microdemocracies developed, philosophers at the time understood the utility of government serving a small population. Aristotle stressed that a democracy should be small enough so that all citizens could assemble and hear a speaker; in other words, smallness would enhance participation. Similarly, Rousseau noted that democracies should be small, cohesive political units composed of like-minded citizens.[3] Whether a quirk of geography or not, the unit of political life was the city, and men were "political animals" of the city.

The ancient Greek city-state was not only a unit of government, but also a club in which "true" membership was achieved through birth, although the city could "adopt" members by general consent. This society, however, was a democracy of aristocrats with a strong economic class structure. (The Greek cities excluded women and, of course, slaves from citizenship.) Aristotle, who clearly understood the connection between politics and economics, described the acquisition and use of wealth, money, commerce, and exchange in *The Politics*, his survey of the Greek political system. He also noted the need for a labor force of slaves or workers "so economically dependent on him as to make their free status positively worthless."[4]

Although Aristotle believed a class structure could benefit society, he did caution against the acquisition of too much wealth:

> Money-making then, as we have said, is of two kinds; one which is necessary and acceptable, which we may call administrative; the other, the commercial, which depends on exchange, is justly regarded with disapproval, since it arises not from nature but from men's dealings with each other.[5]

Rather than calling for the imposition of economic equality on the classes, Aristotle suggested that individuals be taught the proper attitude toward wealth and that society should "equalize appetites [more] than property, and that can only be done by adequate education under the laws."[6] But, recognizing the reality of inequality among classes, he said that stability would result if society would "ensure that those who are by nature a superior class should not wish to get more than their share, and that the inferior should not be able to do so; and that means that they should be weaker but not downtrodden."[7]

Because direct taxation was rejected as a sign of tyranny, except in the case of military needs, government was financed by the wealthy. In fact, Aristotle stressed the importance of community patronage: large-scale private expenditures for communal purposes. These large expenditures obviously gave patrons a large amount of decision-making power in government, as well as in the arts.

THE ARTS IN GREECE, FIFTH CENTURY B.C.

The artistic climate of ancient Greece has been described by Michael Straight: "The arts in Plato's time were one means by which great men conveyed great truths of their time to the great majority of their people."[8] Poetry, music, dance, and drama were offered in worship to the Greek gods at the great state-sponsored festivals.

For example, the most prominent festivals honored the mythological Dionysus, son of Zeus, in the City of Dionysia, Athens, beginning around the thirteenth century B.C. Associated with fertility, wine, and revelry, Dionysus was the focus of two festivals each year: a wine-press festival took place in January or February, and the major festival, lasting as long as six days, was held in March or April.

Part of the festivals were dramatic competitions, with first, second, and third prizes, held under the auspices of the city-states. Each dramatist submitted a tetralogy (set of four plays): three tragedies, usually about one event, and a lighter piece, known as a satyr play. Each poet in the contest was assigned by lot a leading actor and a patron, a wealthy man who as part of his civic duties paid all the expenses of the production. The financial responsibilities of the state included supplying the theatre, awarding a prize to the author, and paying the actors. Music competitions were also held, and, since the cult of Dionysus was associated with the aulos, a double-reed instrument, the festival included aulos contests.

Initially, there was no admission fee. Later a small fee was charged and, since attendance was practically compulsory and considered "an act of civic worship,"[9] poor citizens were given the necessary entrance money. Nearly 17,000 persons could be seated in the giant open-air, semicircular Theatre of Dionysus. With vital support from the state, drama reached an astonishing level of excellence; ancient Greece produced great writers of tragedies—Aeschylus (b. 525 B.C.), Sophocles (b. 496 B.C.), and Euripides (b. 484 B.C.) and a writer renowned for his comedies, Aristophanes (b. 448 B.C.).

Because ritual was a very important part of public life, the ritual drama of that time flourished. Society and the state were not separate entities; Greek political thought equated individual good with state good. The "calm and clear rationalism of the Greek mind" easily accepted the moral influence of the state. Both Plato and Aristotle, who spent most of their lives in Athens, considered the positive furtherance of goodness as the mission of the state and therefore supported the festivals as an important part of public affairs.

In addition, the city-state's elaborate spectacles included a variety of attention-getting devices (for example, mock earthquakes, and supernatural visitations), utilizing the latest music and scenic effects. Kenneth Cavander has described these events:

> The overall intention of these activities—as with any parade, festival, gala, Mardi Gras today—was to project the image of the community outwards, give it form and life, color it, incarnate it. This—the expression of one unusual state's culture at a specific historical moment—is what we now call "Greek Drama."[10]

Because the majority of the Athenian population was nonliterate, these festivals were most important in projecting and reinforcing society's "body of shared myth."[11] Ancient Greek society—where art was an integral part of a coherent community, a central event bringing people together—met Straight's conditions for a flourishing culture. (See Chapter 1.)

THE ROLE OF PARTICIPATION

Active Participation

As already noted, political participation in Athens was open only to a minority—women and many adult males were excluded. The city-state was small in population and territory; it was a "face-to-face" society that fostered a high degree of genuine popular participation in its citizens, a place where boys grew up in contact with public life and received a healthy dose of political education. Aristotle, in fact, equated citizenship with participation in democracy: "I suggest that what effectively distinguishes the citizen from all others is his participation in Judgement and Authority, that is, holding office, legal, political, administrative."[12]

Any citizen could assemble—in what was called the Assembly—to vote on a variety of issues following an open debate. Officials and members of the smaller councils were chosen by lot with restricted terms. Attendance at Assembly was generally 6,000 in the fifth century B.C. and substantially more in the fourth century B.C., with an average of 30,000 men eligible.[13] Members of juries, which decided court cases, were citizens.

Often, because all citizens were allowed to participate, bitter conflicts developed. Thucydides, Plato, and Aristotle thoroughly examined the democratic process and found it to be unstable. Corcoran has explained the difference between Greek political theorists and those of today: "Many contemporary democratic thinkers insist democracy doesn't really exist today, but that it ought to, while classical Greek thinkers had no doubt that it existed but shouldn't."[14] Much of this instability was fostered by class struggles arising in the cities, creating Aristotle's "government of the poor":

> Tyranny, it has been said, is that form of monarchical rule which is despotically exercised over the political association called the state; oligarchy occurs when the sovereign power is in the hands of those possessed of property, democracy when it is in the hands of those who have no accumulated wealth, who are without means.[15]

Political decisions in Athens were made collectively; the individual was absorbed into the community. The Greeks were not acquainted with the value of respect for the individual; instead, the city and the citizens essentially were viewed as one. From our modern perspective, we might consider all of the Greeks as slaves.[16]

A more detailed examination of participation in the arts[17] and political participation is in order. Although Greek children grew up in a society where politics permeated everyday life, their exposure to the arts was much less rigorous. Only boys from the wealthy class received formal schooling where the arts were an integral part of the curriculum. Of the three areas of instruction (gymnastics [diet, medicine, exercise], literature, and music), Plato believed that music appealed to youth and would instill in the young mind "a growing love of righteousness." Art should always "bring lessons of courage to the spirit," he stressed, and suggested reforming literature and music to make sure that it did. As noted in Chapter 4, arts education helps to develop self-esteem, reinforcing the psychological conditions for a participatory society.

Yet, scholars know that the adult artist did not fit comfortably in the Greek political system (ancient Greece was the first civilization to write extensively about its artists): "Ever since democracy became a clear political conception in the city-state of Athens, democratic philosophers have been faced with the anomaly of the artist."[18] Poets and philosophers, although associated with the aristocracy, worked at the whim of their wealthy employers. Greek democracy, which attempted to foster creative expression from individuals, also was very anti-individualistic. Only men could be citizens within the political system, and only men could perform in major arts events, such as plays.[19] Obviously, active participation in the arts in ancient Greece was extremely limited.

Passive Participation

Being an audience member was by far the most prominent means of arts participation in Athenian society. This passive participation, however, was quite different than that of today's arts audiences. The Greek audience was more democratic, composed of citizens from all classes and often subsidized by the government, while twentieth-century U.S. audiences are composed primarily of the upper classes. And there is the difference of political participation: Greek arts events so represented the prevailing myths and values of Greek society, which were also the "official, government-approved" myths and values, that participation through attendance was akin to voting in totalitarian societies, with high voter turnout.[20] The choice of the plays was in the hands of the Greek state, as the political ballot is often really in the hands of the totalitarian states.

The main Greek festival, generally held once a year, can be compared to our presidential elections or the election of the top official of a communist state; each has a period of anticipation and an aftermath of recollection:

> We should remember the Greeks' practice of exposing themselves to one tragic trilogy and one comedy on but a single day each year. High art is meant for rare festivals, where anticipation is followed by exhilaration and the aftermath is meditation and recollection in tranquility.[21]

For the Greek audience, the plays were part of an annual program of "self-affirmation and social purification," which also included the Olympics and other games.[22] The audience was democratic, yet the dramatic material was for political education—an "authoritarian interpretation of the national myth."[23] Even the chorus provided an educative function; it served as the "ideal audience," giving the appropriate reaction to the action on stage. By imitation, the audience in the theatre, which often contained former chorus members, reacted accordingly. The reaction in most cases was that of a "typical citizen." In Greek society, audience members made very few decisions.

Patrons, however, were decision makers in their role as sponsors of the various festivals. Wealthy citizens considered their generosity as an act of political participation—even a civic duty. They believed the arts gave coherence to society,[24] reinforced society's values, and transmitted its culture. The arts helped the Greeks—according to Parsons' theory (see Chapter 3)—transmit, learn, and share their culture.

Using the background set forth in this chapter, how would our theory of participation apply? Because the Greek political unit was small, direct participation by male citizens was at a relatively high level (Pateman would obviously have liked the franchise extended to women), but, as noted, this high level of participation often created instability. Clearly, the kind of participation reinforced by Greek society heightened the tendency toward instability rather than tempering it. Greek democracy relied on majority rule, and, although discussion was encouraged, individual choices and decisions were always of lesser importance than the collective decisions of the state. With no recognition of minority needs, collective decisions were not always easy for all citizens to accept.

This system of participation paralleled the kind of participation reinforced by the Greek arts festivals. Although mass audience participation was encouraged, it was the kind of participation that submerged individual choices and decisions to the appropriate collective emotions of the state.

Clearly, the theory of arts participation did apply to Greek society: participation in the "other sphere," the arts, helped to reinforce the psychological and political skills necessary for participation in government. Ironically, this brand of mass, passive participation, could eventually breed instability and the ultimate breakdown of the system.

Notes

1. Dahl, *After the Revolution?*, p. 5.

2. Robert A. Dahl and Edward R. Tufte, *Size and Democracy* (Stanford, CA.: Stanford University Press, 1973), p. 4.

3. In *Size and Democracy*, Dahl and Tufte analyzed studies of participation in democracies of varying sizes and found that citizens in smaller democracies do not necessarily feel more effective and that no relationship exists between size of unit and voter turnout (p. 44). (See Chapter 9.)

4. J. A. Sinclair, Introduction, Aristotle's *The Politics*, J. A. Sinclair, trans. (Baltimore: Penguin Books, 1970), p. 16.

5. Aristotle, *The Politics*, p. 46.

6. Ibid., p. 74.

7. Ibid., p. 77.

8. Straight, *Twigs for an Eagle's Nest*, pp. 50–51.

9. Dewey, *Art as Experience*, p. 328.

10. Kenneth Cavander, "Imagining the Greeks," *American Theatre*, September 1984, p. 12.

11. Ibid., p. 42

12. Aristotle, *The Politics*, p. 102.

13. M. I. Finley, *Politics in the Ancient World* (New York: Cambridge University Press, 1983), p. 73.

14. Corcoran, "Limits," p. 15.

15. Aristotle, *The Politics*, pp. 116–117.

16. Sartori, *Democratic Theory*, p. 266.

17. In the *Poetics*, Aristotle discussed the performing "arts" of his era, which included: epic poetry, tragedy, comedy, dithyrambic poetry, flute playing, lyre playing, dancing, and even the playing of the shepherd's pipe. All, he said, involved imitation: "For as there are persons who, by conscious arts or mere habit, imitate and represent various objects through the medium of color and form, or again by the voice, so in the arts above mentioned, taken as a whole, the imitation is produced by rhythm, language, or 'harmony,' either singly or combined." (*Aristotle's Poetics*, S. S. Butcher, trans., Introduction by Francis Fergusson [New York: Hill and Wang, 1963], pp. 49–50). (See Chapter 3.)

18. Read, *To Hell With Culture*, p. 1.

19. Women did participate in the visual arts. One Athenian vase shows a male painter with two male assistants and a woman assistant, probably a member of the family. Women artists (except Sappho, an early poet) never achieved individual fame, but even the subordinate role on the vase "must have been a significant step on the road to equality" (Janson, p. 109).

20. Robert S. Friedman has noted that empirical evidence shows mass nonparticipation in democracies and large participation in autocracies, where participation is more a form of obedience to the rules (Robert S. Friedman, "Participation in Democracy: A Theory of Democracy and Democratic Socialization," Ph.D. dissertation, Princeton University, 1973, p.6), while George F. Will refuted the theory that high voter turnouts were an index of social health. In his article in the October 10, 1983 *Newsweek* (p. 96), Will provided the examples that in two presidential elections in Germany in 1932, 86.2 and 83.5 percent of the electorate voted. In 1933, 88.8 percent voted in the Assembly election which was swept by the Nazis.

21. Jacques Barzun, "A Surfeit of Art," *Harper's*, July 1986, p. 49.

22. Cavander, "Imagining the Greeks," p. 42.

23. Hauser, *The Social History of Art*, p. 100.

24. Unfortunately, the arts in twentieth-century American society give coherence only sporadically—the Vietnam Veterans Memorial for

a brief period helped to draw society's attention to those who died in Vietnam; the movie *Platoon* during its national run brought the Vietnam experience closer to large numbers of people. (See Chapters 7 and 8.)

Nineteenth-Century American Democracy and the Arts

The theory of participatory democracy and the arts can also be tested by examining later historical permutations of the democratic political system. The microdemocracy of ancient Greece served as the only model of democracy for theorists for some two thousand years, but with the American and French revolutions, when large nation-states began experimenting with democratic principles, political philosophers began to revise their democratic models. By the nineteenth century, theorists were beginning to take the idea of a macrodemocracy seriously.

In Chapter 2, several models of American democracy were examined. This chapter, focusing on the Jacksonian era, named after President Andrew Jackson, uses as its theoretical foundation Dahl's model of Populist Democracy, which has as its central principle pure majority rule. In theory, decision making under this political system was to be left entirely to the majority.

JACKSONIAN DEMOCRACY: AN OVERVIEW

Immediately following the Revolution in 1776, Americans were busy with the mechanics of establishing a democratic government, yet a widespread democratizing movement did not exist until the second quarter of the nineteenth century. Americans, by that time, had lived under their government long enough to feel confident in suggesting major changes. Arthur Schlesinger, Jr., in *The Age of Jackson*, stated that the Jacksonians believed society was a struggle between the producers (farmer and laborers) and the nonproducers (the business community). The growing industrialization of the nineteenth century began to foster monopolistic tendencies in businesses, and the working man, confident in the "right to the full proceeds of this labor,"[1] believed government should intervene to restore competition.

Although the growth of capitalism had rightfully destroyed the aristocracy based on land ownership, the business community had served its purpose and was wrongfully in a position of power. The people believed it was their turn to rule. This sentiment was expressed in the *United States Magazine and Democratic Review* of 1837: "We have an abiding confidence in the virtue, intelligence, and full capacity for self-government, of the great mass of our people, our industrious, honest, manly, intelligent millions of free men."[2] These noble sentiments, however, did not translate into viable political power:

> But precisely the greatest weakness of the new politics was that for all its talk of democracy and its flattery of the common man[3] who allegedly ruled under it, its definition of democracy was concerned not with the common man's rule, but with his voting opportunities, while its practice effectively denied him either great influence or any realistic chance of exercising it.[4]

Despite the actual lack of power, the Jacksonians remained optimistic and stubbornly maintained their typically American feeling of equality. Additional characteristics of the Jacksonian personality, vast accounts of which exist in the journals of European visitors, included generosity, curiosity, insecurity, a hatred of criticism, and a value of materialism. Americans were considered "self-reliant, versatile, ingenious"[5]; "clever, but not profound"[6]; inveterate joiners; and great chewers of tobacco (and, what was worse, "notorious spitters").[7] Jacksonian Americans, above all, exalted the *potential* of democracy.

During this adolescent period in the history of the United States, a young Frenchman began his epic journey among the Americans and wrote a work that has become a classic in the literature of American political theory. In writing *Democracy in America*, Alexis de Tocqueville sought to examine closely the strengths and weaknesses of a political system that he considered would play a dominant role in the future.

Tocqueville arrived in the United States in May 1831 and, although spending only a period of nine months in the country, he was able to compile "an unparalleled abundance of description, analysis, and prophecy concerning almost every aspect of the American scene."[8] Tocqueville deduced one fundamental principle pervading all aspects of U.S. society: "equality of condition is the fundamental fact from which all others seem to be derived and the central point at which all my observations constantly terminated."[9] (Tocqueville, however, did not mean that democracy, the political institution, was a synonym for "equality." He realized that the French term, *democratie*, which does mean "equality," was taken into English as "democracy," and, under-standing the possible confusion, thought of changing the title of his second volume to "Equality in America."[10]) From the fundamental concept of social equality flow two opposing streams described by Tocqueville as individualism and the tyranny of the majority. In-dividualism, while promoting freedom of choice, could also foster isolationism and anarchism. In the opposite direction is the pull of the majority:

> I know of no country in which there is so little independence of mind and real freedom of discussion as in America. . . .[11] In the United States, the majority undertakes to supply a multi-tude of ready-made opinions for the use of individuals, who are thus relieved from the necessity of forming opinions of their own.[12]

These two streams of individualism and mass conformity have been described by Ward:

> The brilliance of Tocqueville's argument is that he sees the kind of vaunted individualism and self-reliance of the egalitarian democracy, and how that flips over easily into a conformitarian, mass public opinion which has enormous repressive weight on the individual because he cannot deny the majority its right without denying his own.[13]

Participation in Jacksonian Democracy presented this dilemma.

As a moderating force to the tyranny of the majority, Tocqueville observed several buffers. One of the most important was participation in political activity in local communities:

> When the central government which represents that majority has issued a decree, it must intrust the execution of its will to agents, over whom it frequently has no control, and whom it cannot perpetually direct. The townships, municipal bodies, and counties form so many concealed breakwaters, which check or part the tide of popular determination. If an oppres-sive law were passed, liberty would still be protected by the mode of executing that law; the majority cannot descend to the details and what may be called the puerilities of administrative tyranny.[14]

Another buffer was the formation of associations, invariably follow-ing the same form of democratic government as the national model:

The Americans made associations to give entertainments, to found seminaries, to build inns, to construct churches, to diffuse books, to send missionaries to the antipodes; they found in this manner hospitals, prisons, and schools. . . . Wherever, at the head of some new undertaking, you see the government of France, or a man of rank in England, in the United States you will be sure to find an association.[15]

Dahl noted that the associations referred to by Tocqueville within the family, educational institutions, and cultural organizations serve to moderate the tyranny of the majority, but he stressed that other associations—political parties, various interest groups, business firms, trade unions, and so on—could cause instability. According to Dahl, associations are essential to basic human needs for sociability, intimacy, friendship, individual growth, and the preservation of culture, as Tocqueville believed, but Dahl warned that associations have a tendency to stabilize injustice and distort the public agenda.[16]

Tocqueville also noted the strength of religious beliefs so apparent in the United States: It must never be forgotten that religion gave birth to Anglo-American society. In the United States, religion is therefore mingled with all the habits of the nation and all the feelings of patriotism, whence it derives a peculiar force.[17] Throughout his two volumes, Tocqueville weaves the thread of religion: "It runs through those two volumes like a minor chord. Every time he talks about equality or self-interest, you will find some reference to religion within the next dozen pages. It's sort of a reflex tic."[18] In *The Genius of American Politics*, Daniel J. Boorstin devoted an entire chapter to the importance of religious thought in America. He noted that a majority of Americans belong to a church; that a town without a church is a rarity; and that chapels are among the most expensive buildings on university campuses. Boorstin, however, was careful to note: "Intellectually speaking, 'religions' are unimportant in American life; but Religion is of enormous importance."[19]

Religion also provided a powerful principle underlying the free enterprise system, which was in its infancy under Jacksonian Democracy. The Protestant work ethic actually encouraged the growth of free enterprise: "Thus, the founding religions in America have mattered enormously in this way. They gave and still give the impetus to economic exertion."[20]

In *The Selling of the President 1968*, Joe McGinnis noted the continued influence of "Religion": "The American voter, insisting upon his belief in a higher order, clings to his religion, which promises another better life; and defends passionately the illusion that the men he chooses to lead him are of finer nature than he."[21] Religious belief offered consolation to the nineteenth-century individual for the inequities and injustices of everyday life. In other societies this consolation could also come from the arts:

> For as we say, art gives creative expression to a society's ideals by allowing its members an objective unofficial view of themselves and their culture, and it makes possible communication across the barriers of social hierarchy. And by projecting freewheeling definitions of the diversity and complexity of American experience it allows for a more or less peaceful adjustment between the claims of "inferiors" and "superiors"—a function of inestimable value to a society based, as is ours, upon the abstract ideal of social equality.[22]

But the arts as described in the next section, were not so prevalent and accessible as to be able to fulfill that function during the Jacksonian era.

THE ARTS DURING THE JACKSONIAN ERA

As Boorstin wrote, "On the whole, the fine arts in the United States had been the least American of the expressions of this transatlantic civilization."[23] Most respected visual artists painted portraits and historical scenes in the European tradition; unique American subjects, however, began to appear in nature paintings (such as John James Audubon), in works depicting the grandeur of the American continent (such as Thomas Moran), and in artwork focusing on Indian life (such as George Catlin). In general, though, American artists and patrons still looked to the European academies and museums for their ideas about art. Horatio Greenough, who has been called the first American professional sculptor, worked for eight years in a studio in Florence to complete his statue of George Washington, which Congress commissioned. Placed in the Capitol in 1843, the statue "depicted the nation's hero in the undress of a Greek god."[24]

Growth of the fine arts in America may also have been hampered by the religious foundation permeating the country:

> The religion professed by the first emigrants, and bequeathed by them to their descendants—simple in its forms, austere and almost harsh in its principles, and hostile to external symbols and to ceremonial pomp—is naturally unfavorable to the fine arts, and only yields reluctantly to the pleasures of literature.[25]

A strong Puritan heritage produced a reluctance in many Americans to enjoy the visual and performing arts, and, in many cases, hampered creativity in literature through censorship.

Despite the rather apathetic public attitudes to the fine arts, many prominent authors and artists became very supportive of U.S. politics and publicly associated themselves with the Jacksonian party. The writings of Nathaniel Hawthorne, James Fenimore Cooper, and Washington Irving supported the argument that the development of "a powerful native literature, dealing fearlessly in truth and reality, seemed to lie in a bold exploration of the possibility of democracy."[26] In her analysis of the political thought of James Fenimore Cooper, Patricia Elaine Curry noted that fictional literature can provide a unique look at political theory: it differs from political philosophy "not in its completeness, or its coherence, but primarily in its methods of cognition, its language, the glasses it employs in viewing experience."[27]

Of all the literary arts, poetry has the strongest relationship to democracy. Poetry represents "an assertion of the self,"[28] wrote Robert Penn Warren in *Democracy and Poetry*, and it has the special capability of praising or criticizing our achievements in democracy. Perhaps the greatest defender of Jacksonian Democracy was the poet Walt Whitman:

> We know, well enough, that the workings of democracy are not always justifiable, in every trivial point. But the great winds that purify the air, without which nature would flag into ruin—are they to be condemned because a tree is prostrated here and there in their course?[29]

In his doctoral dissertation, "Walt Whitman: A Study in Politics and Literature," Edward McKinley Wheat reminded us that Whitman wrote *Leaves of Grass* as an "epic for democracy—an instrument of education for citizenship in the polis."[30] Because of Whitman's unique view of the actualities and potentialities of American democracy, Wheat considered him a "political philosopher of the first rank." Whitman saw what democracy could become, but "the possibility that it might never be attained despite the great potential of the American context gave his work its point and urgency."[31]

Although American literature, and the visual arts to some extent, prospered under Jacksonian Democracy, the performing arts did not achieve great excellence; the Americans, it seems, had "little time for the cultural side of life."[32] Although known as the "golden age of the actor," with such well-known performers as Edwin Forrest, Mary Ann Duff, John McCullough, and Ira Aldridge, the first great Negro tragedian, nineteenth-century theatre produced very little quality playwriting. Americans, with their overly simplified view of life, encouraged the production of plays involving stock characters and simple morality, and melodrama flourished. This form of theatre, so easily understood, appealed to the practical Jacksonian mind.

Music, like drama, suffered from a democratization of taste: "One heard less and less of good taste and more and more of progress."[33] Gilbert Chase, in his history of American music, described two men who exemplified the conditions of American music during the nineteenth century. Both were leading impresarios of music and excellent promoters: P. T. Barnum, who brought Jenny Lind to the United States, was also the great promoter of the American circus, and Lowell Mason, a composer of sacred music, was a self-made successful American businessman. Barnum and Mason provided music for the masses—one appealed to the "frivolity of the public," the other attempted to "uplift" the public. But neither succeeded in elevating American music to the lofty heights of the sounds produced in Europe. Because the United States had few performing groups of their own and continued to look to Europe, troupes of singers and dancers travelled annually across the Atlantic to perform in the Park, National, and Bowery theatres. In her book on the history of American dance, Agnes DeMille reinforced a major reason artists were brought to the United States: "We kept on from habit bringing European talent to satisfy our snobbishness."[34]

Both music and drama conformed to Tocqueville's description of the arts in America. In a democracy, he concluded, there is always a multitude of persons whose wants are above their means and who are willing to have "imperfect satisfaction." (Today's "imperfect satisfaction" example is television.) In an aristocracy, persons would rather go without, and the artisan sells his workmanship to the few at high prices; in a democracy, he might sell his craft to the many at lower prices "to produce with great rapidity many imperfect commodities."[35] Furthermore, Tocqueville believed Americans prefer the useful to the beautiful:

> Democratic nations . . . will therefore cultivate the arts which serve to render life easy in preference to those whose object is to adorn it. They will habitually prefer the useful to the beautiful, and they will require that the beautiful should be useful.[36]

Tocqueville, however, was not entirely pessimistic concerning the role of the arts in a democracy, asserting "not that, in democracies, the arts are incapable, in case of need, of producing wonders."[37] Only, however, if the customer appears ready to pay for time and trouble.

Nineteenth-century Americans, however, were content with their democratic brand of culture: "the Real in place of the Ideal."

THE ROLE OF PARTICIPATION

Active Participation

Political participation in the Jacksonian era, as in ancient Greece, was limited to adult, white males. But, according to Tocqueville, who did not speculate on the possible effects of extending the vote to women or blacks, but did offer a profile of American women and speculated on future racial problems in the country following the abolition of slavery. Even with such a limited citizenship, political activity was everywhere:

> The political activity which pervades the United States must be seen in order to be understood. No sooner do you set foot upon American ground, than you are stunned by a kind of tumult. . . . Everything is in motion around you; here, the people of one quarter of a town are met to decide upon the building of a church; there, the election of a representative is going on; a little further, the delegates of a district are posting to the town in order to consult some local improvements; in another place, the laborers of a village quit their ploughs to deliberate upon the project of a road or a public school.[38]

While Tocqueville observed political activity in local communities across the country, another form of participation was available in the nation's capital: watching Congress proved to be a lively diversion during the nineteenth century. This same hobby, watching Congress, can be done in the twentieth century either at the capital or via C-SPAN. (See Chapter 8.) Interestingly, Tocqueville noted that this political agitation was evident in all social classes, a "universal movement which originates in the lowest classes of the people and extends successively to all the ranks of society."[39]

In addition to all the discussing, voting, and other political activities described by Tocqueville, Americans were, of course, busy forming their numerous associations, which functioned democratically in a manner similar to the various levels of government. Voluntary organizations were established to found schools and universities; to support fledgling cultural groups; to build churches, hospitals, and libraries; and to encourage local business and trade. Where, in other countries, government fulfilled these functions, in the United States citizens' groups handled these tasks and applied the skills for a democracy. Although Jacksonian citizens were given all this opportunity for political participation, their decision-making power at the higher levels of government was more perceived than actual. Often actual power remained with shrewd, ambitious, and wealthy politicians who could manipulate the common man.

On the one hand, the Jacksonian era has been pictured as a time of agitated political activity with citizens scattering here and there, forming associations, discussing, voting, and generally believing that their participatory behavior gave them a certain amount of decision-making power. Was the picture of arts participation similar? Unfortunately, the vigorous political activity that impressed Tocqueville was not evident in the arts. With a vast educational system not yet in place, most children received very little schooling in the fundamentals of reading and writing, let alone in "less useful" areas like the arts. In general, development of self-esteem was not assisted by formal arts education. Arts activities for the young, if any, involved folk crafts, through which children learned to become self-reliant and independent—important traits in a Jacksonian democracy. Such fierce individualism has been closely allied with twentieth-century democracy, according to a former chairman of the National Endowment for the Arts: "When a society emphasizes the arts, it emphasizes the value of the individual, of individuality. Where the arts flourish, so does that consummate political system centered on the individual—democracy."[40]

In the Jacksonian era, adults often dabbled in the amateur area of folk crafts and sometimes mixed in the fine arts to create "sources of modes and motives for vernacular improvisation."[41] This mixture of the fine and folk arts, although offering little opportunity to hone participatory skills, did, in its own way, express the churning political experimentation with democracy. Ralph Ellison described the fermentation of art and democracy as

helping to clarify and make bearable the endless contentions of democracy, and they were the unconscious underside of the conscious political efforts that were being asserted to incarnate democracy. Thus the vernacular mingling of the fine and folk arts occurred unnoticed in the process of nation-building.[42]

Many professional artists, as noted earlier, welcomed participation in politics. According to Schlesinger, "A surprising number of writers were themselves active in politics or the government service."[43] His examples include George Bancroft (a Massachusetts party boss and later Polk's Secretary of the Navy); Orestes Brownson (an officeholder under Van Buren and a candidate for Congress during the Civil War); Washington Irving (in the diplomatic service); and Nathaniel Hawthorne (an officeholder under three presidential administrations).

Passive Participation

The system of active arts participation provided little reinforcement of the skills necessary for political participation; the system of passive participation for audience members provided even less. As noted, a large portion of the live performing arts events featured European artists, and Americans trooped to the theatre, symphony, and opera with a fascination of European culture and upward mobility—attitudes counter to the principles of democracy that heightened socioeconomic class differences. In short, the arts had yet to become major events uniting society and reaffirming the "American myth"—which was then still being formed.

However, passive participation by patrons was on the upswing. The nineteenth century saw the founding of many of America's major orchestras and opera companies with the sole assistance of wealthy patrons. This system of private patronage gained momentum and continued into the twentieth century, until the economic conditions of the 1920s forced the public sector to take a larger role in supporting the arts.

How would the contributions of the nineteenth-century arts sphere be viewed in relation to our participatory theory? Quite possibly like this: active participation in arts did aid in the development of self-esteem, thus laying a foundation for the psychological conditions necessary for a participatory society, but active participation in the fine arts was so sporadic and often only available to the wealthy that little benefit to society was derived. In addition, because the art world was so unorganized, very few formal institutions, associations, or unions existed for individuals to learn participatory skills. This seemingly chaotic arts activity, however, fostered individualism so vital to American democracy and symbolized the "forms of freedom which allow the American people to gauge their progress as they move toward and away from the fulfillment of their democratic ideals."[44]

The citizens of the nineteenth-century United States had little history upon which to reflect, nor had they developed a sense of tradition; thus they were not a total community. But Americans then did not long for a strong, artistic culture. They had other things on their minds and were optimistic about their future. This attitude was summarized by President Andrew Jackson in his Farewell Address:

Our growth has been rapid beyond all former example, in numbers, in wealth, in knowledge, and all the useful arts which contribute to the comforts and convenience of man; and from the earliest ages of history to the present day, there never have been thirteen millions of people associated together in one political body who enjoyed so much freedom and happiness as the people of these United States.[45]

Jackson obviously was pleased with the successes of democracy, but, as noted earlier, the poet Walt Whitman realized that democracy under Jackson had not reached the heights that were possible. He stated:

We have frequently printed the word Democracy. Yet I cannot too often repeat that it is a word the real gist of which still sleeps, quite unawakened, notwithstanding the resonance and the many angry tempests out of which its syllables have come, from pen and tongue. It is a great word, whose history, I suppose, remains unwritten, because that history has yet to be enacted.[46]

Whitman also recognized an important missing ingredient:

I say that democracy can never prove itself beyond cavil, until it founds and luxuriantly grows its own forms of art, poems, schools, theology, displacing all that exists, or that has been produced anywhere in the past, under opposite influences.[47]

The democratic society Whitman envisioned—with its own brand of art—was clearly an ideal, and the poet might argue that the twentieth-century United States is not much closer to that ideal than it was in his time. Because the arts were one of the weaker threads woven into the fabric of society, they were therefore one of the weaker means through which society transmitted its basic ideas and beliefs. Only in the area of folk art did democracy seem to triumph.

Notes

1. Arthur M. Schlesinger Jr., *The Age of Jackson* (Boston: Little, Brown and Co., 1945), p. 316.

2. Joseph L. Blau, ed., *Social Theories of Jacksonian Democracy* (New York: Bobbs-Merrill, 1954), from the Introduction of the *United States Magazine and Democratic Review*, October 1837, p. 320. The use of the term "freemen" is ironic, for many white and all black men were

excluded from citizenship. Thompson (*The Democratic Citizen*) provides four qualifications for citizenship in a democracy: participation, discussion, rational voting, and equality (Thompson focused on "equality of participation").

3. The glorification of the common man seems to be a durable thread running throughout the history of American democracy and is even more evident in today's mass culture. A 1985 profile in the *Washington Post* analyzing the popularity of actor Jack Nicholson described him as "epitomizing the peculiar paradox of the American ideal; the world's greatest nation dedicated to one common man." (Paul Attanasio, "Jack Nicholson, Genuinely," *Washington Post*, June 14, 1985, p. C9).

4. Edward Pessen, *Jacksonian America* (Homewood, IL: The Dorsey Press, 1969), p. 179.

5. Glyndon G. van Deuson, *The Jacksonian Era 1828–1848* (New York: Harper & Row, 1959), p. 1.

6. Schlesinger, *The Age of Jackson*, p. 18.

7. Ibid., p. 23.

8. Richard D. Heffner, Introduction, *Democracy in America* by Alexis de Tocqueville (New York: The New American Library, Inc., 1956), p. 9.

9. Tocqueville, *Democracy in America*, p. 26.

10. John William Ward, "Tocqueville and the Meaning of Democracy," *Tocqueville's America 1982*, Washington Seminar (Dallas, Texas: The LTV Corporation, 1982), p. 5.

11. Tocqueville, *Democracy in America*, p. 117.

12. Ibid., p. 148.

13. Ward, *Tocqueville and the Meaning of Democracy*, p. 9.

14. Tocqueville, *Democracy in America*, p. 123.

15. Ibid., p. 198.

16. Dahl, *Dilemmas of Pluralistic Democracy*, p. 36.

17. Ibid., pp. 144–145.

18. Ward, Tocqueville, p. 11.

19. Daniel J. Boorstin, *The Genius of American Politics* (Chicago: University of Chicago Press, 6th ed., 1964), p. 136.

20. George Kateb, "Religion and Politics," *Tocqueville's America*, p. 125.

21. Joe McGinnis, *The Selling of the President 1968* (New York: Pocketbooks, 1970), p. 19.

22. Ralph Ellison, Introduction, *Buying Time: An Anthology Celebrating 20 Years of the Literature Program of the National Endowment for the Arts*, Scott Walker, ed. (St. Paul, MN: Graywolf Press, 1985), p. xiv.

23. Daniel Boorstin, *The Americans: The Democratic Experience* (New York: Random House, 1974), p. 503.

24. Ibid.

25. Tocqueville, *Democracy in America*, p. 158.

26. Schlesinger, *The Age of Jackson*, p. 370.

27. Patricia Elaine Curry, "The American Experience Through a Glass Darkly: Three Case Studies in the Political Thought of John Locke and the Novels of James Fenimore Cooper," Ph.D. dissertation, Indiana University, 1973, p. 173.

28. Robert Penn Warren, *Democracy and Poetry* (Cambridge, MA: Harvard University Press, 1975), p. 3.

29. Walt Whitman, "American Democracy," *Brooklyn Eagle*, April 20, 1847, quoted in Schlesinger, p. 389.

30. Edward McKinley Wheat, "Walt Whitman: A Study in Politics and Literature," Ph.D. dissertation, University of California-Santa Barbara, 1975, p. viii.

31. Ibid., p. 252.

32. Margaret Fuller, quoted in van Deuson, *The Jacksonian Era 1828–1848*, p. 2.

33. Gilbert Chase, *America's Dances* (New York: McGraw-Hill, 1966), p. 53.

34. Agnes DeMille, *American Dances* (New York: Macmillan Publishing Co., 1908), p. 31.

35. Tocqueville, *Democracy in America*, p. 171.

36. Ibid., p. 169.

37. Ibid., p. 171.

38. Ibid., p. 108.

39. Ibid., p. 109.

40. Livingston Biddle, quoted by Roscoe Drummond, "Boosting the Arts," *Christian Science Monitor*, October 1, 1980.

41. Ralph Ellison, Introduction, *Buying Time*, p. xxiv.

42. Ibid.

43. Schlesinger, *The Age of Jackson*, p. 374.

44. Ellison, *Buying Time*, p. xxv.

45. Andrew Jackson, "Farewell Address," at the Inaugural of Martin Van Buren, 1837, quoted in Blau.

46. Walt Whitman, "Democratic Vistas," quoted in *To Hell With Culture* by Herbert Read (New York: Schocken Books, 1964), p. 11.

47. Ibid., p. 36.

Twentieth-Century American Democracy

Before testing the theory of participatory democracy and the arts in today's American political system, we should examine the system as it evolved from the early nineteenth-century model examined in the last chapter. By the mid–nineteenth century, the antislavery movement and the Civil War dampened enthusiasm for Jacksonian Democracy. Furthermore, expanding industrialization and the rise of an unstable mass population—which grew, in part, because of increased immigration—placed great stress on democratic theory. In essence, America's hybrid version of democracy has been a constantly changing experiment, especially since the two world wars.

THE AMERICAN HYBRID MODEL OF DEMOCRACY: AN OVERVIEW

Chapter 2 outlined models of American democracy, according to Dahl's descriptions, and Chapter 6 discussed his model of Populist Democracy in relation to the arts and the Jacksonian era. This chapter begins with one of Dahl's models to describe twentieth-century American democracy.

An underlying concept of Dahl's hybrid model (see Chapter 2)—a model most appropriate to the current U.S. political system—is that the "tyranny of the majority" no longer exists. Political commentator George F. Will has addressed the issue as well:

Well, what we have is a country now so lumpy with interest groups that we have devised a rather soothing. . . view of what politics consist of in this country. That is, if you accept Madison's view of the swirl of self-interested people in different factions,

you certainly solve the political problem . . . and it is tyranny. . . .
Because you will not have, as indeed we never had in this country,
a stable tyrannical majority.[1]

American government functions with the varying rule of minorities,
and all active and legitimate groups can make their views heard at
some crucial stage in the decision-making process. Under "tyranny of
the minority," numbers do not always matter; "its intensity, who's
paying attention, who's reading the *Federal Register*"[2] matters more.

Although late to the game of using political skills to influence the
system, arts groups have become most successful in acting as an
extremely effective minority. (See Chapter 3 and Chapter 4.) Their
intensity was particularly evident in 1981, following the release of the
Reagan administration's first budget, which called for a 50 percent
decrease in funding for the National Endowments for the Arts and
Humanities. Joining in a strong national coalition, all the major advocacy groups successfully orchestrated an intense grassroots lobbying effort[3] that persuaded Congress to reject the proposed funding
decrease.

Yet, as important as associations are to American society in general,
and to the political decision-making process specifically, they tend to
have disadvantages. In *Dilemmas of Pluralistic Democracy*, Dahl outlined a variety of defects of associations, including stabilizing injustice
and distorting the public agenda. (See Chapter 2.) While the role of
interest groups continues to be debated, other aspects of American
democracy that may have even greater effects on the political system
should be examined. The rest of this chapter provides an overview of
some of the emerging problems associated with the macrodemocracy
in America today and how these problems affect individuals and their
political participation.

PROBLEMS OF TWENTIETH-CENTURY AMERICAN DEMOCRACY

Historian Daniel Boorstin has outlined a number of problems with
contemporary American democracy that are examined below. In
Democracy and Its Discontents, Boorstin states that the major failure of
American democracy is its success: "There is an obvious cure for
Failure—and that is Success. But what is the cure for Success? This is
a characteristically American problem."[4] Boorstin provided a survey
of democracy in America today, not to "dispraise American
democracy—one of man's most amazing and surprising achievements
on this earth—but rather to help prevent us from being disillusioned."

We can accomplish this, he said, only if we make an honest, ruthless effort to see the price tag that history has placed on our civilization."[5]

Boorstin's inventory begins with "the disease of communication." According to Boorstin, the rapid expansion in the means of communication is the "most important single change in the human consciousness" in the last century. Today the technology of communication is everywhere; at anytime we are no more than a short distance from a radio, television, or telephone. He called this "the disease of communication."

Communication around the world can be instantaneous, and billions of people can be witnesses to a single event. Neil Armstrong's walk on the moon in 1969, witnessed on television by two billion people, was one of the first in a series of now-frequent events seen instantaneously by billions of people across the world. Typically an American phenomenon, these mass electronic events, ranging from the 1985 Live Aid concert to raise money for the starving in Africa to the Super Bowl and the summer and winter Olympic Games, often bring a sense of unity to the country. One particular event, the subject of a CBS television *Sunday Morning* profile (February 20, 1983)—was the mini-series *The Winds of War*, based on the book by Herman Wouk. The show was viewed by 140 million Americans over the week it was aired, and "sometimes in three-hour stretches, this strangely and wonderfully diverse nation was almost united."

In *Media: The Second God*, Tony Schwartz described the power of the electronic media: "God-like, the media can change the course of a war, bring down a president or a king, elevate the lowly, and humiliate the proud, by directing the attention of millions on the same event and in the same manner."[6] For millions to learn of the assassination of President Lincoln took months; Schwartz indicates that by the time eight months had passed, only 85 percent of U.S. citizens knew. Yet, millions learned of President Kennedy's death within minutes of the shooting and by nightfall virtually the entire country was in mourning.

Closely tied to the rapid expansion of the techniques of communication has been the change in our concept of the phenomenon of "public opinion." In reviewing Tocqueville's observations of the previous century, Richard Reeves noted the "technologically driven speedup of democracy," compared to "the slow buildup of public opinion that Tocqueville had seen."[7] Public opinion today can be measured quite accurately and no longer has the negative connotation associated with "mere opinion." Today, the common belief is that responsible citizens all have opinions and should express them. More than thirty years ago, Bernard Berelson helped lay the foundation for today's extensive use of public opinion research. Uniting democratic theory and public opinion research, Berelson demonstrated that "opinion studies can help a democracy not only to know itself in a topical and immediate way but also to evaluate its achievement and its progress in more general terms."[8]

National pollsters—like Louis Harris, who has conducted the periodic survey *Americans and the Arts* since 1973—are courted by politicians and testify before congressional committees. Harris, who is a member of the board of the American Council for the Arts, has testified before the House Interior Appropriations Subcommittee on the results of his surveys. At a 1985 meeting with members of the Congressional Arts Caucus, following Harris's appearance before the subcommittee, various U.S. Representatives requested copies of his questionnaire to send to their constituents. Even if no specific action took place following these polls, at least many constituents must have appreciated being asked their opinions.

In addition to "the disease of communication" and changes in our concept of public opinion, the third item on Boorstin's inventory of American democracy is the tremendous growth of advertising, which he calls "the rhetoric of democracy." Early advertising was to educate and inform; advertising today is to persuade. In a country where a democratized standard of living is important, advertising attempts to persuade everyone that everything is available for all—a condition not helpful to stability. Advertisers, not concerned with the stability issue, continue to pay exorbitant sums, particularly on television, to promote their products (for example, companies have paid tens of thousands of dollars per second for television commercials aired during the Super Bowl). Simple products to fulfill basic needs are no longer the only items advertised; businesses have learned to create needs for "perpetually unsatisfied" consumers whom they educate to have "unappeasable appetites."[9] George F. Will has proposed that perhaps Madison Avenue may be the Main Street of America:

> Madison Avenue, named after the great definer of a self-interested policy, is devoted to inculcating envy and restlessness and dissatisfaction; devoted to shortening, if you will, the ability to defer gratification, inciting people to want more. And it certainly is, I think, an important element in making the American economic system and American society tick.[10]

Even public broadcasting has not been immune to the power of advertising. Concerned with the increased funding provided to public broadcasting by large corporations and the influence these funds might have in programming, Rep. Edward Markey (D-MA) stated that "the idea of increased advertising on public television and radio deeply concerns me."[11] Following Markey's remarks in the *Congres-*

sional Record was an article from *TV Guide* that specifically discussed public broadcasting and oil companies. For example, Mobil Oil spent approximately $20 million and Atlantic Richfield spent $15 million on public broadcasting during the 1970s, when such support was recognized by only a single line of type at the beginning and end of programs. By the beginning of the 1980s, however, stations were allowed to display corporations' logos. The obvious concern now became "whether a corporation, simply by making a contribution, has a subliminal impact on the kinds of programs public broadcasting will undertake."[12]

The tremendous expansion of communications, including the new capabilities for measuring public opinion, as well as the unprecedented growth of advertising, has helped to create a "mass culture"—one that fosters tremendous growth in what has become known as the popular arts. These popular arts, particularly those available via the electronic media, did not exist until the emergence of a mass society in the 1700s. Prior to the eighteenth century, serious artists created for, and were financially dependent on, a minority. With the growth of population during the eighteenth century and its concentration in cities, the popular arts began to flourish: "We could say that the popular arts are more 'democratic,' since they are accessible to larger numbers of people and that 'high art' tends to be 'aristocratic,' the province of the more cultivated."[13] (See discussion of elite theory in Chapter 4.) By the mid–eighteenth century, many artists began to create, for profit, the kind of art this mass public wanted.

By the mid–nineteenth century, mass society was rapidly developing, and the mass medium of newspapers helped to spread popular culture. The advent of radio, television and film in the twentieth century established the popular arts more securely. Curtis B. Gans, who has made an extensive study of popular culture, presented arguments in favor of cultural democracy, a society of "aesthetic pluralism" in which each "taste public"—high culture, upper-middle culture, lower-middle culture, low culture, and quasi-folk low culture—has its own standards, and in which society provides "subcultural programming" to satisfy the standards of every public. In 1985, however, Gans updated his research to note changes in American culture and modified his original classifications.[14] He described the emergence of a new taste public that seemed to cut across and blend upper and lower-middle culture. Similar to the upwardly mobile categories of the VALS system described in Chapter 3, this new taste public "is less interested in symbols than in goods; more in a set of hobby-like activities than in the traditional arts" and it feels no need to revere high culture. Gans also noted that the emergence of this new "middle culture," whose arts interests are so varied, coupled with an expansion of the arts categories enjoyed by a large portion of the American population, lends support to John Dewey's notion that the arts with the most validity for the greatest part of the population are not considered arts at all.

With this trend increasing, the lines between high and popular culture will continue to blur. In other countries, high culture has been centralized and organized, but in the United States, high culture is the least centralized. Popular culture, which thrives on advertising, the "rhetoric of democracy," has become our "centrally organized mass-produced folk culture,"[15] or, as Christopher Lasch noted: "the masses had thrown off ancient folkways only to fall victim to modern advertising."[16] American democracy has produced this folk culture, which is discontinuous and self-destructive; the problem remains for Americans to find new ways to create continuity in their overall life experience.

INDIVIDUAL CONSEQUENCES OF TWENTIETH-CENTURY AMERICAN DEMOCRACY

Twentieth-century American macrodemocracy, saturated with a plethora of communications media peppered with constant advertising, has the capacity to overwhelm the individual, possibly affecting his ability to participate in the worlds of art and politics. Living in this type of macrodemocracy has a variety of everyday consequences.

As an individual moves through the daily tasks demanded by twentieth-century life, he encounters the problem of attenuation—the thinning or flattening—of experience. That is, technological advances that make everyday life so much easier have also deprived us of the charms of the unexpected—"life is punctuated by commas and semicolons rather than periods and exclamation marks."[17] Ownership of property is one example of an experience that has been attenuated. The American ideal of property was initially based on John Locke's ideas expressed in his essay *On Civil Government* (1690). According to Locke, property is the mixing of labor with an object, and no government has the right to take it away; in a simple society, "there was something poignant and characteristic about the experience of ownership."[18] Today, however, we have new forms of property: shares of stock (corporate property); installment and credit ownership; and the rise of franchising. The concept of property ownership has become vague, no longer as poignant as Locke described.

To the average American, experiencing the arts also has become attenuated: the arts "pour down on us in an incessant barrage."[19] Our magazine racks are cluttered with literature appealing to the thousands of segmented interests—testament to the "Tocquevillean structure of American culture—an array of fragmented interest groups."[20] The constant bombardment of television images shortens attention spans and leaves little in the way of visual images to surprise. In his comprehensive study of the inner workings of the management of network television, Todd Gitlin described the tremendous hypnotic effect of the medium: "Television has probably rewired the collective nervous system, making discontinuity the norm of perception, shortening the collective attention span down toward the vanishing point."[21] Young people, so accustomed to MTV (the cable music channel) now expect a video presentation with each new release of a popular song.

Another everyday consequence of American macrodemocracy is the decline of congregation. Technology has brought most of our necessities to our homes. We no longer must go—to use Boorstin's phrase— "like Rebecca to the well to get water." We have become more isolated. Only through the electronic media do we achieve a sense of national unity, but this unity is too often sporadic and short-lived.

From the beginning of American colonization, "people desperately tried to create communities," stated historian James Oliver Robertson in *American Myth, American Reality*.[22] Even as our nation grew, the predominant symbol of real community was—and still remains—the rural, agrarian small town. Most Americans, however, live in urban or suburban settings, where they have a series of partial communities: the home community, the extended family community, the work community. Large corporations today often transfer executives, a situation making the corporation the only stable community in the life of the individual. Michael Novak, in *The Spirit of Democratic Capitalism*, described these fragmented communities as "communities of the spirit,"[23] where individuals find the company of workmates and friends who share the same values more comfortable than sitting down to Thanksgiving dinner with family members whose politics they abhor. Lacking the closeness and community of family, the only connection among these alternate communities is in the mind and experience of the individual. The individual is free to construct a unique community, but this freedom also reinforces his anonymity in U.S. society.

Furthermore, lack of a regular and lasting community experience does not benefit a society seeking to create a flourishing culture as one of its top priorities. (See Michael Straight's societal conditions for a flourishing culture in Chapter 1.) In this aspect, American macrodemocracy is most different from the Greek microdemocracy examined in Chapter 5. Robertson suggested that American spectator sports function, like the Greek arts festivals, as rituals to reinforce society's myths. Calling the participants "communicants," he noted that the uninitiated would have difficulty understanding the procedures, ceremony, and excitement that seem to reinforce the ideal of democratic participation. These mass events "aim at the creation and maintenance of the ideals of community in the midst of the fragmentary forces of urban life."[24]

Another problem of twentieth-century American democracy is the rising sense of momentum and the accompanying lack of control felt by the individual. The development of atomic power is one graphic example; scientists developed it, but could not stop government from using it destructively. The increased momentum of a democratizing society, although enriching experience, continues to dilute it.[25]

Yet another problem of today's society is the popular fallacy that democracy is attainable. Aristocracy, monarchy, and even totalitarianism present ideals that are more easily attainable. Democracy, however, is a process, not a product. Our society is better at "reaching for" than "finding." Every seeming solution becomes a problem in itself (for example, mass production of the automobile has helped to create traffic jams). In summary, having taken an inventory of American democracy and discussing its everyday consequences, Boorstin also provided a view of what American democracy needs to do to remain a vital and optimistic force. His suggestions, as well as the ideas of other writers, are discussed in Chapter 9.

THE EFFECT ON PARTICIPATION

Chapter 3 highlighted the sociological perspectives of participation in the arts and the various cycles of participation as societal values have changed. In simpler societies, the relationship of these values to participation was easier to observe, but in a society as complex as that of the twentieth-century United States, these relationships have become more complicated.

National political participation in the American macrodemocracy often becomes an overwhelming task for the individual. In a country of more than 240 million people, one person can begin to feel very ineffectual. Communication, which is beneficial by bringing information about candidates, often brings too much, and the individual voter becomes confused. Candidates begin to sound alike; issues are blurred; and the citizen begins to think his single vote does not matter.

Voting trends, in fact, indicate that voters feel alienated from the political process. With the exception of a slight upturn in 1984, voter turnout for presidential elections has steadily declined since 1960, when 62.8 percent of the voting-age population voted. The 1960 percentage was the highest since voting privileges were extended to women in 1920. In the 1988 election, however, only 50 percent of eligible voters exercised their right to vote, the lowest turnout since 1924 when the figure was between 43 and 49 percent.[26]

Contributing to the low turnout rate in presidential elections is the increased sophistication of technology. Although not instantaneous, the electronic system tabulating votes in our presidential elections provides quick results to television stations. This, along with the varied time zones across the country, has an effect on voter participation on the West Coast. For example, in the case of a perceived landslide, voters often decide their vote would be inconsequential, they don't vote, and overall participation declines. A case in point: early during the 1980 election evening, many Carter supporters had heard that Reagan was the projected winner; thinking their vote wouldn't matter, they stayed home and watched the Reagan victory.

Turnout for the 1986 primary elections was the lowest in more than twenty years and countered the light 1984 upturn. According to a survey by the Committee for the Study of the American Electorate,[27] a nonpartisan research organization, the average turnout for the most contested races was 10.3 percent, compared with 11.8 percent in 1982 and 18 percent in 1966, the earliest year for which these statistics exist. Gans, director of the committee, explained the low turnout: "voters more and more think their votes don't make any difference because no one seems to be able to solve seemingly intractable problems"[28]

More than twenty years ago, President John F. Kennedy, hoping to prevent such a cycle of decreasing voter turnout, established a commission to study what he believed was an extremely low rate of political participation.[29] The commission's recommendations, presented shortly after Kennedy's death, included:

The abolition of poll taxes and literacy tests
The enfranchisement of minorities and youth between the ages of
     18 and 20
Shortening the time between the close of registration and voting
Voter outreach programs
Establishing an election day holiday
Mail registration
Bilingual ballots
Liberalization of state and local residency tests

Two decades later, virtually all the recommendations have been implemented in whole or in part, with the exception of an election day holiday, and only twenty states have mail registration. And yet the United States remains "the lowest participating democracy in the world with the occasional and possible exceptions of Switzerland and India."[30]

Gans has said the primary reason for declining voter participation is that a smaller percentage of the electorate believes in the efficacy of their ballots. Gans also has noted that nonvoters "tend not to participate in any other form of political, civic, religious or social activity."[31] Citizens who react to a macrodemocracy by not voting fit into four categories, according to Gans:

(1) The largest group is comprised of chronic nonvoters who tend to be in the underclass: poor, young, less educated, unemployed, minority, either rural or urban. They also tend not to participate in other social, religious, or civic activities.

(2) The second group is comprised of approximately 20 million citizens who have dropped out of the political process, like those in group one. Their demographics are similar to group one, but 40 percent of this group is educated, middle-class, professional, and living in the suburbs. According to Gans's survey, they were the most alienated and most adamant that their vote no longer had any efficacy.

(3) Group three is comprised of the young—the lowest participating group in America who "are becoming socialized to participate at a slower rate than previous generations, and their interest in politics as a group is substantially lower than the rest of the nation's."

(4) The fourth category involves approximately one-tenth of the nonvoters who still perceive themselves to be blocked by impediments beyond their control: intimidation at the polls, insufficient places to register, too short a registration period, and so on.

Most importantly, Gans has stressed that voting is a very complex act: "Participation is a product of our upbringing and schooling, of the laws and rules governing the political process, of the issues of the day, the forces within our society, the influences of the media and the quality of our lives."[32] Fine-tuning the Kennedy commission's recommendations would help slightly, as Gans has said, but in general, movement toward the participatory society envisioned by Pateman would be even more beneficial.

Ironically, as dismal as the statistics are for voter turnout at the national level, the very technology that has caused the "disease of communication" has often made it easier for individuals to participate in local decisions. One example is interactive cable television, which allows the viewer to communicate back to the program. The first use of this technology was the Qube two-way cable system in Columbus, Ohio. Viewers were able to answer general polling questions or specific questions about the program they were watching. Their "votes" were tabulated almost instantly and displayed on the screen.[33]

In *Media: The Second God*, Schwartz pointed to a recent experiment in Alaska using electronic town meetings. Through a combination of telephone and television, viewers were able to see the moderator and speakers, as well as to ask questions and vote. According to Schwartz, "More people watched the television town meeting than have participated in all town meetings since the founding of the state of Alaska."[34] Voting in regular elections was approximately 23 percent, while voting in town meetings neared 66 percent.

The city of Santa Monica, California, has also experimented with direct citizen communication by computer. Through the Public Electronic Network, individuals with a home computer could send letters to City Hall.[35]

A final example of the impact of technology on political participation is the televising of the proceedings of the U.S. House of Representatives and Senate. Since the first images of congressional debate beamed across the country by C-SPAN (Cable-Satellite Public Affairs Network), a small audience quickly grew to a quarter-million regular viewers by 1984, only five years after the House of Representatives authorized this use of television. C-SPAN celebrated its tenth anniversary in 1989 with a potential audience of 41.5 million (up from 3.5 million in 1979.)[36] Even more surprising than number of viewers has been the emergence of "a devoted national cult of Congress-watchers" or "C-SPAN junkies"[37] who are fascinated by the everyday mechanics of government in action.

Not only did television change the clothes, hairstyles, and manner of speaking of the members of Congress in chambers, but it also increased the use of "special orders," the longer periods of time for speakers to discuss topics seemingly unrelated to specific legislation. During the first few years of C-SPAN coverage, a small group of Republicans persisted in using special orders to tell a national audience of the "abuses" by Democratic majority in Congress. Their vehement speeches were so effective in reaching a large number of potential voters that former Speaker of the House Thomas P. O'Neill, Jr. ordered the cameras to pan the chamber to show home viewers that the speakers, who acted as if the chamber were full, were talking to no one but the television audience.

With the addition of the daily Senate proceedings on the airwaves in 1986, Americans are now able to watch both legislative bodies in action. This unique form of passive political participation is very similar to the passive arts participation discussed in Chapter 4 and could lead to varying degrees of more active participation as viewera begin to take more interest in the functioning of the national government. One regular C-SPAN viewer attached importance to the regular broadcast of Congress:

I think more people are going to learn about this, and that is going to make a big difference in our democracy. I think we'll find out that C-SPAN is the most important thing that's happened to democracy since the invention of moveable type.[38]

While C-SPAN has the potential to change the participation habits of only those Americans receiving cable or satellite, it clearly is one of the best examples of the positive impact of technology on national politics. Democracy in twentieth-century America has become a "spectator event," Richard Roderick noted. Roderick, who has assigned his classes at the University of Texas to watch C-SPAN, said that if the network continues to expand its audience, "it could eventually recreate real participatory democracy."[39]

America's cultural community, too, has become a sort of "spectator event"; how technology has affected the arts is still open to debate.

Chapter 4 presented findings from the 1987 Harris survey *Americans and the Arts*: Arts participation, particularly passive participation as an audience, increased from 1975 to 1984, with slight decreases being noted in the 1987 survey. Active individual participation, which rose sharply from 1975 to 1980 and increased slightly in 1984, declined less than passive participation in 1987. Of particular interest, however, is the growing role of television and VCRs (video cassette recorders). Attendance at live performances was preferred, in most cases, to watching such entertainment on television (67 percent attended live theatre, compared to 53 percent who watched it on television; 60 percent attended live pop concerts, compared to 57 percent who watched them on television; 35 percent attended opera, compared to 20 percent who viewed it on television). However, in the case of attendance at classical music concerts, 31 percent attended live concerts, while 41 percent watched them on television.

Many of the increased number of television viewing hours can be attributed to the growth of cable television and the use of VCRs. The 1984 Harris survey found 47 percent of all households had cable television and 17 percent had VCRs. Of high attenders of live performances, Harris found 21 to 28 percent own VCRs. This figure is consistent with the results of this book's 1986 survey of individuals greatly involved in both politics and the arts (28 percent own VCRs). (See Chapter 8.) By 1987, cable ownership had increased to 53 percent, but VCR ownership had skyrocketed to 55 percent. Harris noted that because fewer households subscribe to cable, and those that do tend to be less educated and less arts-oriented than VCR owners, the latter technology holds more promise for increasing arts participation.[40]

The effect of this increased use of technology on arts participation, however, is still a matter of debate. In 1981, Jon Goberman, director of Media Development for the Lincoln Center in Washington, DC, presented a speech entitled "Cable—Destiny or Destination?" in which he explored the electronic future of the arts and enumerated several fallacies. Cable does not, he stressed, ensure new audiences for the arts: "Right now, and for the future, we're in no better position with cable than we are with the networks, indeed, worse, because cable has neither the programming revenues to deal with us, nor the occasional guilt of the networks."[41]

Another fallacy: the arts are an unlimited resource for broadcasting. According to Goberman, once you have programmed blockbuster hits and major stars, audience drops off by 50 to 75 percent, and even though viewers say they want more cultural programming, they only want more movies. He noted that surveys indicate a desire for more ballet and chamber music, but "I think that's the result of the fact that [we have greatly] underestimated the capacity of the American public to lie about the arts."[42]

Perhaps advertising, "the rhetoric of democracy," and its sister discipline, public relations, have persuaded people that they should like cultural activities and that a dose of ballet or opera via cable would be easier to take. Whatever the reason, the effects of technology on individuals and their arts participation levels are still being debated.

Like participation in politics, participation in the arts is complex, influenced not only by demographic factors, but also by the particular problems of American macrodemocracy enumerated in this chapter. Chapter 8 looks more closely at the arts in mid–twentieth century America and the particular role of participation.

Notes

1. George Will, "American Politics Today," in *Tocqueville's America 1982*, p. 18.

2. Ibid., p. 28.

3. This lobbying effort was also responsible for an increase in membership of the newly formed Congressional Arts Caucus. Members of the House of Representatives who joined the caucus were able to tell their constituents that they were—at the very least—keeping them informed about issues in the arts.

4. Daniel Boorstin, *Democracy and Its Discontents* (New York: Random House, 1974), p. xi.

5. Ibid. p. xiv.

6. Tony Schwartz, *Media: The Second God* (Garden City, NY: Anchor Books, 1983), pp. 2–3.

7. Richard Reeves, *American Journey* (New York: Simon & Schuster, 1982), p. 244.

8. Bernard Berelson, "Democratic Theory and Public Opinion," *Public Opinion Quarterly*, Fall 1952, p. 330.

9. Christopher Lasch, *The Culture of Narcissism* (New York: W. W. Norton & Company, 1978), p. 72.

10. Will, "American Politics Today," p. 18. Marshall McLuhan, however, viewed ads with a more benign attitude: "Ads of our times are the richest and most faithful daily reflections that any society ever made of its entire range of activities" (*Understanding Media* [New York: New American Library, 1964], p. 206).

11. Hon. Edward J. Markey, *Congressional Record*, July 21, 1981, p. E3616.

12. John Weisman, "Why Big Oil Loves Public TV," *TV Guide*, June 20, 1981, inserted in the *Congressional Record*, July 21, 1981, p. E3617.

13. William M. Hammel, *The Popular Arts in America: A Reader* (New York: Harcourt Brace Jovanovitch, 1972), p. 1.

14. Gans in Wyszomirski and Balfe, *Public Policy*.

15. Boorstin, *Democracy and Its Discontents*, p. 306.

16. Christopher Lasch, "Mass Culture Reconsidered," *Democracy: A Journal of Political Renewal and Radical Change*, Vol. 1, No. 4, October 1981, p. 10.

17. Boorstin, *The Americans: The Democratic Experience*, p. 306.

18. Boorstin, *Democracy and Its Discontents*, p. 109.

19. Jacques Barzun, *The Use and Abuse of Art* (Princeton: Princeton University Press, 1975), p. 145.

20. Todd Gitlin, "New Video Technology: Pluralism or Banality," *Democracy: Culture vs. Democracy*, Vol. I, No. 4, October 1981, p. 68.

21. Todd Gitlin, *Inside Prime Time* (New York: Pantheon Books, 1983), p. 334.

22. James Oliver Robertson, *American Myth, American Reality* (New York: Hill & Wang, 1980), p. 215.

23. Michael Novak, *The Spirit of Democratic Capitalism* (New York: Simon & Schuster, 1982), p. 137.

24. Robertson, *American Myth, American Reality*, p. 256.

25. Ibid., p. 108.

26. "Experts Say Low 1988 Turnout May Be Repeated," *New York Times*, November 11, 1988, p. 17.

27. The Committee for the Study of the American Electorate was founded in 1976 by a bipartisan, tax-exempt research corporation to study the causes and cures of low and declining voter participation. The organization is based on the fundamental premise that "while there may be no optimal level of voter participation, the level of voting is a barometer of the well-being of American democracy and that only with a high level of sustaining and thoughtful voter participation can the United States reach its full potential as a democracy" ("Non-Voter Study '85 '86," a publication by the Committee, 1986).

28. Curtis B. Gans, quoted by James R. Dickenson in "Voter Turnout Falls to Record Low," *Washington Post*, September 9, 1986.

29. Curtis B. Gans, "Remobilizing the American Electorate," unpublished paper for the Thomas P. O'Neill, Jr. Symposium, Boston College, October 5, 1985.

30. Ibid., p. 2.

31. Gans quoted in "An American Habit: Shunning the Ballot Box," *New York Times*, January 31, 1988.

32. Gans, "Remobilizing the American Electorate," pp. 6–7.

33. Schwartz, p. 156.

34. Ibid., p. 157.

35. "Computers Are Linking Citizens and City Hall," *New York Times*, March 5, 1989.

36. Warren Weaver, Jr., "C-Span on the Hill: 10 Years of Gavel to Gavel," *New York Times*, March 28, 1989, p. 10.

37. T. R. Reid, "Congress: Best Little Soap Opera on Cable," *Washington Post*, April 29, 1984, p. B1.

38. Aileen Weber, quoted by T. R. Reid. Ibid., p. B4.

39. Richard Roderick, quoted by Jeanne Saddler, "The Eyes Have It: U.S. House Sessions Are a TV Addiction," *Wall Street Journal*, June 13, 1984, placed in the *Congressional Record* by Sen. Howard Baker (June 13, 1984, p. S7035). Baker highlighted the importance of the "participatory element" to American society in his proceeding statement.

40. Harris survey, *Americans and the Arts V*, p. 23.

41. John Goberman, "Cable—Destiny or Destination?" *ACUCCA Bulletin*, No. 84, May, 1981, p. 3.

42. Ibid.

8

Participation in the Arts: Mid–Twentieth Century America

Chapter 3 introduced systems diagrams depicting the interrelationships between individuals and institutions participating in the arts. With Figure 3.3 in mind, this chapter describes today's American system of arts support, as well as the role of economics and the levels of active and passive arts participation.

THE AMERICAN SYSTEM OF SUPPORT FOR THE ARTS

Chapter 7 illustrated the complexity of mid–twentieth century American society and the many problems of our macrodemocracy. This chapter relies on that background information to develop a "larger culture" framework in which the production-distribution-consumption system functions.

Critical study of the patterns of group action within a social system is called functional analysis. Although it is an abstraction, a social system reflects observable and empirically verifiable behaviors of the actors and is "a complex of stable, repetitive, and patterned action that is in part a manifestation of the culture shared by the actors, and in part a manifestation of the psychological orientations of the actors (which are in turn derived from that culture)."[1] In the twentieth-century American arts system, a stable, repetitive, patterned action is the production, distribution, and consumption of art. Components of the system (artists, producers, audiences, government agencies, etc.) are actually subsystems themselves, and their actions can be analyzed in terms of their contribution to maintaining or disrupting the system's stability. An action is functional if it maintains stability, dysfunctional if it disrupts stability. Although "no agreed upon criteria exist for establishing linkages between the components of a system, and no standard formulas can uncover the precise contribution that a given repetitive form of action makes to the stability of a system,"[2] a functional analysis of the American system of arts support can help us understand this complex social phenomenon.

Components of the System

Figure 8.1 illustrates the components of the American arts-support system. Although similar to Robinson's diagram (Figure 3.3), it includes the additional component, arts advocate, that is part of the theoretical discussion of arts participation in Chapter 4.

Background: Growth of the Public Component

For most of our country's history, the arts have depended heavily on private funding. Except for military bands, the U.S. Library of Congress, the Smithsonian Institution, and a few commissions to

Figure 8.1

Systems Diagram of Twentieth-Century Arts Participation

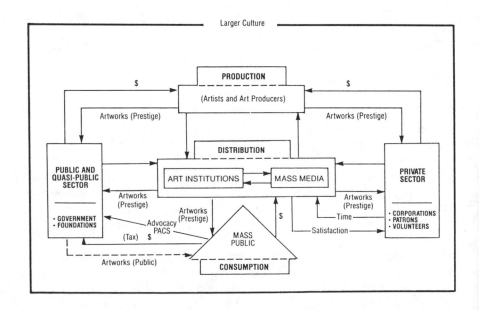

oversee art projects for public buildings, the federal government has paid little attention to cultural activities. And, in general, state and local governments have followed a similar example. "For the most part, the only interest that politicians took in the arts until this century was in the design and glorification of their working quarters, whether they were in the capital of the nation or in state capitals, county seats, cities, or towns."[3] However, as American society has matured, cultural concerns have figured more prominently in public policy.

This gradual process can be traced in a number of ways. Because this book intertwines politics and the arts, an appropriate method to provide a historical overview of the slow acceptance of the arts as a legitimate item on the public policy agenda is to trace the appearance of cultural concerns in the platforms of our political parties.[4]

Political Party Platforms. Platforms act as "one barometer of opinion in American political history,"[5] and give important clues to society's collective ideas on various topics. Political scientist Gerald M. Pomper has conducted extensive analyses of party platforms and has shown that they can be used to predict public-policy changes. According to Pomper's research, platform promises, or pledges, are kept at a very high rate: for the period from 1944 to 1966, more than half of all pledges were fulfilled by direct congressional or executive action; nearly three-fourths of all promises were kept by full action, executive action, similar action, or appropriate inaction; and only one-tenth were completely ignored. Furthermore, 85 percent of all bipartisan pledges (those contained in both the Republican and Democratic party platforms) were fulfilled.[6] For the period from 1968 to 1978, a time of much political turmoil, the percentages were only slightly lower: Two-thirds of all pledges were still fulfilled.[7] According to Paul David, this impressive record was made possible because the platforms offered a series of "coherent proposals that were currently ready for public debate and definitive national action."[8]

Indeed, the history of national party platforms provides a useful barometer of changing attitudes in the United States regarding government support of the arts, in particular, public encouragement for greater individual participation in cultural activities.

At their national nominating convention in 1840, the Democrats were the first to construct a platform and adopt it, and since then, party platforms have emerged every four years—a testament to their perceived value, if only as general policy statements. However, no mention of American cultural concerns was made in any party platform until 1912, when the Progressive party noted in its platform the need for conservation of "human resources"—a rather general concept that could include "artistic resources," although "greater arts participation" was not specifically mentioned. In 1920, the Republican platform included a similar statement referring to human resources, and the 1928 platforms mentioned the new technology of radio, later allied with television and film, in discussions of American technological arts. Motion pictures found their way into the Prohibition party's platform of 1932:

> We favor federal control at the source of the output of the motion picture industry to prevent the degrading influence of immoral pictures and insidious propaganda connected therewith.[9]

The Prohibition party repeated its call for federal censorship in 1936. In 1940, the Republicans approved censorship in the form of radio licensing.

The year 1948 saw the first specific statement in any party platform concerning culture:

> The Progressive Party recognizes culture as a potentially powerful force in the moral and spiritual life of a people and through the people, in its growth of democracy and the preservation of peace, and realizes that the culture of a democracy must, like its government, be of, by, and for the people.
>
> We pledge ourselves to establish a department of government that shall be known as the Department of Culture, whose function should be the promotion of all the arts as our expression of the spirit of the American people, and toward the enrichment of the people's lives, to make the arts available to all.[10]

This was the first four-year policy statement that recognized the value of arts to the growth of democracy, and, most importantly, the need for greater participation by making the arts "available to all."

Although the Progressive party suggested a Department of Culture, actual implementation of that idea came nearly two decades later, in 1965, with the creation of the National Endowments for the Arts and Humanities (NEA and NEH). Not until 1960 had a major political party placed the arts on the public agenda, when the Democratic platform included an "arts plank," that is, a statement specifically concerned with issues affecting the arts. That platform called for the encouragement of participation and appreciation of our cultural life and the creation of a federal advisory agency for cultural resources: a suitably vague statement that served as a building block for later arts planks.

For example, in 1964, the Democrats set forth an arts plank with two specific goals: the creation of an arts advisory commission and the establishment of a national performing arts center—the John F. Kennedy Center for the Performing Arts in Washington, DC. The Republicans, however, were not ready to add the arts to their agenda until the early 1970s.

In 1972, 1976, and 1980, the Democrats and Republicans included an arts plank in each of their platforms—an indication that Americans believed more strongly that government should become directly involved with cultural activities, although the call for greater arts participation appeared only sporadically. In 1984, the Democratic platform, with nearly 45,000 words, was designed to unite the Democrats in electing a president; consequently, its arts plank only contained general statements about the arts in a few nonspecific pledges.[11]

The 1984 Republican platform was the product of a rather disorderly drafting process, of which a very conservative wing of the party seized control, and contained no subsection entitled "arts and humanities." Cultural concerns were a mere afterthought in the education section; following several paragraphs on technology, mention of the arts and humanities was in four sentences emphasizing private-sector support and greater access. These four sentences, despite their seemingly casual placement, were important: they reinforce Parsons' theory that society's values can be transmitted through the arts (see Chapter 3) and emphasize the importance of widespread participation.

In 1988, the Democrats settled on a brief platform of less than 5,000 words, in sharp contrast to their 1984 statement. They seemed to be urging voters to vote democratic because "this time we have a small agenda and promise to keep government out of your way." Since they were attempting to stay away from special interests, no arts plank was included, and cultural concerns received only a token note in the paragraph discussing education, where the Democrats pledged to "expand support for the arts and humanities."

The 1988 Republican platform, although still a relatively conservative document, contained a specific arts plank, but emphasized private support ("We will support full deductibility for donations to tax-exempt cultural institutions in order to encourage the private support of the arts and humanities"). In short, the Republican and Democratic statements of 1988 signaled a return to a more conservative viewpoint; participation was not a major concern. However, in general, national party platforms have come to recognize the arts as a matter of public policy and, specifically, a vehicle for transmitting values, such as greater participation.

Arts Legislation. In general, over the last two decades, government legislation concerning the arts has taken a course parallel to national party platforms by encouraging gradual public-sector involvement and greater participation. Lawrence Mankin has examined three distinct periods of government involvement with the arts in the twentieth century: the Relief Period (1933–1943), the Period of the Great Scare (1938–1958), and the Period of Promise beginning in 1965.[12]

When Franklin Delano Roosevelt became president on March 4, 1933, there were 10,000 unemployed artists. On May 12, 1933, he signed the Federal Emergency Relief Act, which provided the foundation for the Works Progress Administration (WPA) of 1935. The first official announcement of the Federal Artists Project, under the WPA, occurred on August 2, 1935, and outlined the employment program in the fields of art, music, drama, and writing.[13] By 1938, the program had employed more than 20,000 artists (3,622 in art; 10,005 in music; 3,786 in theatre; and 3,023 in writing).[14] The Relief Period had begun. Problems arose within this agency, particularly with theatrical productions, and the project was terminated; however, the Federal Arts Project established a precedent for the national government's support of the artist as worker. Furthermore, the program was the most prominent example of the federal government directly financing active participation in the arts.

Government-funded art in the 1930s also caused its share of active participation. Like the *Tilted Arc*, profiled in Chapter 4, many paintings, as well as theatre pieces, provoked controversy. The Treasury Department's Fine Arts Section, which was separate from the Federal Arts Project, also commissioned art, with many works installed in post offices and courthouses. Karal Ann Marling studied the murals produced during this period and suggested that they chronicled popular taste. Often, to avoid having the artwork cause dissension and political participation, the agency "caused offensive murals to disappear from view." On the other hand, if the public liked a painting, the agency allowed "highly regarded murals to sprout satellites and appendages."[15] In general, the program accommodated public opinion.

One case, described by Marling, however, generated considerable political activity over several years. In 1938, Vermont artist Stefan Hirsch completed *Justice as Protector and Avenger*, a mural installed in the Aiken, South Carolina, courthouse. The style, composition, and even the skin color of a figure depicted in the mural so offended the county judge that he called it a "monstrosity." Eventually, following much active political participation on the part of those who agreed with the judge, as well as from those defending the artist and mural, came a compromise: a tan velvet curtain was used to cover the painting whenever court was in session.

While the early to mid-1930s was a period of much government-sponsored arts activity—often causing active political participation when the art offended enough people—the period between 1938 and 1958 saw an even greater intertwining of arts and politics, but of a different kind. Members of the American cultural community—particularly those involved with film—endured much scrutiny under the period Mankin named The Great Scare. The U.S. House of Representatives Un-American Activities Committee (HUAC) investigated "subversive influences" in the entertainment business, but failed to produce any legislation. The committee, unconcerned with promoting artistic freedom or freedom of thought, presided over an era during which government efforts toward the arts were totally misdirected.

This was an era when participation in certain cultural activities prompted political investigation, which in turn caused certain artists to become even more politically involved. It provides one of the best examples of a time when artists were forced into intense political participation—often forced to make choices that could send them, or others they named, to prison. Victor S. Navasky has compiled a comprehensive chronicle of the period. With the Cold War as background, Navasky has painted a clear picture of the complicated intermingling of the American cultural and political communities. Responding to international tensions, the HUAC joined the national war against communism, but "its attempt to cleanse the cultural apparatus can be understood only within the larger framework of the efforts to cleanse the political apparatus."[16]

The HUAC chose to target the entertainment industry for several reasons. Hollywood, with its glitter and excitement, was a highly visible target. In 1936, the Communist party set up a movie-industry branch, to try to keep anti-communist propaganda out of films, at the very least.[17] In addition, politicians continued to investigate the entertainment industry because they succeeded in getting artists to "name names."

As the decade of the 1960s approached and discussion of cultural policy became more frequent, arguments for a federal arts agency began to gain support in Congress. One of the most compelling was the need to democratize the arts, and the "legacy of the New Deal projects became increasingly important to the drive for a new arts program."[18]

According to Mankin, the third phase of government and arts' relationship began in 1965 with the formation of the National Foundation on the Arts and Humanities, which established NEA and

NEH. This Period of Promise began with a declaration of purpose, which has remained essentially unchanged for twenty years. The original declaration has been modified only slightly, during several periods of congressional reauthorization, and did not contain the phrases in italics below, which were added in 1985 and highlight recent attempts to strengthen arts education and broaden access. Greater participation seemed to be gaining favor with public policy makers:

The Congress hereby finds and declares—

(1) that the encouragement and support of national progress and scholarship in the humanities and the arts, while primarily a matter for private and local initiative, is also an appropriate matter of concern to the Federal Government;

(2) that a high civilization must not limit its efforts to science and technology alone but must give full value and support to the other great branches of scholarly and cultural activity in order to achieve a better understanding of the past, a better analysis of the present, and a better view of the future;

(3) that democracy demands wisdom and vision in its citizens and that it must therefore foster and support a form of education and *access to the arts and the humanities* designed to make people *of all backgrounds and wherever located* masters of their technology and not its unthinking servant;

(4) that it is necessary and appropriate for the Federal Government to complement, assist, and add to programs for the advancement of the humanities and the arts by local, State, regional, and private agencies and their organizations;

(5) that the practice of art and the study of the humanities requires constant dedication and devotion and that, while no government can call a great artist or scholar into existence, it is necessary and appropriate for the Federal Government to help create and sustain not only a climate encouraging freedom of thought, imagination, and inquiry, but also the material conditions facilitating the release of this creative talent;

(6) that museums are vital to the preservation of our cultural heritage and should be supported in their role as curator of our national consciousness;

(7) that the world leadership which has come to the United States cannot rest solely upon superior power, wealth, and technology, but must be solidly founded upon worldwide respect and admiration for the Nation's high qualities as a leader in the realm of ideas and of the spirit;

(8) *that Americans should receive in school, background and preparation in the arts and humanities to enable them to recognize and appreciate the aesthetic dimensions of our lives, the diversity of excellence that comprises our cultural heritage, and artistic and scholarly expression;* and

(9) that, in order to implement these findings, it is desirable to establish a National Foundation on the Arts and the Humanities.[19]

With the above declaration, the United States took a giant leap into the world of art patronage, and "not since the American Revolution had there been so clear a public statement by any Congress of the need for government to foster the quality of life."[20]

During the twenty years following approval of this declaration, support for NEA and NEH grew steadily under both Democratic and Republican administrations, and the agencies' budgets increased as well. Although minor adjustments were made in the legislation authorizing NEA and NEH, their purposes and activities remained the same.

Two major public policy initiatives during the 1970s and 1980s illustrate the degree to which the arts have permeated the public agenda.

Originating as a job training and employment program in 1973 under the Department of Labor, the Comprehensive Employment and Training Act (CETA) began a formal partnership with the arts community by the appointment of a national CETA/arts coordinator in 1978.[21] From the program's beginning, artists and cultural projects received CETA funds. In the late 1970s a strengthened partnership resulted in more than $200 million of government funds to the arts. By 1980, some 600 projects in approximately 200 locations benefited more than 10,000 artists and support personnel. This unique program, the largest artist employment program since the Federal Artists Project of the 1930s, was eventually terminated under the Reagan administration, yet it clearly illustrates how society can recognize unemployed artists as workers in need of assistance and the arts as part of the economy. Once again, direct arts participation was financed by the public.

The second major initiative occurred during President Reagan's first term, when the program's twenty-year record and the need for the National Endowments were questioned. The fiscal 1982 budget contained the following explanation of a proposed 50 percent decrease in funding for NEA and NEH:

Reductions of this magnitude are premised on the concept that Federal policy for arts and humanities support must be revamped.

In recent years, the Endowments have spread Federal financial support into an ever-wider range of artistic and cultural endeavor. This action will place more emphasis on the role of private philanthropy and State and local support for arts and cultural activities. Moreover, in view of the current economic crisis requiring reductions in programs critical for life support, funding for artistic and cultural pursuits is a relative low priority budget item.[22]

In response to the uproar this statement created in the nation's arts community, with its growing advocacy network (see Chapter 4), President Reagan created a task force to investigate the endowments and recommend changes. In October 1981, the Presidential Task Force on the Arts and Humanities presented its report, stating that: "The National Endowments are sound and should remain as originally conceived."[23] The Task Force also found:

The Endowments should emphasize the advancement of American culture through the support of both institutional and individual efforts. The Endowments' encouragement of greater access to, and participation in, the humanities and the arts should be governed by this principle.

Most importantly, the task force recognized the power of the arts to transmit American culture and that extensive participation in the arts is important to society.

With the task force reaffirming these benefits, later Reagan budgets called for less drastic funding decreases, while each decrease requested was successfully defeated by a sympathetic Congress, responding to the growing grassroots advocacy. With a less confrontational attitude toward NEA and NEH, the Bush administration has requested generally level funding.

The Extent of Public Support

The previous discussion has set the stage for a quantitative description of the current system of public support for the arts. This public financial support can be provided directly by grants to artists and institutions or indirectly through various tax deductions.

Direct Public Financing. In 1980, the Federal Council on the Arts and Humanities, an agency established to promote coordination among federal programs in the arts and humanities, published *Cultural Direc-*

tory II, listing more than 300 federal programs, activities, and resources offering assistance to individuals, institutions, and organizations. From the Appalachian Regional Commission to the Veterans Administration, the volume detailed the extensive involvement of our government with cultural activities. Although the directory contained no estimate of the entire amount provided by all of these programs, the following indicates the amount, prior to any across-the-board decreases mandated by deficit-cutting measures, provided for three major cultural programs in fiscal year 1990 (in millions of dollars):

National Endowment for the Arts	171.255
National Endowment for the Humanities	159.300
Institute of Museum Services	22.675

To that total of more than $350 million could be added funds appropriated to the Smithsonian Institute, the National Gallery of Art, the Historic Preservation Fund, and the Commission of Fine Arts. The budgets of these agencies would bring the total federal commitment to approximately $600 million. Furthermore, if all other minor initiatives from other departments and agencies were included, the figure would rise to somewhere between $750 million and nearly $1 billion.

Although much of this money is spent indirectly to support cultural concerns, the National Endowment for the Arts is a major source of direct grants to both individuals and institutions. Most of these grants must be matched with private funds; consequently, public money has the ability to "leverage" large amounts of individual or corporate funds. Since 1976, for example, "challenge" grants (requiring a match of three private dollars to one public dollar) of $250 million have encouraged almost $1.8 billion in private-sector funds.

Public funding, however, does not flow from only the federal government. Under the NEA's legislation, a portion of the funding is required to go to each state through the network of state arts agencies. Although the states preceded the federal government in placing the arts on the public agenda,[24] they use the NEA as their model; these "little NEAs" (the oldest of which is in Utah, founded in 1899) copy the federal agency in both philosophy and grant-making procedures,[25] but the relationship of appropriations from state legislatures to their respective arts agencies does not always follow the federal model. A 1982 study from the State University of New York at Binghamton showed that between 1976 and 1980 state arts appropriations were not affected by changes in federal funding.[26] Each agency also received funding from its state legislature. According to a survey by the National Assembly of State Arts Agencies, fiscal 1988 legislative appropriations for state arts agencies increased 13.1 percent over fiscal 1987 to more than $244 million.[27] (See Appendix B.)

Sanctioned by purpose (4) of the NEA's authorizing legislation, regional arts agencies form a support layer between the state and national levels and also receive a combination of state and federal funding. Unique to the system of public funding, these eight publicly designated, private, nonprofit organizations function in a manner similar to the arts agencies at the state level and provide additional grants to arts organizations within their jurisdictions. (See Appendix C.) The regional organizations seem to have emerged naturally from within the system itself: "It is as though, for once, governmental regionalism had been allowed to develop in a natural, organic way—from the regions themselves."[28]

Total cultural funding by local governments is difficult to ascertain. The network of local arts agencies, the first of which was established in Winston-Salem, North Carolina, in 1949, spans the country and numbers between 1,500 and 2,000. Each of these local organizations has a similar purpose, but each "has a distinct flavor of its own—a uniqueness that represents its history, its environment, its city."[29] A 1985 study comparing support for the arts in eight countries estimated that local public support in the United States was approximately $300 million.[30]

In addition to the network of public support described above, various unique funding methods are instituted periodically by states and local governments. Among a handful of states, in 1981 Oregon passed a "tax checkoff" for the arts in which taxpayers indicate how much of their tax refund they would like transferred to the Arts Development Fund for grants to cultural organizations,[31] while Massachusetts began an arts lottery to provide additional funding for cultural organizations.

Appendix D illustrates the extent of public support for the arts in the United States, including direct, as outlined above, and indirect, as discussed below. Although an extensive network of national, state, regional, and local arts agencies provides nearly $750 million in direct funding to cultural organizations, indirect public funding transfers even more.[32] Appendix D also compares direct and indirect funding in seven other countries. Except for the United States, the predominant form of support is direct budget allocation. In West Germany, for example, three main types of subsidies are used: fixed percentage of costs, variable percentage of costs, and lump sum (grants).[33]

Indirect Public Financing. By allowing individuals to deduct charitable contributions from their federal taxes, the government is in effect paying a percentage of the gift. In the case of donations to cultural organizations, the amount of revenue forgone is three times the amount of direct public support.[34] This "forgone revenue" would be nonexistent without the legal sanction of a federal income tax.

As in all societies, taxation in America has played a greater role as the nation developed: "To the citizen of the modern state, taxation, however disagreeable it may be, seems natural."[35] In the usual course of development, citizens make voluntary contributions to the state for public services; later the government must ask citizens for gifts; and finally the stage of compulsory taxation becomes necessary. Following excise taxes, customs fees, and various other forms of obtaining revenue, an income tax is added to the menu. The first income tax in the United States was instituted during the Civil War (1861) and was in effect until 1872. Concern for equity prompted Congress to allow certain deductions, but a deduction for charitable contributions was not among them. Following the repeal of the 1861 tax, Congress did not attempt to enact another income tax until the 1890s. This tax, however, was ruled unconstitutional by the Supreme Court in 1895. To overcome this ruling, a constitutional amendment was proposed in 1909 and ratified in 1913; the Sixteenth Amendment reads: "The Congress shall have power to lay and collect taxes on incomes, from whatever source derived, without apportionment among the several states and without regard to any census or enumeration."

The Revenue Act of 1913 officially instituted the income tax and included deductions for interest paid, taxes paid, and casualty losses, but not for charitable contributions. (The charitable contributions deduction had been proposed and rejected.) The deductions allowed under the Revenue Act of 1913 were intended to refine gross income to net income by subtracting expenses and losses incurred in pursuit of income. Refining gross income is one rationale for the use of deductions. A second rationale is the use of deductions to attain broad social or economic goals: "the deduction allowable for philanthropic contributions is commonly regarded as a means of stimulating socially desirable expenditures. . . ."[36] Congress feared that the high taxes imposed at the beginning of World War I would cause a decrease in charitable giving and consequently passed the Revenue Act of 1917, which established a charitable contributions deduction of up to 15 percent of net income.

Between 1917 and 1969, "the only substantive changes in the law were in the direction of greater encouragement of giving."[37] An additional Revenue Act in 1918 extended the deduction to trusts and estates; the charitable contributions deduction, with a 5 percent ceiling, was extended to corporations in 1935; the ceiling for individuals was increased to 20 percent in 1952 and 30 percent in 1954; and a carryover provision was introduced in 1964. The Tax Reform Act of

1969 tightened provisions for individuals and foundations, but overall philanthropy was not greatly affected. Few major tax changes involving charitable contributions were made during the 1970s, but in 1982 a special deduction was instituted for taxpayers who did not itemize. With the Tax Reform Act of 1986, however, this provision was eliminated, and, in addition to several provisions involving appreciated property, the tax code began removing incentives for giving. Today, advocates for charitable giving, including the major arts advocacy organizations, are monitoring trends in donations and considering legislative changes, because art contributions to American museums "have declined substantially since the Tax Reform Act of 1986."[38]

The degree of incentive provided by the tax code is still a matter of debate (see next section), but the amount taxpayers deduct can be documented. For 1982–1983, Schuster estimated that support for the arts via tax expenditures was divided as follows:

	$1,750 million	(individuals)
	126 million	(corporations)
	180 million	(foundations)
	300 million	(property taxes)
TOTAL	$2,356 million	

He noted that the total does not include figures from states that allow a charitable contributions deduction, funds involved in untaxed appreciated property, or the revenue from nonprofit cultural organizations exempt from sales taxes. If these are included, between two and three billion dollars is generated for cultural organizations by the indirect incentive of our tax code—unlike any other legislated tax system in the world. Schuster's research indicates that "all European countries are quite envious, at the moment, of the American tradition of private support," which is reinforced by our tax code.[39]

Recognizing the important role tax legislation plays in relation to cultural activity, a 1986 Canadian report on funding the arts there included fourteen recommended changes involving taxes. Among the suggested changes were: tax credits for donations to charities; income-tax deduction of 125 percent for donations to arts endowment funds; special tax considerations for bequests to arts endowments; and exclusion of gifts of cultural property from the alternative minimum tax.[40]

The above overview of the public component of the arts support system shows how vital the combination of direct and indirect public financing has been, and with the growth of the advocacy component to prime the pump of public financing, that component will probably remain strong. Private-sector support is described in the next section.

The Extent of Private Support. Until the twentieth century, cultural activities in the United States were almost entirely financed by private sources; however, as noted, public financing has gradually been accepted as an important component in the arts support network. With implementation of the income tax in 1913 and the subsequent deduction for charitable contributions, private financing has become more noticeable, and rough statistics have become available.

No solid national giving statistics began to appear, however, until research was conducted by the American Association of Fund-Raising Counsel (AAFC) in the mid-1950s. Each year since 1955, AAFC has published *Giving USA*, detailing contributions by individuals, bequests, and gifts from foundations and corporations. AAFC figures show that Americans gave more than $104 billion to nonprofit organizations, institutions and agencies in 1988.[41] Because AAFC also analyzes these figures according to distribution, trends in giving to the arts can be traced. The following chart shows the total contributions to cultural organizations since 1970:

	Amount (billions)		Amount (billions)
1970	$ .663	1980	3.15
1971	1.01	1981	3.66
1972	1.10	1982	4.96
1973	1.26	1983	4.21
1974	1.20	1984	4.50
1975	1.56	1985	5.08
1976	2.27	1986	5.83
1977	2.32	1987	6.31
1978	2.40	1988	6.82
1979	2.73		

The total donated to cultural organizations in 1988 represented 6.5 percent of all philanthropy and an increase of 8.08 percent. In compiling the figures for cultural giving, AAFC utilizes the research provided by several organizations that belong to the advocacy component of the systems diagram: Theater Communications Group annually surveys the nation's professional nonprofit theatres; the American Symphony Orchestra League monitors professional orchestras; the Association of Art Museum Directors and the American Association of Museums collects data from museums; and Dance/USA surveys major professional dance companies. Also included in AAFC's figures are contributions to public broadcasting provided by the Corporation for Public Broadcasting, an agency which distributes federal funds to public radio and television stations.

The relationship of these and all other contributions to the incentives provided by the tax code has been the subject of many research studies. Although the charitable contributions deduction was initially enacted as an incentive to prevent donations from declining after rates were raised during World War I, that same incentive effect was ignored during the 1940s when the standard deduction was instituted. The underlying assumption of lawmakers was that "giving is so ingrained a habit that loss of a tax advantage would not blunt the impulse of generosity."[42] Congress was not worried about charities losing gifts from taxpayers who did not itemize, because giving was "a habit," although little statistical evidence existed to support this idea.

During the 1950s, data relating to charitable contributions began to be compiled. In addition to statistics compiled by AAFC on amount of giving, the organization began to collect specific statistics concerning giving by individuals. For example, an early study[43] published in 1959 analyzes city families' patterns of giving to religious and private welfare organizations. An important conclusion of this study was that the lowest income classes contribute a larger percentage of their income than do middle- and high-income givers. These patterns are consistent with the results of a 1988 Gallup Survey indicating Americans of low and moderate income are more generous than their well-to-do neighbors. (Households with incomes below $10,000 gave 2.8 percent of their incomes, while $50,000–100,000 households gave only 1.5–1.7 percent.)[44] Other studies have also shown that low-income givers contribute primarily to religious organizations, while high-income givers tend to support educational and cultural institutions.[45]

Statistics concerning the amount contributed by each income class, as well as the character of the recipient organization, are relatively easy to compile compared to the problem of determining if an incentive effect exists. A major attempt to analyze this effect was made by Michael K. Taussig in 1965. His research, later published in the National Tax Journal[46] in 1967, was based on a large cross-section of individual tax returns of 1962—a sample of 103,386. Taussig employed regression analysis of the data and discovered that: (1) the size of the family unit (with incomes below $100,000 AGI) influenced level of giving; (2) a positive relationship existed between age and level of giving except in the highest income class; (3) a negative but weak relationship existed between heavy medical expenses and charitable giving; and (4) the level of capital gains was negatively related to level of giving.

In addition, Taussig's research showed that a significant incentive effect existed only for those taxpayers in the highest income categories. These income classes also had a higher than average proportion of individuals donating property. According to Taussig, the charitable contributions deduction is most effective in encouraging gifts of property.

A 1977 study[47] by Michael J. Boskin and Martin Feldstein examined data on philanthropic activity by households below $30,000 (not included were households below $1,000). The 1974 National Study of Philanthropy collected the data. The charitable contributions deduction lowers the individual's net cost of giving if the taxpayer itemizes (that is, net cost per dollar to donor equals one minus the marginal tax rate). If the elasticity of total giving with respect to this net cost is absolutely greater than one, the charitable deduction causes donees to receive more in additional gifts than the Treasury Department forgoes in revenue.

Boskin and Fledstein found that charitable contributions are "quite price elastic throughout this range income."[48] Price elasticity of charitable giving is the percentage increase in the amount given to charity per percentage-point decrease in the price of giving. For example, if a 30 percent decrease in the price of giving induces a 30 percent increase in the *amount* of giving, price elasticity is one. If a 30 percent decrease in the price of giving induces a 45 percent increase in the amount of giving, the price elasticity is one and one half. The higher the price elasticity, the more increased giving occurs per dollar of foregone revenue. (See the discussion on elasticity in Chapter 4.)

A deduction for charitable contributions has been criticized on three grounds:[49] impropriety, inefficiency, and inequity. The impropriety argument states that the charitable contributions deduction violates the principle of horizontal equity; taxpayers with the same amount of income pay different taxes if one chooses to make a charitable contribution. This argument is based on the premise that a charitable gift is a personal expenditure and should have no impact on tax liability. The second criticism states that the charitable contributions deduction is inefficient because it does not distinguish between gifts that need an incentive and gifts that would be made anyway. Finally, the inequity of the charitable contributions deduction is in violation of vertical equity—the benefit of a deduction is based on a taxpayer's marginal tax rate.

Boris J. Bittker refutes these three criticisms: the deduction is compatible with a measure of taxable income, because, in society's judgment, those who contribute to charity should be distinguished from those who do not; proof that the deduction is an efficient method of creating an incentive is not conclusive, therefore, the deduction should not be eliminated for this reason only; and no inconsistency exists between deductions and progressive tax rates, which can be adjusted to account for the effect of the deduction. In fact, Bittker believed, increasing the charitable deduction may even create a greater redistribution of income; low-income givers contribute to churches where they are members, but high income givers contribute to educational and cultural institutions that have a greater potential to benefit all income levels. Feld et al., however, have shown that redistribution occurs mostly from high-income to moderately high income groups.

The above discussion of the incentive effect of the tax deduction for charitable giving demonstrates the complex interrelationship between the public and private components within the arts support system and how the tax system can increase or decrease the participation of patrons. The following section examines the functioning of the entire structure by highlighting the principal internal component of economics.

The Role of Economics

The major components of the American system of arts support, the public and private sectors, function within the context of external and internal conditions. Chapter 7 discussed the external conditions—the atmosphere of society itself. Like the larger culture, where "politics and economics have become inextricably joined,"[50] money is the principle internal condition of the arts support system. This section examines the functional and dysfunctional roles taken by economics and its relationship to the arts.

The "advantageous relationship" between arts and economics has been examined by John Kenneth Galbraith, who noted that the oldest relationship between arts and economics is the financial support of the artist—the first of Galbraith's four categories. His other three relationships are:

the expanding role of art in a modern standard of living and a consistent factor in economic activity;
the role of art objects in capital stock of modern communities; and
the relationship of art and general industrial achievement.

Because "the artist has an increasingly important relationship to economic success in the modern economy and the successful solvency of its participant enterprises,"[51] government perhaps should pay more attention to the first of Galbraith's relationships. The mandate for the economic well-being of the artist is in Purpose (5) of the NEA's authorizing legislation: "It is necessary and appropriate for the Federal Government to help create and sustain not only a climate encouraging freedom of thought, imagination, and inquiry, but also the material conditions facilitating the release of this creative talent."

In the United States, with the exception of a few large annual fellowships from the National Endowment for the Arts, artists are rarely supported entirely with public funds. Corporations and foundations provide even less money directly to creative individuals; consequently, the artist must depend on the marketplace. For the system to function properly with respect to artists, individuals would have to purchase sufficient art at fair-market value for artists to make a living. In twentieth-century America, unfortunately, the public appetite is not sufficient to support all the individuals who wish to be considered artists, but system equilibrium is maintained by these individuals earning income with jobs in other professions.

In the case of performers, the distribution of art generally occurs through institutions, and if the system is functioning properly, enough people would pay sufficient admission to provide adequate income for the performing artists and support personnel. Often, however, in the performing arts an "economic dilemma" develops. First analyzed by Baumol and Bowen in their class study, *Performing Arts: The Economic Dilemma* (1966), the system of arts production, although of service to the community, cannot take advantage of advances in technology like other services: "From an engineering point of view, live performance is technologically stagnant."[52] The amount of labor to produce a manufactured product continues to decline, but the labor and number of performers required to produce a play remains the same. In an inflationary society, this situation presents a critical dilemma. The severe predictions of Baumol and Bowen's "cost disease" failed to develop, however, over the twenty years since their study was published. In a 1979 reassessment, Baumol attributed the ability of the arts to maintain financial stability to "a very real growth in administrative efficiency and similar benign developments, which are desirable ways to combat the cost disease."[53] Both artists and institutions have become more business oriented since the Baumol and Bowen study—a testament to the fact that they are beginning to take the arts/economics relationship seriously. This recognition from the artist's side helps to maintain the stability of the system and the proper functional role of money.

A second relationship of the arts to economics is the value of the cultural industry in generating additional spending throughout the economy. Known to arts advocates as the economic impact of the arts on society, this relationship has been studied in many contexts over the past twenty years. One of the first studies was sponsored by the National Endowment for the Arts in Baltimore, Maryland, in 1977.[54] This was followed by six additional case studies in Columbus, Minneapolis/St. Paul, St. Louis, Salt Lake City, San Antonio, and Springfield.[55] Statewide studies soon began to appear, and a regional study of New England's arts was published by the New England Foundation for the Arts in 1981.[56] In almost all the studies, an input/output multiplier to determine the "ripple effect" of a dollar spent on the arts was used. The multiplier concept is "based on the well-established economic theory concerning the fact that money spent on any commodity or service recirculates in the local or regional economy to varying degrees before finally leaving the area."[57] Depending on the sophistication of the research and the area studied, multipliers can range from 2 to 4, or even more. (See Appendix E for a partial list of economic impact studies.)

To illustrate the wide range of economic impact studies generated in the arts community, a sampling of several follows:

A study of out-of-town visitors to the King Tut Exhibit at the Metropolitan Museum of Art (May 1979) found that 80 percent of the visitors came to the city directly to view the exhibit; 65 percent ate or planned to eat in a restaurant; 6 percent spent at least one night at a hotel; 23 percent spent money on taxis, 23 percent on buses, 16 percent on subways; and 49 percent spent money on shopping.[58]

A 1980 update of the impact of the arts on the Oklahoma City area measured the impact of 34 arts agencies, organizations, festivals, shows, programs, and events and found that the amount of total expenditures resulting from both direct and secondary impacts was nearly $50 million.[59]

The arts had a $5.6 billion impact on New York City-New Jersey metropolitan area economy, according to a 1983 report by the Cultural Assistance Center. Furthermore, more than $2 billion in personal income and more than 117,000 jobs were generated.[60]

The magnitude of the economic impact of the arts in Texas was studied by Peat, Marwick, Mitchell & Co. in 1984. The statewide multiplied impact is at least $1.7 billion per year, of which approximately 44 percent is economic activity associated with nonprofit organizations. Every dollar spent statewide by arts or arts-related organizations generates an average of $3.35 in economic activity.[61]

The nonprofit arts in Michigan have an economic multiplier of 1.5, according to a 1983 study by Touche Ross. The nonprofit arts industry received $133 million in total revenue; expended $130 million for wages, goods, and services; and generated $3 million in excess revenue over expenses. The $130 million expended generated $195 million in total economic impact.[62]

To add to the data presented by the numerous local, state, and regional studies, the NEA has begun to research the arts as part of our Gross National Product. NEA Research Division Note #13 (November 6, 1985) provides these general observations:

Consumer admission expenditures in 1984 for performing arts events reached more than $2 billion for the first time (.25 percent of the GNP).

Consumer expenditures for radio and television sets, records, and musical instruments represented .84 percent of the GNP.

Consumer expenditures for books and maps represented .25 percent of the GNP.

Consumer admission expenditures to motion picture theatres peaked in 1978, declined for three years, rose strongly in 1982, and continued to rise in 1983 and 1984, reaching .11 percent of the GNP. Consumer admission expenditures to spectator sports remained about level at .08 percent of the GNP.

Although a national economic impact report is not feasible, the above statistics can be helpful in tracing the relative importance of the culture industry in our mass economic system. In this category of the arts/economics relationship, the cultural community functions to maintain financial equilibrium within the entire system of society. Eliminate the arts and jobs would be lost in many sectors of society.

A third relationship, according to Galbraith, is the role of art objects in the capital stock of society. Art has become a major object of investment. Wealthy persons are now advised not only by stock and real-estate brokers, but also by art consultants. "No great and solemn difficulties in this development as regards either to the artist or investor,"[63] Galbraith said. The investment builds the capital values in established works of art, but the financial rewards often go not to the artist, but to those who sell or inherit the work. In many cases, art is bought at one price and then sold at a much higher price. The original buyer receives the appreciation on the sales. In every state but California the artist receives no additional compensation following these transactions. In California, which has enacted a "resale royalties act," the artist would receive a small percentage from resales over $1,000.[64]

However, established painters often do receive great financial rewards that can impede changes in legislation to benefit artists of all income levels. Since 1969, for example, when an artist donates a work, the only tax deduction he may receive would be equal to the cost of his materials. Between 1969 and 1986, buyers of the same work were able to receive a tax deduction equal to the fair market value when the work was donated (in 1986, tax regulations were tightened to allow only a deduction equal to the original purchase price of the work, if the taxpayer was subject to the alternative minimum tax). Donations of original works, particularly manuscripts since 1969 and paintings and sculpture since 1986, to public institutions have declined because of these regulations. One reason lawmakers have been reluctant to change the 1969 provision pertaining to creators is that they feel it would benefit wealthy artists the most. The myth that artists should be poor still remains, but as Galbraith asserted, "the adverse effect of money on artists has been greatly exaggerated."[65] Raphael, Michelangelo, Rubens, Picasso, and others were great artists despite their wealth. In the relationship between artist and investor, who often risks large amounts of money on unknown artists, the risks are great; however, the investor, the artist, and society can all benefit in this relationship: "We should encourage investment in art and the arts and worry not at all about the enrichment of artists or the losses to investors."[66]

The importance of the artist as designer in environmental planning, as well as industrial development, is a fourth relationship of arts to economics. From the perspective of urban planning and design, "the arts are among the most positive forces at work in the modern city."[67] The tools of environmental planning (historic preservation, architectural design, urban design of parks and plazas, public art, and art surrounding urban transportation systems) are as much the tools of the artist as the economist.[68] Furthermore, although the scientist and engineer are the forerunners in technological achievement, the artist is becoming a growing part of the American national product and is also vital to industrial progress: "After utility comes design; after things *work* well, people want them to *look* well [sic]."[69] Galbraith noted that design depends on the availability of artists and the depth and quality of a country's artistic tradition; he provided the example of Italy, whose strong artistic tradition survived two world wars. In time of economic crisis, the industries that survive are those with a solid artistic tradition—textile design, dress manufacture, advertising, filmmaking, theatre. These industries may be even less vulnerable to competition and modern economic disasters than industries like steel, coal, or automobiles. Galbraith even suggested that cities that best survive are those that coexist with a strong artistic tradition. Furthermore, this artistic tradition also preserves and cultivates small businesses, where flexibility lends itself to creative endeavors.

To Galbraith's list of relationships must be added a uniquely political one: the existence of PACs (Political Action Committees) for the arts. Growing from organizations established in the 1940s by labor unions who were barred from contributing to campaigns from union treasury funds, PACs made their way into the corporate structure and during the 1970s into trade, membership, and health organizations. Since 1972, the number of PACs increased fivefold, while the number of corporate PACs increased fifteen times.[70] Although tightly regulated by the Federal Election Commission (FEC), PACs have proven to be a powerful factor in the American political system. In 1984, 3,525 PACs were registered with the FEC; by 1987, 4,100 were registered,[71] and that figure climbed to more than 4,800 by 1988. Contributions in 1987 and 1988 to House, Senate, and presidential candidates reached $340 million.[72]

In 1982, the first arts PAC was formed; but the political Fund for the Arts and Humanities, with its low-key marketing and small staff, quickly went out of business by 1983. During the same period, ArtPac was founded by Rubin Gorewitz, a New York financial counsel to several major artists and sculptors. ArtPac seeks to promote "legislative reforms for the community of artists and creators, and to help offset the ominous threat to artistic and literary freedoms."[73] The "ominous threat" was more a marketing tool than a reality to entice individuals to contribute. Most arts advocacy groups have remained isolated from ArtPac, because of their concern that funds raised by ArtPac could be contributed directly to cultural organizations for a greater benefit. For this reason, arts PACs are viewed by some individuals as dysfunctional to the entire system.

In summary, the system's internal financial condition is intricate; equilibrium results when money flows smoothly from both public and private sources; art exchanges hands; artists and support personnel receive adequate compensation; and the artistic tradition is recognized as an integral part of the culture. The next section presupposes a system in equilibrium as described above and highlights participation.

THE EFFECT ON PARTICIPATION

The previous section discussed the two most important components of the American arts system, showing that the flow of money is a vital force. The system is now examined through "a window of participation."

Active Participation

The equilibrium of the system today provides opportunity for professional artists to continue their active participation. (See Figure

8.1.) Many of these creative individuals receive large financial rewards, while others fall into the middle- and low-income categories. Still others find themselves outside the system and unable to earn an adequate income through active arts participation. Proponents of the elite theory of art would say that great artists will emerge despite their economic conditions and that poverty stimulates creativity. But the argument can be made that the benefits derived from increasing active participation are worth an increased level of public and private financial commitment. By including more professional artists within the safety net of an adequate income level, the self-esteem of the individual would be heightened, thus contributing to the psychological conditions necessary for a participatory society. Furthermore, the stronger the community of active professional artists, the greater the chance of assuring a thriving artistic culture.

Active amateur participation also brings benefits to society. Under the current system, very little public or private support is available to allow individuals a chance to actively experience the arts. (See Figure 8.2.) The system is biased toward a large, passive audience. For adults, a personal financial investment must be made to participate—purchase of a musical instrument, private music lessons, classes in painting or singing. A positive trend, however, is the growing availability of arts classes sponsored by community arts agencies or "open universities." "With or without public subsidy," amateur participation has been growing since the late 1970s.[74] As noted in Chapter 4, increased amateur arts activity raises self-esteem, allows the individual experience in decision making, and makes him more likely to be willing

Figure 8.2

Systems Diagram: Active Amateur Participation

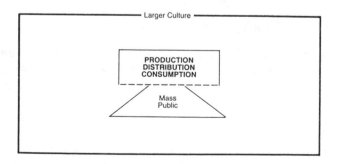

to participate as an audience member for the professional side of his art.

The current equilibrium of the system also provides very little for formal arts education. (See Figure 8.3.) The strongest benefit from the arts education of children again is in the area of self-esteem. Decision making is also strengthened when children are involved in creative activities. Increased attention to this component, in turn, would create a more educated electorate willing to pump additional public and private funds into the system, thus raising the level of active professional participation with more opportunity for passive audience participation.

Active participation in the area of support personnel follows the pattern of the professional and amateur artist, although supply and demand are generally more evenly distributed. With the exception of specialized technical people in the performing arts, the number of persons involved with production and distribution of art is adequate to service consumption needs. With sufficient compensation, these people also develop self-esteem and, within their own art (set design, lighting, etc.) make creative choices that benefit decision making capability. To keep the system sensitive to the material conditions necessary for professional artists, the support personnel include unions. As noted in Chapter 4, these unions also provide excellent training in the skills of political participation.

Figure 8.3

Systems Diagram: Arts Education

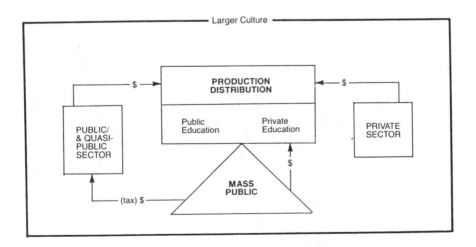

One area of growing active participation is in the advocacy component of the system (Figure 8.4). Chapters 3, 4, and 8 described this component in various contexts and noted the numerous opportunities for training in political skills. As the public arts support network expands, the number of arts advocates increases. The advocacy groups working at the national level have been highlighted, and nearly every state now has a citizens' group lobbying at the state level for greater state arts appropriations. In a 1983 study of these groups, however, Joseph Wesley Zeigler discovered that existence of a citizens' advocacy group did not always correspond to an increase in state appropriations to the arts.[75] In nine states without advocacy organizations, Zeigler found greater growth in arts funding than the overall percentage growth. From 1979 to 1983, funding grew 99 percent in Delaware, Florida, Idaho, Kansas, Maine, New Hampshire, Rhode Island, Vermont, and Virginia (states without advocacy organizations) and 435 percent between 1977 and 1983, in contrast to the overall growth of 58 percent and 126 percent in all states and ter-

Figure 8.4

Systems Diagram: The Active Arts Advocate

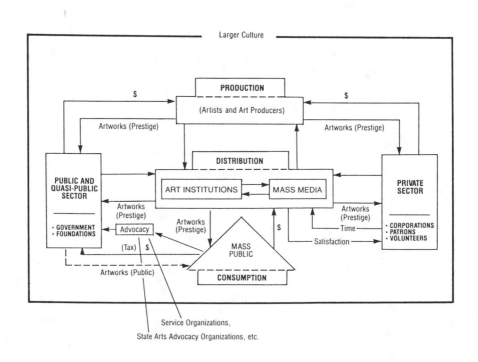

ritories. Zeigler has suggested that the lack of an advocacy group may be related to the character of the state (Delaware is so small that political lobbying can be done informally; Rhode Island has a powerful Democratic party favorable to the arts) or to the simple fact that the governor is supportive of the arts and an advocacy group is not needed.

The survey conducted as part of this book provides a profile of heads of state advocacy efforts in 1986, as well as executive directors of public arts agencies receiving state appropriations. These people are actively involved in both arts and politics, and I hypothesized that their participation profile would show high levels of participation in several areas. These results are discussed in the last section of this chapter.

Another segment of the population whose participation profile should be studied is professional politicians themselves. Although the Congressional Arts Caucus has conducted no formal surveys, at various times it has surveyed its members regarding arts participation and interest. An informal survey in 1981 was sent to caucus members (then numbering approximately 130) to determine the strength of their interest (by relative degrees from 1 to 5) in various areas (jazz, country music, musical theatre, opera, etc.), if they played a musical instrument, and in which artistic activities they participated. Of the fewer than one-third who returned a questionnaire, very few played an instrument and arts interests centered around "3." No pertinent participatory research was gleaned from that survey, with the exception that the elected officials showed no strong interest in a particular artist or art.

A second survey was conducted in 1986 (membership was then about 190). With only 25 caucus members responding, the survey was then sent to all members of the House of Representatives. This step increased responses by 24. Active arts participation calculated from the survey (from "marginal" to "accomplished") included: 18 photographers, 16 singers, 6 visual artists, 9 writers, 3 actors, and 22 musicians. One cautious hypothesis resulting from this information is that, of all the arts, music and photography are the choice of persons whose participation level in politics is high.

At the state legislative level, a similar but more controlled survey was conducted by the Illinois Arts Action Coalition. In 1984, more than 200 political candidates running for seats in the Illinois General Assembly were surveyed. Of the 83 persons who responded, 55 percent were Democrats, 45 percent were Republicans. Sixty-five percent were from the Chicago area and 35 percent from "downstate."[76] In the first section of the survey candidates were asked about their arts participation. They tended to be involved mainly as passive participants of an audience (79 percent attended theatre; 71 percent music concerts; 48 percent art exhibits; 44 percent film; 28 percent dance). Section 2 asked for comments on arts opportunities in the candidates' communities. A majority (58 percent) rated the opportunities good or excellent. Most deficiencies were noted in the area of dance (24 percent) followed by theatre (19 percent).

Nearly all respondents consider the arts important or essential to the quality of life in Illinois (98 percent), while 97 percent believe the arts are a critical selling point to prospective new industries. When asked if the state should require arts education, most of the candidates felt that such a decision should be left to local school boards (only 12 percent would mandate specific arts courses).

The candidates were also asked questions about public support for the arts. A large number (20 percent) were unfamiliar with the programs of the Illinois Arts Council, but 95 percent believed the current amount of funding was appropriate or slightly less than needed. Finally, the survey listed options to raise public funds for the arts. Of the options (an arts lottery, an appropriation from the horse-racing tax fund or the hotel/motel tax fund, an appropriation based on a portion of lottery proceeds, or an income tax checkoff) only the tax checkoff received much support (60 percent indicated that it was a good idea).

In addition to active participation by individuals, a second category of active arts participation involved political participation in relation to the creation of a work of art. How does the current system relate to that category? In the case of the monuments and memorials, most activity centers on the public sector at the national and state levels, although when government bureaucracy moves too slowly, the private sector forms a committee and begins fundraising. Clearly, the current system provides enough opportunity for the artistic creation of monuments and memorials and is flexible enough to accommodate public opinion in the process. The Vietnam Veterans Memorial is the ultimate example: the system used the creative talents of artists, was flexible enough to survive the political participation resulting from the creation of the art, and was able resolve the conflict with the addition of a second work of art.

Public art, on the other hand, may still be considered dysfunctional to the system by those who find specific works offensive. Procedures for choosing artists continue to be revised with more emphasis on local involvement. No national legislation exists for allocating a certain percentage of the cost of public buildings for art (the program is still only a policy of the General Services Administration), and the practice varies widely in states and cities. Until the public becomes more accustomed to public art, each new work has the potential to stimulate political participation. Ironically, to support the hypothesis that participation in the arts leads to a participatory society, the way public art is handled under the current system should not be changed.

Passive Participation

Chapter 4 described three types of actors in passive arts participation: the audience, the volunteer, the patron. How does the current arts support system function with respect to these areas?

Chapter 3 profiled passive audience participation in twentieth-century America, as well as research from Harris surveys showing that audience size has increased. Figures from the National Endowment for the Arts' Public Participation Survey indicate the following numbers of adults who attended performances in 1982 (estimated in millions)[77]:

Jazz Performances	14.8–16.3
Classical Music Performances	20.5–22.5
Opera Performances	4.7–5.5
Musical Plays or Operettas	29.6–31.4
Plays (non musical)	18.7–20.3
Ballet Performances	6.2–7.2
Art Museums or Galleries	35.2–37.3

Although audiences are increasing, their demographics are difficult to change:

> To summarize the unambiguous trends, the social composition of the arts audience is far more elite than the general public, and the center of the audience is more elite than its periphery. Education and, to a lesser degree, income are good predictors not only of who consume the arts but of the intensity of their consumption.[78]

Education continues to be the key to expanding the arts audience.

A 1969 study of visitors to art museums in four European countries noted similar results with regard to educational level. The following table shows percentages of each educational category who visited art museums in each of the four countries[79]:

	Greece	Poland	France	Holland
No educational qualifications	.02	.12	.15	—
Primary education	.30	1.50	.45	.50
Secondary education	10.05	10.40	10.00	20.00
Higher education	11.50	11.70	12.50	17.30

In addition to size and demographics of audience, research is being conducted on barriers to attendance. The 1982 NEA study on Public Participation in the Arts[80] indicated that "not enough time" is the most frequently cited barrier to more attendance for all age groups (mentioned by 43 percent), except those over 65. "Too expensive" ranks second, with 29 percent of the adults mentioning it. "Art form not available" was cited by 27 percent of the 18-to-34 age group; also 27 percent of the 35-to-49 age group; 29 percent of the 50-to-64 age group; and 25 percent of those over 65. The fourth most frequently mentioned barrier is "too far to go," followed by "poor performance time," "lack of motivation," "no one to go with," and "transportation problem." Little can be done within the arts support system to change "not enough time," but "too expensive" can be handled by financial adjustments of the various components. Members of the arts distribution system should analyze the NEA findings regarding barriers and make adjustments accordingly in an attempt to democratize the audience.

Research by DiMaggio and Useem indicates that this democratizing process has been slow or even nonexistent since 1960. After evaluating audience composition data for several different periods between 1960 and 1976, they found: the proportion of men in the performing arts audience has changed little (varying from 30 to 50 percent); that audiences are not getting younger (the median age remains between 33 and 41); the proportion of the audience with at least a college education did not decline over time (ranging from 63 to 65 percent); the audience still contains a majority of white-collar workers (between 59 to 65 percent); and median audience income remains above $20,000. DiMaggio and Useem pointed to an absence of discernible democratization of the American performing arts audience during the period studied, and they suggested that this situation is "related both to elite resistance to democratization and to entry problems facing non-elites."[81] Elite resistance is related to the reaffirmation of social and cultural status and may be most crucial for the upper middle class who aspire to join the elite. Other barriers include lack of information about arts events, lack of training to ensure appreciation, and unfamiliarity with social conventions of attendance. Because cultural resources are "very inequitably distributed," according to DiMaggio and Useem, they suggest the establishment of more "outreach" programs for underserved segments of the population, participatory-oriented arts activities, and more arts programs in schools. Their suggestions for increasing audience participation parallel mine for increasing active amateur arts participation.

The second category of passive arts participation is the volunteer, whose demographic profile is similar to the typical audience member. A survey by the American Council for the Arts in which sixty volunteers were sent questionnaires yielded the following: with a return rate of 45 percent, the survey indicated that the majority of the volunteers had postgraduate education, lived in larger cities, and had a high level of active arts participation. Seventy-four percent were involved with United Arts Funds, 55 percent were on arts boards (22 percent were on school boards), and 40 percent worked on political campaigns. According to this survey, volunteers are "highly educated, civically involved movers and shakers whose tastes and views are establishment oriented."[82] With few tax incentives to increase volunteer effort and a lack of leisure time, passive arts participation as a volunteer is not highly reinforced by the overall system.

Passive participation as a patron, however, is reinforced several ways. For the very wealthy, major gifts to cultural organizations give the donor great decision-making power. An entire art gallery could be named after the patron, or he could dictate the choice of theatrical productions. Donors of smaller gifts often receive recognition by having their names printed in the program or on plaques. Subscribers may even be asked to vote on their choice of a series of plays. In addition to decision making ability and recognition, patrons may derive a feeling of satisfaction that they are contributing to the common good of society. Finally, the entire American system of patronage is reinforced by a tax code in which our government helps defray the cost of the gift with a tax deduction.

SURVEY RESEARCH OF A SPECIFIC COMPONENT

Because this study combined politics and the arts, I constructed a survey to look at a small segment of the arts participants whose work involved participation in both the political and cultural realms. (See Figure 8.4 for a systems diagram depicting this small population.) I hypothesized that a profile of these persons would provide a small bit of empirical evidence that high arts participation is correlated with high political participation. Figure 8.5 is a copy of the cover letter to the survey questionnaire pictured in Figure 8.6.

Figure 8.5

Cornwell Survey Cover Letter

July 18, 1986

Dear

     I am writing to request your assistance with
research I am conducting in conjunction with my Ph.D.
dissertation: "Democracy and the Arts: The Role of
Participation." This research is the culmination of my
work in the Public Communication program of the Department
of Communication Arts and Theatre at the University of
Maryland -- a program which is complementary to my current
position with the Congressional Arts Caucus.

     Because you are among those persons who demonstrate
a high degree of participation in areas relating to both
the arts and politics, your answers to the enclosed survey
would be most helpful.

     If you wish to receive a copy of the results of
this survey or would like more information on my research,
please check the appropriate box on the back of the form.

     Thank you for your assistance.

     Sincerely,

     Terri L. Cornwell
     Legislative Director

Enclosure

    The survey was sent to 103 directors of state arts councils and arts
advocacy organizations. Five questionnaires were returned because of
address changes, so the total sample was 98. Seventy-three responses
were received—a rate of 74 percent. This high rate was attributed to
the fact that a stamped, self-addressed envelope was enclosed, and the
cover letter indicated that not only was I doing research for a doctoral
dissertation, but that, in my professional position, I was a staff member of the Congressional Arts Caucus, a high-profile advocacy group
with which most participants were familiar.
    According to the results (see Appendix F for complete numerical
results), the typical individual working in a capacity involving arts
advocacy is female, between the ages of 41 and 60, with a graduate
degree. Approximately one-third of the respondents held arts degrees,

Figure 8.6

Cornwell Survey Questionnaire

PARTICIPATION IN POLITICS/THE ARTS
Survey

1. In each of the five columns check the <u>one</u> answer that best describes you:

[] Male	[] Under	[] Undergraduate Degree	[] Arts Degree	[] Work alone
[] Female	Age 26	[] Graduate Degree	[] Business Degree	[] Head staff of 1-5
	[] 26-40	[] Other _____	[] Pol. Sci. Degree	[] Head staff of 6-10
	[] 41-60		[] Other _____	[] Head staff of more
	[] Over 60			than 10

2. Check the area that best describes where you live and check your approximate yearly household income: **(OPTIONAL)**

[] urban	[] less than $15,000
[] suburban	[] $15,001 - $30,000
[] town/rural	[] $30,001 - $50,000
	[] $50,000 and over

3. Rate your level of active participation in the following arts activities (1--lowest to 5 --highest):

	1	2	3	4	5
Singing	___	___	___	___	___
Playing Musical Instru.	___	___	___	___	___
(Which one(s)? _____)					
Painting, Drawing, etc.					
Pottery, Ceramics	___	___	___	___	___
Sculpture	___	___	___	___	___
Theatre	___	___	___	___	___
Photography, Video Arts	___	___	___	___	___
Ballet/Modern Dance	___	___	___	___	___
Folk/Ethnic Dance	___	___	___	___	___
Opera	___	___	___	___	___
Writing	___	___	___	___	___

4. Rate your audience participation level for the following arts events (1--lowest to 5 --highest):

	1	2	3	4	5
Cultural Programs on TV*	___	___	___	___	___
Movies*	___	___	___	___	___
Jazz Music	___	___	___	___	___
Classical Music	___	___	___	___	___
Opera	___	___	___	___	___
Theatre	___	___	___	___	___
Dance	___	___	___	___	___
Museums	___	___	___	___	___

*Do you own a VCR?___ Yes ___ No
If yes, what is its <u>primary</u> use? _____ show rental movies _____ time shifting
_____ show movies you _____ of TV programs
have bought _____ other:_____

5. Rate your level of participation in the following activities related to cultural organizations (1--lowest to 5--highest):

	1	2	3	4	5
Contributing Money	___	___	___	___	___
Volunteering Time	___	___	___	___	___
Serving on a Board	___	___	___	___	___

(OVER)

Figure 8.6 (continued)

6. Rate your level of participation in the following political activities (1--lowest to 5 --highest):

	1	2	3	4	5
Voting in Presidential Elections	___	___	___	___	___
Voting in State/Local or off-Year Elections	___	___	___	___	___
Voting in Primaries	___	___	___	___	___
Contributing Money	___	___	___	___	___
Volunteering Time	___	___	___	___	___
Running for Office	___	___	___	___	___

7. Check the most appropriate response regarding your participation as a teenager in family decisions concerning you:

A Lot of Influence ___
Some Influence ___
No Influence ___
Other ___
Comments: _____

8. Check the most appropriate response regarding your participation in school discussions and debate:

	Elementary School	High School	College
Could and Did Participate	___	___	___
Could, But Did Not Participate	___	___	___
Could Not Participate	___	___	___
Other	___	___	___
Comments:			

Additional Comments on Survey: _____

_____

* * * OPTIONAL * * *

NAME _____

TITLE _____

ORGANIZATION _____

ADDRESS _____

_____

[] I would like a copy of the results of this survey.

Thank you for your assistance. Please send completed survey to:

Ms. Terri L. Cornwell
13007 Brookmill Court
Laurel, MD 20708

(A STAMPED, ADDRESSED ENVELOPE IS ENCLOSED.)

with another 13 percent having two degrees, one of them in the arts. Slightly more than half (56 percent) lived in urban areas with suburban and town/rural areas evenly distributed among the remaining group, while family incomes clustered above the $30,000 range, with nearly half above $50,000.

Surprisingly, active participation clustered in the low range. Interest in the arts seemed to be very high, while time or perhaps talent was lacking. Audience participation, on the other hand was generally high, while other forms of passive participation seemed to vary. Responses to "contributing money" clustered in the middle range, while "volunteering time" and "serving on a board" rated slightly higher. Political participation followed Danielson's pyramidal scheme (see Chapter 2) of fewer responses with respect to the activities taking the most time and effort and more responses toward "easier" activities, like "voting in presidential elections"; however, responses showed greater participation than in the general population. Responses to the home participation question indicated that the persons surveyed tended to come from homes where they were given either "a lot of influence" in decision making or "some influence." A similar profile emerged with the school participation question, with the majority of responses in the "could and did participate" category. The above results are similar to the results of a survey by Marleen Sansone.[83] Of those surveyed, Sansone found 35 percent were "extremely involved" in six or more types of activities: 92 percent were board members, 76 percent were contributors, 68 percent were fundraisers, 63 percent held offices, 48 percent were volunteers, and 39 percent were practicing artists. Furthermore, two-thirds had education beyond a four-year college degree and 59 percent were between the ages 41 and 60. Like the Illinois survey cited earlier in this chapter, more Democrats than Republicans replied (53 percent vs. 27 percent).

In summary, the results of my survey highlight all aspects of active and passive participation outlined in this book with the exception of "professional artist" (respondents were not asked if they were professional artists).

> By definition, all respondents were active participants in the support component (either advocacy organization director or director of a public art agency).
> Their active amateur participation was average or low (probably because of "lack of leisure time" and because much of their time was spent advocating greater opportunities for others to participate in the arts).
> Their passive audience participation was high (the fact that they are often the ones offered free tickets may help).

Their level of volunteering was high.

Their patronage level was high (although no attempt was made to determine amount of giving).

Their political participation level was also high with respect to voting in presidential, off-year, and primary elections; level of contributing money to political campaigns was somewhat lower, while volunteering time and running for office was the lowest.

Family and school participation level also rated high.

Using the profile of the average respondent in this survey to construct a model democratic citizen would yield an individual who learned participatory skills at home, had them reinforced at school, and chose to use them both politically and in the arts as an adult. Pateman's ideal participatory society could be composed of a majority of similar citizens.

The concluding chapter summarizes the theory on arts participation set forth in this book, the implications drawn from the research, and provides recommendations to increase the levels of participation in the arts, thus reinforcing a participatory democratic society.

Notes

1. DeFleur and Ball-Rokeach, *Theories of Mass Communication*, p. 170.

2. Ibid., p. 172.

3. Lynes, *The Lively Audience*, p. 394.

4. An expanded version of this section was originally published as "Party Platforms and the Arts" in Wyszomirski and Balfe's *Art, Ideology, and Politics*, ibid.

5. Kirk H. Porter and Donald Bruce Johnson, ed., *National Party Platforms 1840–1960* (Urbana: University of Illinois Press, 1961).

6. Gerald M. Pomper, *Elections in America*, 2nd ed. (New York: Longman, 1980), p. 161.

7. Ibid., p. 163.

8. Paul T. David, "Party Platforms as National Plans," *Public Administration Review* (May–June 1979): 303–315.

9. Porter and Johnson, *National Party Platforms 1840–1960*, p. 339.

10. Ibid., p. 447.

11. Specific pledges seem to appear more frequently in the platforms of minor parties and eventually make their way into those of the major parties. John Anderson's 1980 National Unity Party Platform, for example, included support for several specific issues: a

White House Conference on the Arts and Humanities and a National Art Bank, among others.

12. Lawrence Mankin, "The National Government and the Arts: A Policy Pastiche," paper prepared for the 1979 Annual Meeting of American Political Science Association.

13. William F. McDonald, *Federal Relief Administration and the Arts* (Columbus: Ohio State University Press, n.d.), p. 129.

14. Joan Garratt, "The Arts Programs of the WPA," Library of Congress Legislative Reference Service, October 10, 1963.

15. Karal Ann Marling, *Wall-to-Wall America: A Cultural History of Post Office Murals in the Great Depression* (Minneapolis: University of Minnesota Press, 1982), p. 3.

16. Victor S. Navasky, *Naming Names* (New York: The Viking Press, 1980), p. 5.

17. Ibid., p. 78. The growing Soviet film industry and its use of anti-American propaganda helped initiate the first joint American-Soviet film conference to discuss each country's image of the other as presented in film. This conference took place in March 1986—fifty years after the Communist party first began to respond to American propaganda in movies made in Hollywood.

18. Ibid.

19. National Foundation on the Arts and Humanities Act of 1965, as amended through December 20, 1985.

20. Fannie Taylor and Anthony L. Barresi, *The Arts at a New Frontier: The National Endowment for the Arts* (New York: Plenum Press, 1984), p. 227.

21. Rae Moore, National CETA/Arts Coordinator, "Message from Rae Moore," in *Putting the Arts to Work*, 1980 conference materials prepared by A. L. Nellum and Associates of Boston.

22. *Fiscal Year 1982 Budget Revisions, Additional Details on Budget Savings* (Washington, DC: Executive Office of the President, Office of Management and Budget, April 1981), pp. 366–367.

23. Presidential Task Force on the Arts and Humanities, *Report to the President* (Washington, DC: Superintendent of Documents, October 1981), p. 2.

24. James Backas, "The State Arts Council Movement," background paper prepared for The National Partnership Meeting, June 1980, George Washington University, Washington, DC, p. 3.

25. Anthony J. Radich, "The Politics and Administration of State Arts Agencies: Four Views," (Denver, CO: National Conference of State Legislatures, 1985), p. 4.

26. John K. Urice and Richard Hofferbert, *State Legislative Funding of, and National Endowment for the Arts Grants to, State Arts Agencies: An Assessment of Relative Impact, Interrelationships, and*

Effects of and Upon Other Variables (Binghamton, NY: Center for Social Analysis, 1982).

27. Annual Survey, State Arts Agencies Legislative Appropriations, Fiscal Years 1987 and 1988, National Assembly of State Arts Agencies.

28. James Backas, "The Regional Arts Organization Movement," background paper prepared for the National Partnership Meeting, June 1980, George Washington University, Washington, DC, p. 1.

29. Robert Mayer, "The Local Arts Council Movement," background paper prepared for the National Partnership Meeting, June 1980, George Washington University, Washington, DC, p. 29.

30. Mark Davidson Schuster, *Supporting the Arts: An International Comparative Study* (Washington, DC: National Endowment for the Arts, 1985).

31. Lois Fishman, "Report on Tax Checkoff for the Arts" (Washington, DC: National Assembly of State Art Agencies, 1983).

32. In his very negative perspective of federal arts funding (*The Ministry of Culture* [New York: Wyndham Books, 1980]), Michael Mooney noted that additional monetary benefits accrue to both artists and politicians, particularly through the many black-tie fundraisers that they both seem to enjoy.

33. Schuster, *Supporting the Arts*, p. 37.

34. Ibid., p. 44.

35. Edwin Seligman, *Essays on Taxation* (New York: Macmillan, 1925), p. 1.

36. Harry Kahn, *Personal Deductions in Federal Income Tax* (Princeton, NJ: Princeton University Press, 1960) p. 1.

37. Edwin D. Etherington, "Effects on Donees," *Tax Impacts of Philanthropy* (Princeton, NJ: Tax Institute of America, 1972).

38. Grace Glueck, "Gifts to Museums Fall Sharply After Changes in the Tax Code," *New York Times*, May 7, 1989, p. 1.

39. Schuster, *Supporting the Arts*, p. 41.

40. The Tax Reform Act of 1986 changed the American rules for the alternative minimum tax to include gifts of appreciated property. The museum community, in particular, is studying the expected negative effect of this change on major contributions of art.

41. *Giving USA*, 1988 report.

42. Etherington, "Effects on Donees."

43. Helen H. Lamale and Joseph A. Clorety, Jr., "City Families as Givers," *Monthly Labor Review*, December, 1959.

44. "Giving and Volunteering in the United States," 1988 Gallup Survey for Independent Sector.

45. Kahn, *Personal Deductions in Federal Income Tax*, p. 81.

46. Michael K. Taussig, "Economic Aspects of the Personal Income Tax Treatment of Charitable Contributions," *National Tax Journal,* March 1967.

47. Michael J. Boskin and Martin Feldstein, "Effects of the Charitable Deduction on Contributions by Low Volume and Middle Income Households," *Review of Economic Statistics,* Vol. 59, No. 3, August 1977.

48. Ibid., p. 354

49. Boris J. Bittker, "The Propriety and Vitality of a Federal Income Tax Deduction for Private Philanthropy," *Tax Impacts on Philanthropy,* Ibid., p. 146.

50. Leon P. Baradat, *Political Ideologies: Their Origins and Impacts* (2nd ed., Englewood Cliffs, NJ: Prentice-Hall, Inc., 1984), p. 83.

51. Ibid., p. 13.

52. Baumol and Bowen, *Performing Arts,* p. 164.

53. William J. Baumol, "Financial Prospects for the Performing Arts: Reports from the Cloudy Crystal Ball," a speech to the Annual Conference of the Association of College, University, and Community Arts Administrators, December 16, 1979.

54. *Economic Impact of Arts and Cultural Institutions: A Model for Assessment and a Case Study in Baltimore,* National Endowment for the Arts, November 1977.

55. Ibid.

56. *The Arts in the New England Economy,* New England Foundation for the Arts, 1981.

57. John Fuller, Scott Kralik, Steve Nichols, Dean Peckham, and James Schwab, "Economic Impact of the Arts: Methods of Analysis," Institute of Urban and Regional Research, University of Iowa, October 1982, p. 2.

58. "A Study of Out-of-Town Visitors to the Tut Exhibit at the Metropolitan Museum of Art," May 1979, Yankelovich, Skelly and White, Inc.

59. "The Economic Impact of the Arts on the Oklahoma City Area Economy, 1980 Update," Arts Council of Oklahoma City, July 20, 1981.

60. "The Arts as an Industry: Their Economic Importance to the New York-New Jersey Metropolitan Region," Cultural Assistance Center, Inc., and the Port Authority of New York and New Jersey, February 1983.

61. "Report on the Economic Impact of the Arts in Texas, Executive Summary," Texas Commission on the Arts, October 1984.

62. "Michigan: State of the Arts, An Economic Impact Study Summary of Findings," Touche Ross, May 1985.

63. John Kenneth Galbraith, *A View from the Stands, Of People, Politics, Military Power, and the Arts* (Boston: Houghton Mifflin Company, 1986), p. 146.

64. Federal resale royalties legislation was introduced by Congressman Thomas J. Downey during the 99th Congress, but it never moved out of committee.

65. Ibid.

66. Ibid. Galbraith noted, however, that along with the encouragement of investment in art, society must take responsibility for the preservation of art.

67. Carole Refkind, "Tourism, the Arts, and the City: Design Strategy," *The Arts and Tourism: A Profitable Partnership* (New York: American Council for the Arts, 1981), pp. 23–25.

68. In *The Affluent Society* (New York: New American Library, 1958), Galbraith stated that "the major social goal of society" (p. 267) should be to expand the class of people who find pleasure in their work. One way to improve the work environment is through artistic design and planning.

69. Galbraith, *A View from the Stands*, p. 149.

70. Joseph E. Cantor, "PACs: Political Financiers of the 1980s," Congressional Research Service Review, February 1982.

71. "Backing Down the PACs," *Washington Post*, April 3, 1987.

72. Berke, Richard L., "Political Action Committees Giving More to Incumbent Democrats," *New York Times*, April 9, 1989.

73. Quoted by Joseph Wesley Zeigler, "Friendly Persuasion: The Arts Arrive on Capital Hill," *American Arts*, July 1983, p. 25.

74. Dick Netzer, *The Subsidized Muse* (New York: Cambridge University Press, 1978), p. 169.

75. Joseph Wesley Ziegler, "Mending Wall," *American Art*, September 1983.

76. "Action Update," November 1984, Illinois Arts Action Coalition.

77. National Endowment for the Arts, *Five-Year Plan 1986–1990*, p. 32.

78. DiMaggio and Useem, "Cultural Democracy in a Period of Cultural Expansion: The Social Composition of the Arts Audiences in the United States" in Kamerman and Martorella, *Performers and Performances*, pp. 217–218.

79. Pierre Bourdieu and Alain Darbel, *L'Amour de L'Amour de l'Art*, Editions de Minuit, Paris 1969, Appendix 5, Table 4 in *Ways of Seeing* by John Berger (New York: The Viking Press, 1973), p. 24.

80. NEA is beginning to research segments of the arts audience to determine if demographics and barriers vary according to art form. In *The American Jazz Music Audience* (Washington, DC: National Jazz Service Organization, 1986), Harold Horowitz listed the four leading barriers to jazz attendance: "not enough time," "cost," "not available," and "too far to go" (p. 4).

81. DiMaggio and Useem in Kamerman and Martorella, *Performers and Performances*, p. 221.

82. Joseph Wesley Ziegler, "The Advocacy Personality," *American Arts*, November, 1983, pp. 22–23.

83. Marleen Sansone, "The Arts and Power: A Study of the Relationship Between Leaders in the Arts and Political Leaders in Connecticut, 1979–1980," M.A. thesis, Goddard College, Vermont, cited by Joseph Wesley Ziegler, "The Advocacy Personality," *American Arts*, November 1983.

9

The Role of Participation: Implications and Recommendations

The interrelationship between the arts and the democratic political system was the impetus for this book. As research progressed, the focus became participatory democracy and how participation in the arts can enhance the particular brand of democracy found in mid–twentieth century America. The preceding chapters have outlined my theory of participation and the arts and tested it in various societies and times. This chapter summarizes and sets forth a number of recommendations.

Beginning with the assumption that a liberal democratic form of government is an appropriate goal and that maximum participation can and should be attained, Carole Pateman theorized that participation in the family, home, and work environments can help society attain these goals. Her analysis of experiments with worker participation in industry led her to state that the psychological underpinnings and skills necessary for individuals to participate can also be obtained in other spheres of society.

Beginning with the assumption that the arts are beneficial to society and that a maximum participatory democracy should be attained, my theory flows from Pateman's. In order to provide a framework for this theory of participation in the arts, a connection with Talcott Parsons' theory of social action was established and, using a systems diagram approach, a historical overview of participation was provided within that framework.

Participation in the sphere of the arts ranges on a continuum from the active professional artist to the passive arts observer, and specific activities are not always easily categorized. For illustration, two categories of active arts participation were defined: the individual who engages in the creative act and the work of art which is so powerful it *causes* political participation. Individuals in the first category include professional and amateur artists, as well as arts support personnel. Of particular emphasis under this category is the importance of arts education. A strong arts education program can increase children's self-esteem, sharpen their decision-making skills, and give them the background necessary to become amateur or professional artists as adults. Arts education is also a vital ingredient in expanding one of the passive categories of arts participation—the audience.

When well-prepared by arts education, both the amateur and professional artists are more likely to participate in art as adults. This participation continues the building of self-esteem and decision-making techniques started in childhood, and, if the professional becomes involved in arts unions, for example, very specific political skills could develop. Political skills also could be acquired by the amateur in association with the growing field of arts advocacy organizations.

Works of art that tend to cause individuals to take part in political participation were also included under the category of active arts participation. Two subcategories were: monuments and memorials and public art. (Any work of art, if it proves offensive to enough people, could cause active political participation in the form of censorship; however, the scope of this study did not include a discussion of censorship in the arts.) Each subcategory was illustrated by an example of art that caused participation. In the description of the steps involved with the design, construction, and dedication of the Vietnam Veterans Memorial, the unusual amount of political participation involved was highlighted. The powerful design of the memorial and the turbulent period in our history that it represented seemed to draw energy and emotion from individuals who otherwise were among the politically apathetic majority. The second subcategory was represented by the public sculpture *Tilted Arc*. Once again, the extremely powerful design and seemingly defiant placement of the art stirred people to make, at the very least, a political decision on whether the piece should remain or be removed.

The discussion of passive arts participation was divided into three subsections: the audience, the volunteer, and the patron. An audience member has the potential to move up the passive participation hierarchy by becoming a volunteer or a patron. Both of these levels entail greater degrees of decision making. Under the current arts support system, analyzed in Chapter 8, the patron, in particular, can exert an enormous amount of decision-making power, if the patronage is excessive.

Under an ideal participatory society, a strong arts education program would prepare adequate and sophisticated audiences for all the arts. This large demand at the consumption level would support a thriving artistic production level. The entire system would then be creating a truly American cultural tradition. One of the essences of this tradition would be the value of participation. Thus, the arts would be an integral part of Parsons' theory in which culture is learned, transmitted, and shared.

Having set forth the theory of arts participation, this theoretical outline was used in discussions of three historical periods when political democracy was predominant: Greece in the fifth century B.C.; America during the Jacksonian era; and the United States today. For each period, a general discussion of the society and the role of participation were provided. Each section was then followed by a discussion highlighting participation.

In ancient Greece, for example, the microdemocracy promoted maximum participation by citizens who were free males born into citizenship. The major arts festivals were an integral part of society's rituals and served to reaffirm the sense of community within the political system itself. Extensive participation was encouraged, but both the political and arts participation was pervaded by a mass mentality perpetuated by the elites, who held the majority of decision-making power. Democracy and the arts in ancient Greece were participatory, but not in the sense that Pateman or I would recommend.

During the Jacksonian era, widespread political participation was encouraged, but mass involvement with the formal arts was not a matter of public concern. Arts activity was individual, eclectic, and widespread at the folk level. This intense folk activity in music eventually emerged in the twentieth century as the truly American genre— jazz. In the field of dance, folk elements merged with classical and created the modern dance forms in which American creativity began to lead the world, while opera, operetta, and theatre combined as the American musical theatre began to blossom in the twentieth century to create yet another new art form.

The most extensive discussion of arts participation in a democracy involved mid–twentieth century American society. After reviewing an appropriate model of the political system and discussing elements of the larger culture that effect participation, various systems diagrams highlighting elements of arts participation were presented. The public and private components, the most important elements of the system, were analyzed, and the effect of the current system on participation was discussed.

The remainder of this chapter looks at the current system again, but proposes changes that would affect the components of the system and modify levels of participation. Implementation of any one of these recommendations would likely move the system toward a more participatory society.

GENERAL RECOMMENDATIONS

The Overall Political System

Because this study depends on a strong foundation of political theory, specific recommendations are accompanied by general suggestions regarding the political system as a whole. With these in place, political participation would increase, a participatory society would be reinforced, and, assuming that society still valued the role of the arts, participation in the arts would increase.

Two categories of changes would affect political participation: mechanical changes in the system and socioeconomic changes in society. One of the first mechanical changes suggested by political theorists to increase political participation in a democracy is to limit the size of the political unit. The problems inherent with a country the size of the United States today have already been discussed and the differences with a society as small as that of ancient Greece have been noted; however, Robert Dahl, who has analyzed studies regarding size and democracy, concluded that participation and sense of effectiveness do not depend to any significant degree on size.[1] But he did stress that the effect of the unit size within a particular country is important—"participation and effectiveness are best achieved in densely populated communes with populations under 8,000."[2] Units of this size, however, may not be optimal to handle other problems. Therefore, Dahl suggested that neither a city-state unit nor a nation-state unit is optimal and that theorists must analyze a collection of interacting units from small primary associations where direct democracy is possible to larger units employing representative forms of government. The current New England town meeting system could serve as the smallest model, as in this description of a 1982 town meeting in Antrium, New Hampshire:

> But it was merely for me the high point of the town meeting, which, to tell you the truth, I found the finest political gathering I have ever attended. . . . As we went through the long day, from 10 to 5, I fell to thinking what a marvelous invention it was—"as near to pure democracy as you dare," said Town Clerk Martin Nicholas, proudly, when it was over. It gives people a sense of control over their own destiny—from repairing the dam at Gregg Lake to giving orders to the White House and the politburo.[3]

The above captures the essence of direct American democracy. The author of that description suggested in her editorial that this kind of meeting should be "exported" to El Salvador. Perhaps it should also be exported to New Jersey, Kansas, and Arizona.

Instituting a change to town meetings must occur at the bottom level of the political system. C. B. Macpherson's model of participatory democracy[4] stresses, too, that direct democracy should occur at the base of the system, while levels above should provide for more representative democracy. Other changes also could take place at the upper levels. Chapter 7 discussed several of these modifications, including easier registration methods, more extensive voter campaigns, even a national holiday on election day. Similar mechanical change could occur in the artistic community: reducing barriers to attendance, instituting "go to the arts" campaigns; or even a day celebrating our national culture.[5]

The second category of changes helpful to increasing participation involves basic socioeconomic modifications. In both the arts and politics, many aspects of participation simply require a minimum amount of money, and in a society with high economic inequality, both political and artistic resources also tend to be distributed unequally. James Leonard Danielson stressed that the levels of participation are greatly influenced by the resources available to the participants and encouraged policies to help redistribute wealth.[6] Dahl noted that the United States lags behind other countries in reducing economic inequalities and suggested that the standard solution is the establishment of "floors and ceilings." Currently, the United States employs minimum floors (social security and free elementary and secondary education) and certain ceilings (limits to campaign contributions). Although unequal economic resources had not been a major issue, Dahl indicated they could become one,[7] and research outlining the distribution of wealth in America during the last half of the 1980s shows that Dahl may have been correct. The current system should, at the very least, be closely monitored to prevent trends toward further inequality, and, if possible, it should be fine-tuned in the direction of eliminating the unequal distribution of political and artistic resources. Perhaps the government should institute "artistic floors" by *requiring* nonprofit arts institutions to offer free or reduced services for certain segments of the population[8] or establish "artistic ceilings" over which wealthy donors may not contribute to lessen the influence of elites.

Another social change to help temper inequalities in the system would be the formation of organizations and coalitions,[9] along with encouragement of participation in other spheres. Political parties should ensure that voter organizations reach all classes and all levels of the political system; arts advocacy groups should also begin to broaden their membership; and businesses should expand opportunities for worker participation. The latter suggestion is also favored by Dahl and Macpherson. With the above mechanical and socioeconomic changes in place, a firm foundation would be laid for increased political and artistic participation. The following sections examine more specific recommendations aimed at various components of the arts support system.

The Public and Private Roles

The focus of this chapter, which has been on the overall political system and its effect on the larger culture, now shifts to the specific components of the arts support system, where additional fine tuning is needed. Because this theory is based on the assumption that participation is good for society and that participation in the arts should be encouraged, part of this task is assigned to government. To gain a clearer picture of the issues involved with allocating some cultural responsibility to government, a brief overview of arguments for and against public support should be examined.

Public Support of the Arts: The Case Against. Ernest Van den Haag, in his article "Should Government Subsidize the Arts?", said that in order to justify government support of the arts, one must show that private funds are not likely to support the arts to the degree or in the manner justified by their social usefulness, while government subsidies can do so. Van den Haag argued that "the arts are not among the activities which contribute enough to social cohesion, national identity, or shared values in the United States to justify support by the government. On the other hand, the activities (most notably sports and rock music) which would deserve support on these grounds scarcely need it."[10] Edward C. Banfield agreed that government has no place in supporting the arts. The two great ends of government—protection of the individual in exercising his rights and the improvement of the individual as a citizen—do not, according to Banfield, justify placing the arts on the public agenda. He noted that some philosophers (Plato, Rousseau) believed that certain aesthetic experiences are bad for society, and, even if art is good for society, government is not the appropriate patron. Like religion, not all activities affecting the public interest merit government action. We do not want a "National Endowment for Religion," stated Banfield.[11] This study, however, is based on the belief that the arts are good for society and that "continuity of culture in passage from one civilization to another as well as within one culture is conditioned by art more than any other one thing."[12]

A second argument suggested by Van den Haag is that government support may even hurt the arts. He discussed the problem of government censorship and argued that subsidies often stifle creativity in the best artists and encourage bad art in the worst. Subsidies may attract people who would not have become artists without government support, and in addition make it harder for true artists to succeed. Kingsley Amis extends this argument by stating that the state-supported artist is likely to be wasteful, irresponsible, and self-indulgent.[13] Baumol and Bowen, among others, however, have shown that interference by private patrons may be even more frequent and detrimental. I would also argue that the National Endowment for the Arts has been carefully constructed and is carefully monitored to alleviate the problems of interference and quality control.

An additional argument against government's involvement with the arts concerns the selection of individuals to sit on panels that choose grant recipients. Amis has claimed these "so-called experts officialize, bureaucratize, and politicize art."[14] This argument can be countered by pointing to the panel selection system, which is tightly regulated. Panelists, who are professionals in the field, not "bureaucrats," serve short terms, are forbidden to vote on grants involving conflicts of interest, and must be representative of all areas of the country.

Van den Haag concluded that the only legitimate area in which government should subsidize the arts is in preservation of art for future generations. His conclusion is supported by Amis: "there is no reason why those who are currently gratified by viewing art should compel others to pay for their gratification."[15] Supporting the viewing of art also brings to light the controversy between the elitists versus the populists. The elitists argue that in an attempt to broaden the arts audience the government continues to "fertilize weeds instead of flowers."[16] As government subsidies increase, elected officials are inclined to see which portion of the money is spent in their districts: "The result is that an increasing percentage of government arts money is being dribbled away on mime troupes, street theatre, supergraphics on the sides of buildings, and hand presses that print up slim volumes of homemade poetry (on the best possible paper)."[17] The arts audience is still elite, according to Banfield. Both he and economist Milton Friedman have agreed that the arts are enjoyed by middle- and upper-income individuals: "What justification is there for imposing taxes on low-income people to finance luxuries for high-income people?"[18] In short, the political power of the elite makes the decision for arts subsidies, according to those opposed to government support; opponents argue that the political power of the wealthy private patron maintains the elite side of the arts, but that the government support encourages access for all.

Public Support of the Arts: The Case For. In 1980, Congressman Ted Weiss, speaking in support of the 1980 reauthorizing legislation, stated that the Endowments "have made an enormous contribution to the cultural well-being of our nation. The arts and humanities are now available to more citizens in practically every community across the country than ever before. The Arts and Humanities Endowments have successfully accomplished their mission and merit the reaffirmation of their roles and purposes that is contained in this legislation before us today."[19] Whether the NEA has been as successful as Weiss remarked is open to debate;[20] however, direct government support of the NEA, coupled with the indirect support of our tax system, has been helpful in a number of ways, which are highlighted by arguments for that support.

In "The Rationale for Public Culture,"[21] Kevin Mulcahy outlined five arguments for government's involvement with cultural support. His economic, social, educational, moral, and political arguments encompass most major claims of other arts advocates. Chapter 8 outlined many of the major points involved with the economic argument, including economic impact studies. Clearly, the arts are an important part of local, state, regional, and national economies, and all levels of government should help ensure their contribution to the system, if not through direct subsidies, at least through policies which are not detrimental.

An additional point concerning the economic argument involves Baumol and Bowen's "cost disease," as outlined in Chapter 8. Although not as catastrophic as the economists originally suggested, the deficits of arts organizations are still a reality: "The argument is simple: If through no fault of their own the arts cannot survive without public support, the necessary support must be provided."[22] Within the past ten years this argument has been expanded in the case of arts organizations within the District of Columbia. Because of their unique location, these groups argue, they do not have available as many private and governmental sources of funding as organizations in other cities and deserve special public support. A 1985 study by the Washington Cultural Alliance comparing major cultural organizations in Washington, DC, to similar groups in eight other cities showed that the District of Columbia organizations raised a higher percentage of their funding from private sources. In addition, the study concluded that these organizations were disadvantaged in obtaining public, nonfederal funds. For a number of years, federal support came in the form of line items in the federal budget for organizations like the National Symphony, the Washington Opera, and Corcoran Gallery of Art, but in 1985 a special funding program, the National Capital Region Arts and Cultural Affairs Program, was approved by Congress to eliminate the continual competition for line-item funding.

According to Mulcahy, the cultural world is "uncomfortable" with his second argument: the arts are important to society. Support for this claim lies in the fact that the arts can be considered "public goods"—items that, when supplied to one individual, can also be enjoyed by others, and items whose supply is not diminished when the item is used. Public goods are often items that should be conserved for future generations:

> We support the arts, the nonprofit sector of the arts world, as a "public good." It's a perfectly good and valid reason. There is no need to hide behind statistics—the art experience is our experience. Learning about art is learning about ourselves, our culture, our values, our goals. Art is not escapism but a discovery, and its abundance and accessibility is a determining factor in the quality of our lives. It is to maintain this that governments are created, and it is on this basis that governments are judged.[23]

This book also has used this argument to highlight the value of the arts in learning, transmitting, and sharing culture, as well as the value of participation in the arts.

The educational argument involves several aspects. Thompson would stress that arts education is a necessary part of the education for citizenship; Mulcahy and most arts advocates would point to the importance of creating an audience receptive to artistic excellence and innovation; and I would add the importance of arts education in the realm of participation. According to economist Tibor Scitovsky, the purpose of arts education is to increase membership in the current elite audience until it no longer just serves an elite; and he has added another reason for arts education: because individuals have an inherent desire for stimulation and because excitement is limited, peoples' increased enjoyment of one source of excitement (the arts) is bound to diminish their demand for other sources (crime, for example).[24]

Mulcahy's fourth argument involves the moral dimension. If the arts perform a ritual function, like the festivals of ancient Greece, they should be supported for moral reasons. Although this book has argued that the arts do not perform this function in our society, in sporadic instances they do. The playing of American marches on the Fourth of July, singing "The Star Spangled Banner" before the World Series, even the purging of emotion brought out by the music used for the intense Vietnam movie *Platoon* (Samuel Barber's "Adagio for Strings")—these all serve a ritual function.

The final argument for public support of the arts is the political argument under which fall several categories. Government should fund cultural activities to broaden access for all citizens; international prestige is bolstered by a strong national culture; and the goal of world peace is reinforced by cultural exchange. In a convocation address at Brown University, the playwright Eugène Ionesco supported the political argument for public arts support: "It is literature and not politics, literature and art alone, that are capable of rehumanizing the world."[25]

Since the focus of this book is the importance of participation in the arts, all arguments—economic, social, educational, moral, political—intertwine with the theory. In all discussions of the systems diagrams, the economic element was highlighted; the social argument provided the foundation for historical perspectives of arts participation; arts education is one of the most important aspects of the theory; the moral argument was most prominent in the discussion of arts participation in ancient Greece; and the political arguments were evident in all discussions of increased audience participation. Obviously, public support of the arts plays an important part in the model of the ideal participatory democratic culture, and the mix of this public and private support is unique to America: "The American system for financing the arts through patchwork (and this in the end may be its primary virtue) meets the most fundamental tests—freedom, diversity, excellence, and vigorous new growth."[26] The model of democratic government that provides for a *careful* blend of direct and indirect government support with a healthy amount of corporate and private philanthropy provides an appropriate model under which American arts could flourish and participation could be maximized: "The need is to carry out the cultural premise of the American Revolution, to see to it that the majority is capable of shouldering the responsibilities that in past centuries were entrusted to elites."[27]

FINE-TUNING THE SYSTEM

The Public and Private Components

The previous discussion outlined arguments for and against government support of the arts. If the argument for government support is accepted, how can the system be most responsive to optimum participation?

As a matter of public policy, regulating the balance of public and private support of the arts can be based on several different models. Paul DiMaggio has provided four: (1) government as leader in cultural support; (2) the private sector as leader in cultural support; (3) an equal partnership of public and private support; and (4) a natural division of labor in which each sector does what it does best.[28] Whichever model is chosen depends on the level (federal, state, local) of decision making; high levels give more decision-making power to the public sector, while low levels give more decision-making power to the private sector.

Economist J. Pen would choose DiMaggio's fourth model with qualifications. He has imagined a "Golden Age" where decision making is as low as possible, but, Pen says, "as a 'very cultural person' you would want the government to help," because a system based purely on marketplace demand does not give the artist enough freedom.[29] Pen would have the decision making of the three levels of government allocated as follows: The federal government should be responsible for the support of great cultural institutions across the country,[30] entitlements to artists, programs ensuring geographic equity, and arts education; the local government should handle all amateur arts; and the state government would have the freedom to assist in any way it wished. This book's analysis of the arts support system is also based on DiMaggio's fourth model in which each sector shares decision-making power.

Although the hybrid model of American democracy, with its patchwork system of support for the arts, does not offer optimum participation, it does offer the greatest flexibility and opportunity for the creation of a climate in which participation can be encouraged and a truly American artistic tradition can develop. To help this vision become a reality, however, various changes have been suggested by individuals involved with cultural policy in both the public and private sectors. For example, the 1986–90 Five-Year Plan of the National Endowment for the Arts contained four general areas in which the NEA expected to focus on improvements and which provide an appropriate framework to focus attention for improvement: individual artists, institutions, audience development, and arts education. Individual artists, institutions, and audience development are discussed as part of this section, and arts education, which I view as extremely important and in most need of improvement, is discussed in the next section.

Because individual artists are the foundation of the entire arts system, they deserve special attention. Although written nearly ten years ago, one of the first major studies to provide a thorough analysis of the public support system and to offer recommendations, *The*

Subsidized Muse[31] by Dick Netzer urged that grants to individual artists be increased. In Chapter 8 I highlighted the importance of economic considerations in the relationship of the artist and society and also suggested that government pay more attention to policy changes affecting the individual artist. Although NEA's purpose is not to ensure minimum income for all artists, individual grants can free the artist for a short period of time to devote energy to creative concerns. Because active arts participation is so important to my theory, the NEA should evaluate its support of programs that continue to train professional artists and possibly expand them.

In the realm of arts institutions, NEA policies during the last half of 1980s were aimed at helping with artistic deficits, providing additional funds for operating support, more grants to emerging organizations,[32] and more support in the area of data collection. All are appropriate policies which attempt to strengthen institutions as the major components of the distribution system of American arts. Netzer, however, cautioned that NEA should subsidize major arts institutions more selectively and minimize or eliminate subsidies for amateur groups. Institutions should also be encouraged to develop or expand "profit-seeking" arts activities and still remain eligible for public support.

In the third area, audience development, federal cultural policy in the late 1980s highlighted enhancement of programs aimed at community arts groups, strengthening professional touring and presenting organizations, and encouraging expanded use of the mass media for arts presentation. Netzer suggested that, in order to foster geographic dispersion, state and local matching grants should be encouraged, but that all levels of arts agencies have more clearly defined roles. (See Pen's comments above.)

Clearly, in support of my participatory theory, NEA should continue to research the composition of arts audiences and evaluate programs in an effort to increase participation across all socioeconomic classes. Innovative programs that attempt to broaden the arts audience should be encouraged. A unique example of a pre-1930 Soviet experiment in expanding the arts audience provides an interesting model. W. D. Kay described an experience of the Russian director Constantin Stanislavsky when theatre performances were free to all who received tickets from their place of work. According to Stanislavsky, the artists found they had to teach the new spectator how to sit quietly, how to come to the theatre at the proper time, not to bring food into the theatre, and "to dress his best so as to fit more into the atmosphere of beauty." Apparently, the experience was extremely rewarding. The new audiences were the best spectators, trembling with expectation of something they had never experienced before, and according to

Kay: "This example may be viewed as an application of Pateman's idea of 'learning to participate by participating'. . . ."[33]

The above recommendations apply to programs of direct government subsidy. They are particularly important to the model of a participatory society set forth in this book and parallel Netzer's views which indicate that public funding is "essential for the preservation, enhancement, and diffusion of our cultural heritage."[34]

Chapter 8 demonstrated that indirect public funding has been more substantial than direct public funding; consequently, changes in this component, therefore, could have more impact on the system as a whole. A major study examining the American tax system that offered recommendations is *Patrons Despite Themselves: Taxpayers and Arts Policy*. Although the authors analyzed the system prior to the 1986 Tax Act which lowered rates and changed rules for donating appreciated property, their findings that the system of charitable contributions tax deductions allows greater decision making in the upper-income categories is still valid. In order to create equity, they have proposed alternatives: the tax credit, the percentage contribution bonus, and the sliding matching grant.[35]

Tax credits allow all taxpayers to subtract the same percentage of any gift directly from tax liability. Of course, the flow of money to charitable organizations would change, religious organizations would receive more and, according to Feld et al., cultural institutions would experience a decrease in contributions of approximately 20 percent. The second proposal from Feld et al. would have the government match the total funds contributed to a charity. (The British system known as a Deed of Covenant is similar to the contribution bonus.) The third proposal, the sliding matching grant, "is designed to achieve a middle ground between the inequity of the existing charitable deduction and the redistribution of funds among charitable sectors that would occur with a tax credit or a percentage contribution bonus."[36] Under this system, the size of the government's contribution would be tied to the percentage of the donor's income given to charity each year. According to Feld et al., this proposal would result in approximately the same amount of total giving with a moderate increase to religion and moderate decrease to culture. Of the three proposals, the authors recommended a tax credit of 30 percent, because it would require only minor changes in existing regulations. In addition, government could easily adjust a tax credit to compensate for any unforeseen losses to charitable institutions. Since this proposal would result in a decrease in contributions, they also recommended that direct government aid be modified accordingly.

In addition, Feld et al. suggested that the indirect benefit accrued as a result of gifts of property in which appreciation is not taxed tends to add to the elitist character of the system. Regulations related to gifts of property were modified in 1986, and gifts to cultural organizations have declined. Finally, Feld et al. noted that the property tax exemption offers the fewest advantages and often rewards arts institutions for spending their money in a way opposed to the public interest. For that reasons, they recommended that it be abolished[37]—with a careful transition period to cushion the blow.

All these changes would make the system more responsive to public policy rather than private interest. If direct government support has the quality of restraint as part of NEA's authorizing legislation, these changes would serve to legislate restraint on the part of private patrons—a quality considered most important by Michael Straight.[38] Furthermore, the entire system would better approximate the ideal model of a participatory arts environment.

The above changes in direct and indirect public support should be mirrored at the state and local levels. In 1982, an arts conference was organized by the Congressional Arts Caucus to discuss local responses to a changing arts environment. The conference, "Arts in Transition: Creative Responses," produced the following recommendations:

> Community planning processes should include greater participation by art interests, from initial planning through implementation.
>
> Tourism development in cities should include arts planning efforts and the participation of artists and others interested in the arts.
>
> City governments should be strongly encouraged to review and revise city codes and zoning ordinances in order to provide a wider range of spaces for the arts.
>
> Local governments should consider the value of incentives that would encourage developers to include artists' living and workspaces in their projects.
>
> Local boards of education should acknowledge their responsibility to arts education through adequate funding and by assuring that the arts are a basic element of the curriculum.
>
> Arts interests and others at the local level should engage in arts roundtables and other vehicles to ensure an exchange of information and collaboration.[39]

Of particular interest to this book are the recommendations to include greater participation by arts interests in community planning and tourism developments, expanded use of cable television, and strengthened arts education. Use of technology and arts education are discussed beginning on page 179.

The United States is not alone in evaluating the role of all sectors of the arts support system. Chapter 8 highlighted a Canadian study that recommended various tax changes to enhance that country's arts support by the year 2000. Perhaps of greater importance is the fact that the study clearly recognized the contributions of all sectors and recommended a 5 percent annual growth: "Arts funding partners— governments, the private sector, consumers, and the art community—should pool their efforts to attain the overall goals that such growth implies."[40] In agreement with my previous recommendations, the study also suggested increased financial support for individual artists, including a goal of 1 percent of the arts in the Canadian art bank for Canadian artists; stronger arts curricula; periods of free admissions to museums for certain populations; and expanded use of technology.

In addition to the above recommendations aimed mostly at the public sector, with the private sector indirectly affected by changes in tax law, certain components of the private sector have suggested areas for improvement. Because the marketplace is not sufficient to support all segments of the arts community and government is unable or unwilling to venture into these areas, the Ford Foundation outlined three priorities in a 1986 working paper:

Development of new works and innovative forms of artistic expression.

Furtherance of pluralism and diversity, encouraging the most talented artists and arts organizations outside the tradition of mainstream culture.

Conservation outside of the visual arts, documentation of performances on film, archival and oral history, and notation.[41]

All three areas would increase participation. Support of innovative forms would benefit the active professional participant; encouragement of pluralism and diversity would broaden the participation of cultural minorities; and conservation would preserve the American artistic tradition through which the value of widespread participation could be transmitted to future generations.

Implementation of any or all of the above recommendations by the public and private components would help fine-tune the system in the direction of greater participation. In the next two sections, two areas that have the most potential for helping to create a participatory society are highlighted: arts education and innovative technology.

Arts Education

Chapter 4 provided a background of current public attitudes toward education in general and arts education in particular. New initiatives began with the publication of *A Nation at Risk* in 1983, which clearly outlined the cultural importance of education: "A high level of shared education is essential to a free, democratic society, and to the fostering of a common culture, especially in a country that prides itself on pluralism and individual freedom."[42] As public opinion became more favorable to changes in education, the 1983 College Board report *Academic Preparation for College* was published and listed the arts as a basic element in education. It also stated that all students should learn to understand and appreciate the unique qualities of each of the arts and urged that the appreciation of different artistic cultures, different styles and historical periods, and the knowledge of the social and intellectual influences in art be taught. All of these suggestions are vitally important to educating individuals to participate as audiences for the arts. Furthermore, active arts participation in one or more disciplines was included as a requirement.

Publication of these reports and the ensuing public interest[43] in strengthening American education led to renewed emphasis on arts education and the commissioning of a report by Congress in 1985 as part of legislation governing the National Endowment for the Arts. This report, *Toward Civilization*, was completed in 1988 and recommended strengthened standards for arts education, including time spent on arts instruction in elementary school and the number of high school courses required.

Combining the decidedly conservative recommendations of *Toward Civilization*—a product of the Reagan era—with the more liberal values of a 1977 report, *Coming to Our Senses: The Significance of the Arts for American Education* provides an acceptable balance serving to increase participation all around. While the 1988 report stressed "cultural literacy" and "hard work and discipline," the 1977 report emphasized "enriching our emotional selves" and "the rich world of personal expression"[44]—all beneficial to the ultimate goal of increased participation. With increased attention to arts education by NEA, the public sector began to move slowly toward increasing funds in that direction. Still, the agency is far from the goal set in 1984 by one of its National Council members, Samuel Lipman: "And so I think we come to some idea of a proper role for the National Endowment for the Arts. It should be *educational*, an attempt to teach rather than to beguile."[45] Although the very conservative Lipman would probably not agree with a number of my other recommendations to increase participation, he probably would agree that arts education is most vital to

American society. The following section, which highlights use of technology, also discusses technology's value in arts education.

The Role of Technology

According to Michael Straight, strengthened artistic education and use of technology are the two means to carry out the cultural premise of the American Revolution,[46] and I believe we have only begun to tap the resources of this "sympathetic technology." For example, for several decades, the Metropolitan Opera has reached millions of listeners with its Saturday afternoon broadcasts, and *Live from Lincoln Center* telecasts also broadened the arts audience, but innovative uses of technology are just emerging.

One recent creative approach attempting to expand the opera audience is the use of "supertitles"—English translations of the foreign texts projected above the stage. Most likely, elitists would argue that this particular device appeals to an unsophisticated audience undeserving of the spectacle of opera but "true or not, a lot of people are coming away from the State Theater this season having heard an opera and, for the first time, having known with some precision what was going on."[47]

Some innovative opera companies are also expanding audiences by involving the talents of rock musicians. In October 1989, the Cleveland Opera presented the world premiere of *Holy Blood and Crescent Moon*, a new opera by rock musican Stewart Copeland. The production attracted a new mix of audience, including a much younger segment who were intrigued by the contemporary music and spectacle.

Supertitles and rock music are just two examples of the use of new technologies to educate new audiences. Both the NEA 1986–90 Five-Year Plan and the Rockefeller Panel Report, ten years earlier, stressed that technology is one of the most powerful resources for arts education. Clearly, the potential of the media arts for expanding educational opportunities in the arts overall is extensive. The use of television and film can bring the professional arts into classrooms at all levels, and active arts participation using these media themselves can be an exciting educational experience. Audience training outside the classroom can be a continuing process through the technological arts, as well. Public radio and television are prime sources for the dissemination of the arts and the development of cultural audiences. Furthermore, a strong public broadcasting system has the freedom and capability to emphasize regional programming.

Of all the electronic media, television, because it exists in nearly every household, is perhaps the best to help preserve, enhance, and diffuse our cultural heritage, and thus broaden participation. Straight has considered television an important means of fostering a general appetite for artistic excellence, as well as enabling serious artists to reach wide audiences, and as the cable industry expands, it has the potential to add to the participation possibilities in both politics and the arts. (See Chapter 7.)

In addition to expanding the audience and broadening participation, new technologies, particularly VCRs, have various unique characteristics that are just beginning to be explored. We are unaware of the enrichment possible with the capability to speed visual images, play them back at slow speed, or stop the action for analysis. Tony Schwartz has reminded us that when the printed word made written replay possible, great leaps occurred in the history of civilization.[48] But television critic Tom Shales has cautioned us that maybe we are entering an era "where there isn't anything worth replaying."[49] And, according to Todd Gitlin:

> Yet if we are serious about living in a democracy, the fundamental responsibility of the media should be to help people better pursue their rights and obligations as citizens not to sell goods, or serve as an amplification system for politicians, or shore up the prestige of the privileged, or sprinkle flakes of celebrity and blips of disconnected fact upon daily life of a society otherwise dedicated to private gain.[50]

Of all the media, television, because of its tremendous power to reach millions of people, has the greatest obligation to reinforce—or at the very least, not interfere with—the skills of democratic participation.

Chapter 7 explored the importance of a sense of community to society and the lack of that sense in twentieth-century America. In ancient Greece, large masses attended the festivals and shared common experiences. These experiences reinforced the values of the society as a whole and served to preserve and transmit the Greek culture. Because our society is a macrodemocracy, many times the size of the Greek microdemocracy, one of the only means of providing similar community experiences to the majority of the American population is through the technological arts. A number of television "events" (such as the Olympics, the Super Bowl, and various miniseries) are periodically seen concurrently by millions, who share in the particular kind of community experience shaped by these events. In discussions of the unprecedented size of the audience viewing the television miniseries *Winds of War*, for example, this concept was affirmed: "And that is the importance of television, really the fact that it enables so many of us to experience something at the same time and have something in common with all of our neighbors."[51]

The sense of community transmitted by television was first noticed during the 1960s as television ownership increased drastically. More and more public events began to be infused with a national community feeling. At the funeral for President John F. Kennedy, the entire country "meditated on death and the mystic of death."[52] The national television audience was able to view the ritual procession with six horses, the seventh carrying no rider with the stirrups reversed, and experience a sense of resolution. The power of television to involve the entire population in a ritual process can be equalled by no other medium. In a review of television programs during the twentieth anniversary of Kennedy's death, Tom Shales referred to Marshall McLuhan, who brought to our attention the power of television to invest an occasion with the character of corporate participation.[53]

Newspaper columnist Ellen Goodman has called this kind of community a "community of viewers" and suggested that television also has the power to make an event larger, yet more personal. She cited the telecast of the last episode of the series "M*A*S*H," noting that we all seem to come together to say good-bye.[54]

National holidays, namely the Fourth of July, are another time for gatherings shared across the airwaves: Congress appropriated funds to telecast each year the tens of thousands of faces on the Mall in Washington, DC, as the National Symphony celebrates America's birthday. The year 1986, the 100th anniversary of the Statue of Liberty, set the stage for an even larger televised event. Although some considered it excessive, the occasion brought millions of Americans together, and, in many cases, those who were not in the viewing audience were able to tape the event and still be part of the community at a later time—another unique aspect of the new technology that needs to be explored more fully.

Extending the sense of community throughout the world is even possible with the use of satellite transmission. The 1985 rock concert "Live Aid," organized to raise money to help those starving in Africa, was seen internationally by millions. The concept of a "world community" was captured at the concert by the musician Sting who performed "Message in a Bottle," a song about one man getting a hundred million responses to his lonely cry for help. That idea of one common message seemed to transmit a "heightened sense of human community."[55]

Although television has the power to produce a sense of community—and help enhance arts education—it has yet to become a truly artistic medium for the masses. The "first significant attempt since the beginning of our modern individualistic civilization to produce art for a mass public" was in the medium of film.[56] Movies are a truly American art form created by American democracy. Television has been successful in capturing the masses on occasion and giving them a sense of community, but film can extend their horizons and give them artistic experiences. Perhaps the combination of film on television has the potential to do both.

From the legacy of the Jacksonian period, where no American art form predominated and individual artistic activity fused polished European art with rough American folk art, has come a period when America is beginning to produce new forms of technological art for the masses. A true combination of Jacksonian freedom and Greek community experience is possible in twentieth-century American democratic society.[57] As film begins to explore American myths, that art form begins to approach this ideal: "Movies could take the function of great art in every epoch: the moral function."[58]

When movie director George Lucas invited author and scholar of mythology Joseph Campbell to a private screening of his films *Star Wars*, *The Empire Strikes Back*, and *The Return of the Jedi*, Campbell's response was: "He found a mythological model out in space—it's an open field. It seemed to me to be the counterpart of the Greek Argonauts. It released the imagination."[59] Campbell calls the myth "a public dream," and the American filmmakers are just beginning to explore the possibilities of giving our dreams expressions. When film begins to more readily fulfill this function, it will help give coherence to American society, which in turn will provide an even richer environment for the production, distribution, and consumption of art.

The fine tuning of the system as outlined in this chapter—mechanical and socioeconomic changes which encourage greater participation and specific modifications to the arts support system—continue the process of enhancing America's participatory brand of democracy. By examining participation in American society and the nourishment it draws from the arts, this book has shown that by strengthening participation in the arts, participatory democracy itself is strengthened—a key concept that was said no better than by President Franklin Delano Roosevelt over fifty years ago:

> The conditions for democracy and for art are one and the same. What we call liberty in politics results in freedom in the arts. Nourish the conditions for a free life and you nourish the arts, too. In encouraging the creation and enjoyment of beautiful things we are furthering democracy itself.[60]

American presidents since Roosevelt have also recognized, although often difficult to describe and rarely articulated during the daily activities of the government, that the relationship of the arts to society seems to be recognized as positive and fundamental. The words of President John F. Kennedy reinforce that belief:

> The life of the arts, far from being an interruption, a distraction, in the life of a nation, is very close to the center of a nation's purpose—and is a test of the quality of a nation's civilization.[61]

By examining how participation in cultural activities benefits society, this book was designed to take the reader down a perhaps unfamiliar path to see how the arts are close to the center of the American purpose. Clearly, exploration of that path has only begun.

Notes

1. Dahl and Tufte, *Size and Democracy*, p. 65.
2. Ibid.
3. Mary McGrory, "Democracy," *Washington Post*, March 21, 1982, p. D4.
4. C. B. Macpherson, *The Life and Times of Liberal Democracy* (New York: Oxford University Press, 1980), p. 108.
5. Numerous commemorative days, weeks, and months pass through Congress as special resolutions. In the past five years, Congress has approved National Theatre Week, National Dance Week, and National Humanities Week, among others.
6. Danielson, "Democratic Patterns of Political Participation," p. 247.
7. Dahl, *Dilemmas*, p. 181.
8. Opponents of government support, however, have claimed that even though "free days" have been offered by various museums, attendance by the target groups is very low.
9. Dahl, *Democracy in the U.S.*, p. 494.
10. Ernest Van den Haag, "Should the Government Subsidize the Arts?" *Policy Review*, Fall 1980, p. 67.
11. Banfield, *The Democratic Muse*, p. 12.
12. Dewey, *Art as Experience*, p. 327.
13. Kingsley Amis, "Government Shouldn't Fund the Arts," *New York Times*, August 31, 1980. Subsidizing the individual artist often causes many problems for the government. Notable examples include the funding of a poetry anthology by the NEA which included a one-word poem, "Lighght!"; and the partial funding of a film showing a chained dog being shot ("Killing for Art?" *Washington Post*, February 8, 1980). Ernest B. Furgurson said that the government should not fund

the individual creative artist: "The man or woman who wants deeply enough to write or compose can make it on his own" ("Government and the Arts," *Baltimore Sun*, March 18, 1979).

14. Kingsley Amis, "An Arts Policy?" *Policy Review*, Winter, 1980, p. 89. James J. Kilpatrick, a vehement opponent of government support of the arts, writes disparagingly of these experts:

> Somewhere in the budget statement sent to the House, the Endowment defines one of its concerns. It is concerned with issues that are "horizontally generic or deeply involved in the processes of many, if not all, responsiveness." At another point, the statement says the Endowment needs "linkage, specific and structure, between the application review process and policy discussion, since it is partially out of the application review process that policy, program and guideline issues emerge." . . . These birds are going to pass judgment on literature? (James J. Kilpatrick, "Artistry in Grants," *Washington Star*, September 6, 1979.)

Kilpatrick has confused the "experts" who write the legislation with the "experts" who pass judgment on art, but his comments express a commonly held attitude.

15. Van den Haag, "Should the Government Subsidize the Arts?" p. 72.

16. Richard Steele, "Populism vs. Elitism," *Newsweek*, October 31, 1977.

17. Tom Bethell, "The Cultural Tithe," *Harper's*, August 1977.

18. Milton Friedman, "Whose Money Is It Anyway?" *Newsweek*, May 4, 1981, p. 64.

19. Hon. Ted Weiss, *Congressional Record*, November 17, 1980, p. H10898.

20. Apparently, a large portion of the population agrees with Congressman Weiss that public support has been appropriate and that more should be expended. According to the 1988 Harris survey, 70 percent of Americans support paying $5 more per year in taxes to assist the arts—a rare exception to the rule of not supporting increased federal spending.

21. Kevin V. Mulcahy, "The Rationale for Public Culture," *Public Policy and the Arts*, Kevin V. Mulcahy and C. Richard Swaim, ed. (Boulder, CO: Westview Press, 1982).

22. Baumol and Bowen, *Performing Arts*, p. 369.

23. Daniel Grant, "Art for Art's Sake Is Reason Enough for Public Support," *Newsday*, June 5, 1983.

24. Tibor Scitovsky, "Subsidies for the Arts: The Economic Argument," *Economics of Cultural Decisions*, pp. 6–25.

25. "Ionesco: The Arts, Not Politics, Bring Peace," *Washington Post*, September 5, 1984, p. B8.

26. Waldemar A. Nielson, "Needy Arts: Where Have All the Patrons Gone," *New York Times*, October 26, 1980.

27. Straight, *Twigs for an Eagle's Nest*, p. 67.

28. Paul DiMaggio, "Can Culture Survive the Marketplace?" *Journal of Arts Management and Law*, Spring 1983.

29. J. Pen, "A Very Economist's Ideas About the Locus of Decision-Making," *Economics of Cultural Decisions*, p. 21.

30. Levine (p. 301) suggested that the government should ensure that everyone is within 25 miles of a great cultural institution.

31. Dick Netzer, *The Subsidized Muse* (New York: Cambridge University Press, 1978).

32. In her study, *The Emerging Arts* (New York: Praeger Publishing, 1980), Joan Jeffri noted that these smaller arts groups began to grow at the same time public funding mechanisms grew, but that research is unclear as to whether they would survive without public funding (p. 131).

33. Kay, "Arts Policy in a Democratic State," p. 18.

34. Netzer, *The Subsidized Muse*, p. 195.

35. Feld et al., *Patrons Despite Themselves*, p. 217.

36. Ibid., p. 219.

37. Ibid., p. 230.

38. Straight, *Twigs for an Eagle's Nest*, p. 72.

39. David Cwi, ed. *Arts in Transition: Creative Responses: Proceedings of the National Conference* (Washington, DC: U.S. Conference of Mayors, 1982), p. 9.

40. *Funding the Arts in Canada*, p. 9.

41. *Ford Foundation Support for the Arts in the United States*, a working paper from the Ford Foundation, August 1986.

42. *A Nation at Risk*, p. 7.

43. The 67th American Assembly in 1984 also included a recommendation for increased support for arts education: "Appreciation of the arts is by and large developed through the educational system. We cannot hope to establish the centrality of the arts to this society or their value to the individual without a clear recognition of this fact." *The Arts and Public Policy in the United States*, American Assembly, 1984.

44. William H. Honan, "Stringency Is Advised in Training About the Arts," *New York Times*, May 4, 1988, p. 28.

45. Samuel Lipman, "Cultural Policy: Whither America, Whither Government?" *The New Criterion*, November 1984, p. 14.

46. Straight, *Twigs for an Eagle's Nest*, p. 67.

47. Bernard Holland, "An Argument in Favor of Supertitles for Opera," *New York Times*, November 5, 1984.

48. Schwartz, *Media: The Second God*, p. 20.

49. Tom Shales, "Replay It Again Sam," *Washington Post*, October 27, 1978, p. L3.

50. Gitlin, *Inside Prime Time*, p. 334.

51. *Sunday Morning*, CBS television, February 20, 1983.

52. Kenneth Cavander, "Heroes When We Need Them," *American Theatre*, Vol. 1, No. 10, February 1985, p. 15.

53. "Camelot Recaptured," *Washington Post*, November 13, 1983, p. L7.

54. Ellen Goodman, "M*A*S*H: Community Affair," *Washington Post*, March 5, 1983.

55. Tom Shales, "On TV—Hype, Hoopla in the Whole World," *Washington Post*, August 15, 1985, p. B2.

56. Hauser, *The Social History of Art*, p. 960.

57. Although not a technological art form, jazz is also becoming a true representation of American expression throughout the world. On the CBS news program "West 57th," jazz trumpeter Wynton Marsalis said, "It is our music," and he stressed that the legacy of jazz is more important than the individuals. ("West 57th," CBS television, April 6, 1987). The unique freedom of the individual jazz player and the overall sense of the music can also be likened to a combination of Jacksonian and Greek democracy where individuals still have freedom of expression within the overall community spirit of the music. This same concept was expressed in a congressional resolution introduced by Congressman John Conyers, Jr., during the 99th Congress. The bill, H. Con. Res. 396, proclaimed jazz an American national treasure and stated that it "makes evident to the world an outstanding artistic model of individual expression and democratic cooperation within the creative process, thus fulfilling the highest ideals and aspirations of our republic" (*Congressional Record*, September 26, 1986, p. E3282).

58. Bruno Bettelheim, "Schools Treat Kids Like Idiots," *Washington Post*, August 19, 1981.

59. Cavander, "Heroes When We Need Them," p. 13.

60. Franklin Delano Roosevelt, 1939, quoted by Congressman Les AuCoin in remarks before the Third Annual National Assembly of Community Arts Agencies Convention, *Congressional Record*, June 24, 1981, p. E3164.

61. The words of President John F. Kennedy, inscribed on the wall of the John F. Kennedy Center for the Performing Arts in Washington, DC.

Appendices

Appendix A

Arts Advocacy Organizations

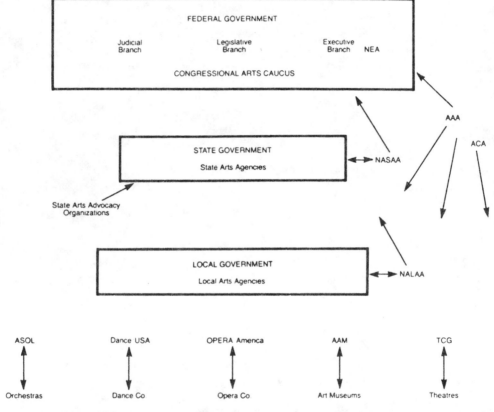

The above chart provides an overview of the American arts advocacy network. The following organizations are involved with federal legislation and appropriations: American Arts Alliance (AAA), American Council for the Arts (ACA), National Assembly of State Arts Agencies (NASAA), National Assembly of Local Arts Agencies (NALAA), Americna Symphony Orchestra League (ASOL), Dance/USA, OPERA America, American Association of Museums (AAM), and Theatre Communications Group (TCG). In addition, citizens in most states have established state arts advocacy organizations to lobby the state legislatures on behalf of the state arts agencies.

State Arts Agencies Legislative Appropriations

TABLE A: FISCAL YEAR 1989 STATE ARTS AGENCY LEGISLATIVE APPROPRIATIONS **UPDATE**

April 1989

	Rank FY89	Spending (¢) FY89	FY88	APPROPRIATIONS ($) FY89	FY88	Percent Change	Line Items
Alabama	48	36.16	32.56	1,476,485	1,319,020	11.9	
Alaska	5	322.94	239.66	1,695,480	1,275,000	32.9	192,780
American Samoa	15	121.62	80.42	45,000	30,000	50.0	
Arizona	40	45.62	40.35	1,545,000	1,323,100	16.7	
Arkansas	43	42.75	42.85	1,021,027	1,016,027	0.4	
California	34	52.79	50.65	14,604,000	13,677,000	6.7	
Colorado	45	39.67	31.86	1,307,561	1,040,647	25.6	
Connecticut	29	65.91	62.63	2,116,547	2,000,000	6.8	
Delaware	14	122.03	108.42	785,900	686,300	14.5	
District of Columbia	2	569.71	567.04	3,544,000	3,544,000	0.0	650,000
Florida	10	173.31	148.27	20,838,063	17,339,509	20.1	12,972,015
Georgia	37	52.20	49.56	3,248,016	3,023,671	7.4	50,000
Guam	9	274.60	267.26	348,748	338,897	2.9	88,660
Hawaii	1	623.00	366.39	6,747,192	3,902,112	72.9	4,619,126
Idaho	50	33.98	19.72	339,200	197,600	71.6	
Illinois	30	64.83	65.63	7,508,679	7,580,975	-0.9	
Indiana	49	35.62	35.78	1,970,305	1,969,472	0.0	
Iowa	52	29.09	25.57	824,659	729,020	13.1	196,590
Kansas	42	43.33	23.71	1,073,023	583,057	84.0	
Kentucky	32	63.53	54.52	2,368,000	2,031,700	16.5	
Louisiana	56	16.30	20.68	727,500	930,581	-21.8	
Maine	36	52.41	43.92	622,114	514,753	20.8	
Maryland	13	131.66	115.60	5,971,010	5,157,002	15.7	2,000,000
Massachusetts	4	333.71	362.50	19,538,727	21,148,270	-7.6	
Michigan	12	135.06	137.99	12,426,006	12,611,306	-1.4	2,554,800
Minnesota	27	74.81	71.93	3,176,596	3,030,438	4.8	992,900
Mississippi	55	18.90	18.61	496,230	421,062	17.8	
Missouri	17	96.28	92.02	4,913,477	4,660,007	5.4	
Montana	22	89.74	89.40	726,062	730,423	-0.5	13,376
Nebraska	33	56.03	38.06	893,177	608,323	46.8	
Nevada	53	26.69	27.96	268,817	270,425	-0.5	
New Hampshire	41	44.02	43.89	465,376	450,848	3.2	
New Jersey	8	296.66	263.61	22,760,000	20,101,000	13.2	1,120,000
New Mexico	39	47.34	47.75	710,200	706,300	0.5	
New York	6	313.95	301.00	55,961,645	53,563,775	4.4	
North Carolina	25	78.05	71.16	5,005,493	4,505,493	11.0	
North Dakota	51	31.77	32.75	213,515	222,416	-4.0	
Northern Marianas	3	407.00	304.56	81,400	60,000	35.6	
Ohio	20	92.95	89.23	10,023,924	9,591,028	4.5	
Oklahoma	24	81.59	50.77	2,669,705	1,678,607	59.0	
Oregon	35	52.54	47.83	1,431,409	1,292,538	10.7	
Pennsylvania	16	106.84	82.22	12,753,000	9,780,000	30.3	
Puerto Rico	7	300.37	247.73	9,834,324	8,110,708	21.2	5,457,797
Rhode Island	11	146.08	109.76	1,440,402	1,070,165	34.5	320,000
South Carolina	21	91.05	82.83	3,118,702	2,800,713	11.3	291,500
South Dakota	38	47.73	46.64	338,411	330,265	2.4	
Tennessee	28	72.22	31.72	3,506,400	1,522,600	130.2	705,000
Texas	54	19.71	20.27	3,309,657	3,382,956	-2.1	
Utah	18	95.39	91.21	1,602,700	1,517,900	5.5	
Vermont	23	83.37	64.73	456,916	350,200	30.4	
Virgin Islands	26	76.89	94.90	84,582	103,919	-18.6	
Virginia	31	63.86	52.05	3,770,625	3,016,781	24.9	
Washington	47	38.69	38.18	1,756,011	1,704,024	3.0	
West Virginia	19	93.98	94.46	1,782,910	1,810,904	-1.5	418,940
Wisconsin	46	39.13	26.67	1,881,400	1,276,000	47.4	250,000
Wyoming	44	42.07	40.12	206,149	203,457	1.3	
		117.9	101.9	268,331,457	242,842,294	10.5	32,893,484

States printed in boldface have had an appropriation change since the October, 1988 survey.
Source: National Assembly of State Arts Agencies.

Appendix C

Regional Arts Organizations

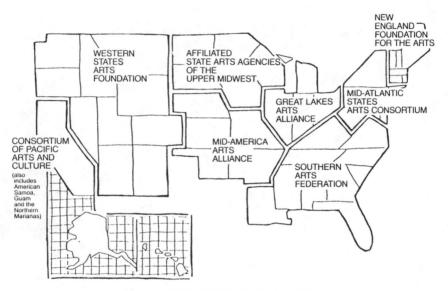

Source: *ACUCAA Bulletin*, September, 1980.

192

Appendix D

Direct/Indirect Government Expenditures for the Arts

Country	Year		Direct Government Expenditure			Total Direct Public Expenditure	Indirect Estimate of Tax Expenditure	Total Public Expenditure
			Nat'l Gov't Expenditure	Reg'l Gov't Expenditure	Local Gov't Expenditure			
Canada (million Canadian $)	1981-82	All Expenditures:	418 (36%)	350 (30%)	389 (34%)	1,157	small	1,157 +
		U.S. Equivalents:	200 (21%)	350* (37%)	389* (41%)	939	small	939 +
Federal Republic of Germany (million marks)	1982	All Expenditures:	114 (2%)	2,011 (41%)	2,752 (56%)	4,877	small	4,877 +
		U.S. Equivalents:	101 (2%)	1,579 (39%)	2,411 (59%)	4,091	small	4,091 +
France (million francs)	1983	All Expenditures:	11,990 (42%)	2,791 (10%)	13,443 (48%)	28,224	very small	28,224 +
		U.S. Equivalents:	3,799 (29%)	637 (11%)	8,761 (60%)	13,197	very small	13,197 +
Great Britain (million pounds)	1983-84	All Expenditures:	256 (33%)	Support for RAAs Included	520 (67%)	776	15 (?)	791
		U.S. Equivalents:	174 (49%)	In other gov't levels	182 (51%)	356	15 (?)	371
Italy (billion lire)	1983-84	All Expenditures:	1,461 (68%)	200 (9%)	500-600 (?) (23%)	2,161	very small	2,161 +
		U.S. Equivalents:	746 (54%)	142 (10%)	500-600** (36%)	1,388	very small	1,388 +
Netherlands (million guilder)	1984	All Expenditures:	1,742 (27%)	309 (5%)	4,332 (68%)	6,384	very small	6,384 +
		U.S. Equivalents:	403 (38%)	74 (7%)	590 (55%)	1,067	very small	1,067 +
Sweden (million kronor)	1983-84	All Expenditures:	2,746 (43%)	431 (7%)	3,190 (50%)	6,367	0	6,367
		U.S. Equivalents:	1,195 (54%)	195 (9%)	841 (38%)	2,231	0	2,231
United States (million dollars)	1983-84	All Expenditures:	266 (38%)	136** (19%)	300 (43%)	702	2,356***	3,058

Notes: (?) Guess
* Not possible to separate U.S. equivalents
** Includes only appropriations to State Arts Agencies.
*** Includes arts and humanities for individual and foundation donations.

Source: J. Mark Davidson Schuster, *Supporting the Arts: An International Comparative Study* (Washington, D.C.: National Endowment for the Arts, 1985). Used with permission.

Per Capita Support for the Arts
(All Government Levels)

Notes on the interpretation of Table 4:

The interpretation of data at this level of aggregation is complicated by the number of assumptions and compromises that are made in arriving at a final figure:

- Public accounting practices differ from country to country, so it is not clear that coverage is the same for all countries. In some cases, for example, social costs for employees such as pensions and health benefits are included, while in other cases they may not be. In Italy, for example, the regional figures apparently do not include any staff costs. Similarly, building rent and maintenance may not be included when they come under another governmental department.

- Generally, capital expenditures have been included though there is no way of being certain that this is true in all cases.

- The use of exchange rates to translate all expenditures into a common currency can hide more than it reveals. Recently, the dollar has been unusually high with respect to all of these currencies, making their expenditures appear artificially low. Ceteris paribus, French expenditures currently appear to be less than half of what they would have been in 1979-80 as a result of changes in the exchange rate alone.

- A calculation based on U.S. Equivalents assumes that they have been adequately identified, but in several cases--municipal expenditures in Italy and provincial and municipal expenditures in Canada--the level of aggregation of the available data made this impossible.

In addition to these technical caveats there are a number of factors that result from the unique situation of the arts:

- Neither national currency figures nor exchange rates can adequately capture real differences between countries in the cost of providing goods and services. It may be that it is simply more expensive to produce opera in one country than in another. This is likely to be particularly true in the labor intensive performing arts.

- It is undoubtedly true that each country has as an element in its arts policy the support of at least one "national" orchestra, one theater, one museum, one ballet, and one opera. At a minimum those costs have to be distributed across the population. For a smaller country, that distribution of costs would lead to a higher per capita expenditure than in a larger country.

- In the final analysis, the differences between countries may reflect differences in the relative importance of the public sector more than differences in the relative importance placed on the arts and culture. Per capita comparisons for other areas of government support would likely show similar differences.

On the other hand, the per capita comparisons in Table 4 are an improvement on previous comparative studies of arts support in four important respects:

- As much as possible, the estimates have been developed through using a common base of comparison, "U.S. Equivalents."

- The analysis has been expanded to incorporate indirect aid to the arts, though, unfortunately, good estimates of tax expenditures are not yet available for countries other than the U.S.

- All levels of government are included in the analysis.

- All primary arts funding agencies have been included: e.g. OAL in addition to the Arts Council of Great Britain, the Department of Communications in addition to the Canada Council, and both ministries in Italy.

Notes on Interpretation of Tables

Country	Year	Per Capita Expenditure on U.S. Equivalents	Notes
Canada	1981-82	$32.00	Estimate is high due to inability to separate U.S. Equivalents from provincial and local data.
Federal Republic of Germany	1982	$27.00	
France	1983	$32.00	
Great Britain	1983-84	$10.00	Includes $.40 tax expenditure.
Italy	1983/1984	$14.00	Based on a guess for local expenditure Estimate is high due to inability to separate U.S. Equivalents from local data.
Netherlands	1984	$29.00	
Sweden	1983-84	$35.00	
United States	1983-84	$13.00	Including estimate of tax expenditure, which is high because available data are based on a broader definition of arts and humanities.
		$ 3.00	Direct government support only.

Sources: Total public expenditure on U.S. equivalents for each country from Table 3. Population data and exchange rates used in the calculations are taken from <u>International Financial Statistics</u>, (Washington, D.C.: International Monetary Fund, January 1985).

Sources: Total public expenditure on U.S. equivalents for each country from Table 3. Population data and exchange rates used in the calculations are taken from *International Financial Statistics*, (Washington, D.C.: International Monetary Fund, January 1985).

Appendix E

Selected Economic Impact Studies

CITY:

Baltimore: "Economic Impacts of Arts and Cultural Institutions: A Model for Assessment and a Case Study in Baltimore," National Endowment for the Arts, November, 1977.

Columbus, Minneapolis/St. Paul, St. Louis, Salt Lake City, San Antonio, Springfield: "Economic Impact of Arts and Cultural Institutions: Case Studies in Columbus,Minneapolis/St. Paul, St. Louis, Salt Lake City, San Antonio, Springfield," National Endowment for the Arts, January, 1981.

Chicago: "A Survey of Arts and Cultural Activities in Chicago," Chicago Council on Fine Arts, 1977.

Duluth: "The Impact of the Fine and Performing Arts on the Duluth-Superior Growth Center Region" by Phillip H. Coffman, Wayne A. Jesswein, Richard W. Lichty, University of Minnesota, November, 1979.

New York City: "The Arts as an Industry: Their Economic Importance to the New York-New Jersey Metropolitan Region," Cultural Assistance Center, Inc. and the Port Authority of New York and New Jersey, February, 1983.

Reno: "A Marketing and Economic Study of Selected Arts Organizations in the Greater Reno-Sparks Area," Bureau of Business and Economic Research, College of Business Administration, University of Nevada, Reno, 1981.

St. Louis: "The Arts in Metropolitan St. Louis" by Betty Crowther and Alfred Kahn, Center for Urban and Environmental Research and Services, Southern Illinois University at Edwardsville, 1981.

Washington, D.C.: "A Cultural Assessment: An Examination of Arts Organizations in the Greater Washington Area," The Community Foundation of Greater Washington, February, 1982.

COUNTY:

Dade County, Florida: "The Economic Impact of Cultural Activity on Dade County," Dade County Council of Arts and Sciences, Miami, Florida, 1981.

Nassau County, New York: "Economic Impact of the Arts on Nassau County," Nassau County Office of Cultural Development, 1983.

Suffolk County: "Art for Art'$ $ake," Suffolk County Office of Cultural Affairs, 1983.

STATE:

Arizona: "The Arts in Arizona: A Study of Economic Impact," Arizona State University, College of Business Administration, Bureau of Business and Economic Research, 1981.

Arkansas: "The Arts are Big Business: An Economic Impact Study of the Arts in Arkansas," Arkansas Arts Council, 1979.

California: "The Economic Impact of the Arts in California: A Policy Perspective" by Leon S. Waskin, February, 1980 (no publisher).

Colorado: "Economic Impact of the Arts in the State of Colorado," Center for Public and Private Sector Cooperation, University of Colorado, 1983.

Louisiana: "Economic Impact of the Arts, Division of the Arts," Department of Cultural, Recreation, and Tourism, State of Louisiana, June, 1980.

Nebraska: "The Economic Impact of Non-Profit Arts Organizations in Nebraska, 1976-1977" by Murray Frost and Garneth Peterson, Center for Applied Urban Research, University of Nebraska at Omaha, August, 1978.

Oklahoma: "1980 Economic Impact Study of the Arts in Oklahoma" by James Pinto, Center for Economic Education, Central State University, Edmond, Oklahoma.

Oregon: "Doallars & Sense of the Arts: Summary of an Economic Study," Oregon Arts Commission, 1979.

South Dakota: "Economic Survey of Non-Profit Arts Organizations in South Dakota" by Mara Lemanis Cunningham, South Dakota Arts Council and the Business Research Bureau of the University of South Dakota, 1981.

REGIONAL:

New England: "The Arts and the New England Economy," New England Foundation for the Arts, 1980.

MISCELLANEOUS:

"A Study of Out-of-Town Visitors to the Tut Exhibit at the Metropolitan Museum of Art," Yankelovich, Skelly & White, Inc., May, 1979.

"The Economic Impact of the Public Visitor to the Seattle Art Museum's Tutankhamun Exhibit," Seattle, 1978.

"Bringing People Back Downtown with a Little Help from the Arts" by Jerry Hagstron, *National Journal*, December 15, 1979.

"The Arts Talk Economics," National Assembly of Community Arts Agencies, December, 1980.

Cornwell Survey Results

— Survey was sent to 103 arts council/arts advocacy org. directors
— 5 were returned by the Post Office
— Total Sample: 98
— Total responses: 73 – 74%
— NOTE: "no answers" account for varying total.

PARTICIPATION IN POLITICS/THE ARTS
Survey

1. In each of the five columns check the <u>one</u> answer that best describes you:

29[] Male   0[] Under 18[] Undergraduate Degree 21[] Arts Degree   16[] Work alone
44[] Female   Age 26 46[] Graduate Degree   3[] Business Degree 12[] Head staff of 1-5
    31[] 26-40 7[] Other _____   4[] Pol. Sci. Degree 5[] Head staff of 6-10
    37[] 41-60   26[] Other   26[] Head staff of more
    4[] Over 60   10 – combination arts & degree than 10
        other degree

2. Check the area that best describes where you live and check your approximate yearly household
income: **(OPTIONAL)**
    41[] urban   1[] less than $15,000
    15[] suburban   9[] $15,001 - $30,000
    13[] town/rural   25[] $30,001 - $50,000
                         34[] $50,000 and over

3. Rate your level of active participation in the following arts activities (1--lowest to 5
   --highest): NOTE: active participation is low — answers clustered around #1.

	1	2	3	4	5
Singing	30	9	11	2	9
Playing Musical Instru.	26	12	5	3	8
(Which one(s)?			)		
Painting, Drawing, etc.	36	10	7	2	4
Pottery, Ceramics	38	4	5	2	0
Sculpture	39	5	2	1	0
Theatre	23	6	9	6	4
Photography, Video Arts	23	7	10	6	3
Ballet/Modern Dance	30	4	8	3	2
Folk/Ethnic Dance	37	1	5	2	2
Opera	41	5	2	1	3
Writing	15	13	12	6	5

"fiber arts" ──→ 1 "current"   1 "formerly"

4. Rate your audience participation level for the following arts events (1--lowest to 5
   --highest): NOTE: Audience participation is generally high.

	1	2	3	4	5
Cultural Programs on TV*	5	11	19	15	17
Movies*	6	10	17	18	14
Jazz Music	14	15	15	18	7
Classical Music	4	7	15	14	29
Opera	20	12	13	7	14
Theatre	3	3	19	22	24
Dance	9	5	19	21	19
Museums	2	3	23	17	38

*Do you own a VCR? 43 Yes 28 No
If yes, what is its primary use? 27 show rental movies   16 time shifting
                                  2 show movies you   of TV programs
                                    have bought   9 other:_____

5. Rate your level of participation in the following activities related to cultural
   organizations (1--lowest to 5--highest):

	1	2	3	4	5
Contributing Money	7	15	15	15	19
Volunteering Time	14	8	10	9	27
Serving on a Board	16	7	8	9	28

(OVER)

197

-2-

6. Rate your level of participation in the following political activities (1--lowest to 5 --highest):

	1	2	3	4	5
Voting in Presidential Elections	5	2	1	1	64
Voting in State/Local or off-Year Elections	3	3	1	6	61
Voting in Primaries	8	0	3	7	53
Contributing Money	7	13	21	11	17
Volunteering Time "0"-1	26	10	15	4	12
Running for Office "0"-2	54	4	1	0	6
"lobbying for the arts"					1

7. Check the most appropriate response regarding your participation as a teenager in family decisions concerning you:

A Lot of Influence _27_
Some Influence _38_
No Influence _2_
Other _____
Comments: _____

8. Check the most appropriate response regarding your participation in school discussions and debate:

	Elementary School	High School	College
Could and Did Participate	44	55	54
Could, But Did Not Participate	8	8	10
Could Not Participate	5	2	1
Other	1	1	0
Comments:			

Additional Comments on Survey: _____

_____

* * * OPTIONAL * * *

NAME _____

TITLE _____

ORGANIZATION _____

ADDRESS _____

_____

[] I would like a copy of the results of this survey.

Thank you for your assistance. Please send completed survey to:

Ms. Terri L. Cornwell
13007 Brookmill Court
Laurel, MD 20708

(A STAMPED, ADDRESSED ENVELOPE IS ENCLOSED.)

Bibliography

Democratic Theory

Almond, Gabriel A., and Verba, Sidney. *The Civic Culture*. Boston: Little, Brown and Company, 1965.

———. *The Civic Culture Revisited*. Newbury, CA: Sage Publications, 1989.

Adler, Norman, and Harrington, Charles. *The Learning of Political Behavior*. Glenview, IL: Scott Foresman & Co., 1970.

Bachrach, Peter. *The Theory of Democratic Elitism: A Critique*. Lanham, MD: University Press of America, 1967.

Baradat, Leon P. *Political Ideologies: Their Origins and Impacts*, 2nd ed. Englewood Cliffs, NJ: Prentice-Hall, Inc., 1984.

Boorstin, Daniel. *Democracy and Its Discontents*. New York: Random House, 1974.

Cnuddle, Charles F., and Neubauer, Deane E. *Empirical Democratic Theory*. Chicago: Markham Publishing Co., 1969.

Cohen, Carl. *Democracy*. Athens, GA: University of Georgia Press, 1971.

Dahl, Robert A. *After the Revolution?* New Haven: Yale University Press, 1978.

———. *Democracy in the U.S.: Promise and Performance*. Chicago: Rand McNally, 1976.

———. *Dilemmas of Pluralist Democracy*. New Haven: Yale University Press, 1982.

———. *A Preface to Democratic Theory*. Chicago: University of Chicago Press, 1966.

———, and Tufte, Edward R. *Size and Democracy*. Stanford, CA: Stanford University Press, 1973.

Danielson, James Leonard. "Democratic Patterns of Political Participation: The Ideal and the Real," Ph.D. dissertation, University of Minnesota, 1971.

Dewey, John. *Democracy and Education*. New York: Macmillan, 1922.

———. *Freedom and Culture*. New York: G. P. Putnam & Sons., 1939.

Downs, Anthony. *An Economic Theory of Democracy*. New York: Harper & Bros., 1957.

Duncan, Graeme, ed. *Democratic Theory and Practice*. New York: Cambridge University Press, 1983.

Easton, D., and Dennis, J. "The Child's Image of Government," *The Learning of Political Behavior*, Norman Adler and Charles Harrington, eds. Glenview, IL: Scott Forseman & Co., 1970.

Kay, W. D. "Arts Policy in a Democratic State," unpublished paper presented at the American Political Science Association Annual Meeting, Washington, DC, 1984.

Lipset, Seymour Martin. *Political Man: The Social Bases of Politics*. Garden City, NY: Doubleday & Co., 1960.

Lucas, J. R. *Democracy and Participation*. Harmondsworth, Middlesex, England: Penguin Books, Ltd., 1976.

Macpherson, C. B. *The Life and Times of Liberal Democracy*. New York: Oxford University Press, 1980.

Mason, Ronald Milton. "Participation and Workplace Democracy," Ph.D. dissertation, The University of Iowa, 1976.

Mill, J. S. *Considerations on Representative Government*. New York: Henry Holt and Company, n.d.

Naisbitt, John. *Megatrends*. New York: Warner Books, 1982.

Pateman, Carole. *Participation and Democratic Theory*. New York: Cambridge University Press, 1979.

Rousseau, Jean-Jacques. *The Social Contract and Discourses*, C.D.H. Cole, trans. New York: Dutton, 1978.

Sartori, G. *Democratic Theory*. Detroit: Wayne State University Press, 1962.

Shumpeter, J. A. *Capitalism, Socialism, and Democracy*. London: G. Allen & Unwin, 1943.

Thompson, Dennis F. *The Democratic Citizen*. London: Cambridge University Press, 1970.

Walker, Jack L. "A Critique of the Elitist Theory of Democracy," *American Political Science Review*, Vol. 60, No. 2, June 1966, pp. 285–295.

Will, George F. "In Defense of Nonvoting," *Newsweek*, October 10, 1983, p. 96.

Sociology and the Arts

Burke, Kenneth. *A Grammar of Motives*. Los Angeles: University of California Press, 1945.

———. *Permanence and Change*. Indianapolis: Bobbs-Merrill, 1935.

———. *A Rhetoric of Motives*. Los Angeles: University of California Press, 1950.

———. *Rhetoric of Religion*. Los Angeles: University of California Press, 1955.

Clignet, Remi. *The Structure of Artistic Revolutions*. Philadelphia: University of Pennsylvania Press, 1985.

Combs, James Everett. "The Dramaturgical Image of Political Man: A Modernist Approach to Political Inquiry," Ph.D. dissertation, University of Missouri—Columbia, 1973.

DeFleur, Melvin L., and Ball-Rokeach, Sandra J. *Theories of Mass Communication*. New York: Longman, 1982.

Dewey, John. *Art as Experience*. New York: G. P. Putnam's Sons, 1934.

Etzioni, Amitai. "Socio-Economics: Humanizing the Dismal Science," *Washington Post*, January 11, 1987, p. C3.

Edmondson, Brad. "Marketing: Who You Are Is What You Buy, "*Washington Post*, October 26, 1987, p. B3.

Faulkner, Robert R. "Orchestra Interaction: Some Features of Communication and Authority in an Artistic Organization," *The Sociological Quarterly*, Spring 1973.

Gans, Herbert. "American Popular Culture and High Culture in a Changing Class Structure," *Art, Ideology, and Politics*, Judith H. Balfe and Margaret Jane Wyszomirski, eds. New York: Praeger, 1985.

Hauser, Arnold. *The Social History of Art*. London: Routledge & Kegan Paul, 1951.

Kamerman, Jack B., and Martorella, Rosanne. *Performers and Performances: The Social Organization of Artistic Work*. New York: Praeger, 1983.

Kirk, John W. "Kenneth Burke's Dramatistic Criticism Applied to the Theatre," *Southern Speech Journal*, Vol. 33, Spring 1968.

Lynes, Russell. *The Lively Audience: A Social History of the Visual and Performing Arts in America 1890–1950*. New York: Harper & Row, 1985.

Parsons, Talcott. *The Social System*. Glencoe, IL: The Free Press, 1951.

———. *The Structure of Social Action*. New York: The Free Press, 1949.

Robinson, John P., ed. *Social Science and the Arts 1984*. Lanham, MD: University Press of America, 1985.

Schlesinger, Arthur M., Jr. *The Cycles of American History*. Boston: Houghton Mifflin Company, 1986.

Democracy and the Arts—Ancient Greece

Aristotle. *The Poetics*, Francis Fergusseon, ed. New York: Hill & Wang, 1961.

———. *The Politics*, T. A. Sinclair, trans. Baltimore, MD: Penguin Books, 1970.

Barker, Ernest. *Greek Political History*. New York: Barnes and Nobel, 1960.

Brockett, Oscar. *History of the Theatre*. New York: Allyn and Bacon, 1968.

Cavander, Kenneth. "Imagining the Greeks," *American Theatre*, September 1984.

Esslin, Martin, ed. *Encyclopedia of World Theatre*. New York: Charles Scribner's Sons, 1977.

Finley, M. I. *Politics in the Ancient World*. New York: Cambridge University Press, 1983.

Forrest, W. G. *The Emergence of Greek Democracy*. New York: McGraw-Hill, 1972.

Grout, Donald Jay. *A History of Western Music*. New York: W. W. Norton, 1960.

Janson, H. W. *History of Art*, 3rd ed. New York: Harry N. Abrams, 1986.

Jacksonian Democracy and the Arts

Blau, Joseph L., ed. *Social Theories of Jacksonian Democracy*. New York: Bobbs-Merrill, 1954.

Chase, Gilbert. *America's Music*. New York: McGraw-Hill, 1966.

Cunliffe, Marcus. *The Literature of the United States*. Baltimore, MD: Penguin Books, 1964.

Curry, Patricia Elaine. "The American Experience Through a Glass Darkly: Three Case Studies in the Political Thought of John Locke and the Novels of James Fenimore Cooper," Ph.D. dissertation, Indiana University, 1973.

de Tocqueville, Alexis. *Democracy In America*. Robert D. Heffner, ed. New York: New American Library, 1956.

Hewitt, Bernard. *Theatre U.S.A., 1668 to 1957*. New York: McGraw-Hill, 1959.

Pessen, Edward. *Jacksonian America*. Homewood, IL: The Dorsey Press, 1969.

Schlesinger, Arthur M., Jr. *The Age of Jackson*. Boston: Little, Brown and Company, 1945.

Tocqueville's America, 1982 Washington Seminar, LTV Corporation.

van Deuson, Glyndon G. "The Jacksonian Era 1828–1848." New York: Harper & Row, 1959.

Wheat, Edward McKinley, "Walt Whitman: A Study in Politics and Literature," Ph.D. dissertation, University of California, 1975.

Whitman, Walt. *Leaves of Grass* (1855), Gay Wilson Allen, ed. New York: New American Library, 1964.

Wilson, Garff B. *Three Hundred Years of American Drama and Theatre*. Englewood Cliffs, NJ: Prentice-Hall, 1973.

Twentieth-Century American Democracy and the Arts

Academic Preparation for College. New York: The College Board, 1983.

The American Jazz Music Audience. Washington, DC: National Jazz Service Organization, 1986.

Americans and the Arts: A Survey of Public Opinion. New York: Louis Harris, 1973, 1975, 1980, 1984.

Amis, Kingsley, "An Arts Policy?" *Policy Review*, Winter, 1980.

———. "Government Shouldn't Fund the Arts," *New York Times*, August 31, 1980.

Anderson, John. "National Unity Party Platform," *Congressional Record*, September 8, 1980.

Annual Survey of Corporate Contributions. New York: The Conference Board, 1986.

Art in the Capitol, prepared by the Architect of the Capitol. Washington, DC: Government Printing Office, 1976.

"Arts and Government: Should They Mix?" *U.S. News and World Report*, March 20, 1980.

Arts and the States. Denver: National Conference of State Legislators, 1981.

"The Arts in Secondary Education," *Bulletin*, National Association of Secondary School Principals, Vol. 73, No. 430, November 1979.

Backas, James. "The Regional Arts Organization Movement," background paper for National Partnership Meeting, National Endowment for the Arts, 1980.

————. "The State Arts Council Movement," background paper for National Partnership Meeting, National Endowment for the Arts, 1980.

Balfe, Judith H., and Wyzomirski, Margaret Jane, ed. *Art, Ideology, and Politics.* New York: Praeger, 1985.

Banfield, Edward C. *The Democratic Muse.* New York: Basic Books, Inc., 1984.

Barzun, Jacques. *The Use and Abuse of Art.* Princeton: Princeton University Press, 1975.

Baumol, William J. "Financial Prospects for the Performing Arts," *Association of College, University, and Community Arts Administrators Bulletin,* March 1980.

————, and Bowen, William G. *Performing Arts: The Economic Dilemma.* New York: The Twentieth Century Fund, 1966.

Berelson, Bernard. "Democratic Theory and Public Opinion," *Public Opinion Quarterly,* Fall 1952.

Berke, Richard L. "Political Action Committees Giving More to Incumbent Democrats," *New York Times,* April 9, 1989.

Berman, Ronald. "Art vs. the Arts," *Commentary,* Vol. 68, November 1979, p. 48.

Bethell, Tom. "The Cultural Tithe," *Harper's,* August 1977.

Beyond Creating: The Place for Art in America's Schools. Santa Monica, CA: The Rand Corporation, 1985.

Boorstin, Daniel J. *The Americans: The Democratic Experience.* New York: Vintage Books, 1974.

————. *Democracy and Its Discontents.* New York: Random House, 1974.

————. *The Genius of American Politics.* Chicago: University of Chicago Press, 1964.

Biddle, Livingston, "The Dream . . . The Reality," *Cultural Post,* Vol. VI, No. 4, November–December 1980.

"Big Business Backing for the Arts at Half-Billion Dollar Mark and Growing," *Christian Science Monitor,* October 30, 1980.

Book Forum: Culture and Money, Vol. VI, No. 1, 1982.

Boren, Susan. "Government Support of the Arts: Should It Be Maintained or Decreased?" Congressional Research Service Issue Brief, November 1981.

Boskin, Michael J., and Feldstein, Martin. "Effects of the Charitable Deduction on Contributions by Low Income and Middle Income Households," *Review of Economic Statistics.* August 1977, pp. 351–354.

Cavander, Kenneth, "Heroes When We Need Them, *American Theatre,* Vol. 1, No. 10, February 1985.

The Charitable Behavior of Americans, A National Survey Conducted by Yankelovich, Skelly, & White, Inc., 1986.

Clotfelter, Charles and Salamon, Lester. *The Federal Government and the Nonprofit Sector: The Impact of the 1981 Tax Act on Individual Charitable Giving.* Washington, DC: The Urban Institute, August 1981.

The Cost of Culture: Patterns and Prospects of Private Arts Patronage, M. J. Wyszomirski and Pat Clubb, eds. New York: American Council Arts, 1989.

Course Offerings and Enrollments in the Arts and the Humanities at the Secondary School Level. Washington, DC: National Center for Educational Statistics, December 1984.

Cwi, David., ed. *The Arts in Transition: Creative Responses*, proceedings of the National Conference, April 23, 1982.

———— and Moore, Susanne. *City Arts Support: Status and Issues.* Baltimore, MD: Cultural Policy Insitute, 1982.

———— and Lyall, Katherine. *Economic Impacts of Arts and Cultural Institutions: A Model for Assessment and Case Study in Baltimore.* Washington, DC: National Endowment for the Arts, November 1977.

————. *How Cities Support the Arts.* Washington, DC: U.S. Conference of Mayors, 1981.

————, ed. *Research in the Arts.* Baltimore, MD: The Walters Art Gallery, 1977.

Daniels, Lee A. "Long Seen as Frill, Arts Education Gains Support," *New York Times,* July 19, 1989.

David, Paul T. "Party Platforms as National Plans," *Public Administration Review,* May–June 1979, pp. 303–315.

DeMille, Agnes. *America Dances.* New York: Macmillan, 1980.

DiMaggio, Paul, Useem, Michael, and Brown, Paula. *Audience Studies of The Performing Arts and Museums: A Critical Review.* Washington, DC: National Endowment for the Arts, November 1978.

"Dividing Up the Federal Arts Pie," *American Artist,* September 1978.

Drummond, Roscoe. "Boosting the Arts," *Christian Science Monitor,* October 1, 1980.

Federal Council on the Arts and Humanities. *Cultural Directory II.* Washington, DC: Smithsonian Institution Press, 1980.

Feld, Alan L., O'Hare, Michael, and Schuster, J. Mark Davidson. *Patrons Despite Themselves: Taxpayers and Arts Policy.* New York: New York University Press, 1983.

The Finances of the Performing Arts. New York: Ford Foundation, 1974.

Fishman, Lois. *Report on Tax Checkoff for the Arts.* Washington, DC: National Assembly of State Arts Agencies, October, 1983.

Five-Year Planning Document, 1986–1990. Washington, DC: National Endowment for the Arts, February 1984.

Ford Foundation Support for the Arts in the U.S., working paper, Ford Foundation, August 1986.

Funding the Arts in Canada to the Year 2000. Government of Canada, June 1986.

Frischner, Linda and Hoffman, Miles, "The Community and the Local Arts Center," *Art, Ideology, and Politics,* Wyszomirski and Balfe, ed. New York: Praeger, 1985.

Furgurson, Ernest B. "Government and the Arts," *Baltimore Sun,* March 18, 1979.

Galbraith, John Kenneth. *The Affluent Society.* New York: 1958.

————. "Guilt by Association," *American Arts,* July/August 1985.

————. *A View from the Stands: Of People, Politics, Military Power, and the Arts.* Boston: Houghton Mifflin, 1986.

Gans, Herbert J. *Popular Culture and High Culture*. New York: Basic Books, 1974.

Garratt, Joan, "The Arts Programs of the WPA," Library of Congress Legislative Reference Service, October 10, 1963.

Giving USA, 1988 Annual Report. New York: American Association of Fund-Raising Counsel, 1989.

Gitlin, Todd. *Inside Prime Time*. New York: Pantheon Books, 1983.

Glueck, Grace. "Gifts to Museums Fall Sharply After Changes in the Tax Code," *New York Times*, May 7, 1989, pp. 1, 17.

Goss, Kristin A. "Value of Objects Donated to Museums Plunged 33 Pct. in 1987; Tax Reform is Blamed," *Chronicle of Philanthropy*, May 2, 1989, pp. 5, 9.

Hammel, William M. ed. *The Popular Arts in America: A Reader*. New York: Harcourt Brace Jovanovitch, 1972.

Henahan, Donald. "Who Supports the Arts Today? And Who Tomorrow?" *New York Times*, November 2, 1980.

Hendon, William S. and Shanahan, James L., ed. *Economics of Cultural Decisions*. Cambridge, MA: Abt Books, 1983.

Honan, William H. "Arts Dollars: Pinched As Never Before," *New York Times*, May 28, 1989, p. H1, 20.

Jeffri, Joan. *The Emerging Arts*. New York: Praeger, 1980.

Joyce, Michael. *Mandate for Leadership*. Heritage Foundation Report on the National Endowment for the Arts and the National Endowment for the Humanities, 1980.

Kay, W. D. "Toward a Theory of Cultural Policy in Non-Market, Ideological Societies," unpublished paper prepared for the Annual Meeting of the American Political Science Association, 1981.

Keller, Anthony, Introduction, "The Arts and Public Policy," *Journal of Arts Management and Law*, Vol. 13, No. 1, Spring 1983.

Keller, Shirley, "The New Volunteer," *American Arts*, July 1981.

"Killing for Art?" *Washington Post*, February 8, 1980.

Kilpatrick, James J. "Artistry in Grants," *Washington Star*, September 6, 1979.

———. Interview on "Agronsky and Company," television program, November 16, 1980.

Kopper, Philip. *Volunteer! O Volunteer! A Salute to the Smithsonian's Unpaid Legions*. Washington, DC: Smithsonian Institution Press, n.d.

Kramer, Hilton. "Reagan Aids Discuss U.S. Role in Helping Arts and Humanities," *New York Times*, November 26, 1980.

Larsen, Gary. *The Reluctant Patron: The United States Government and the Arts 1943–1965*. Philadelphia: University of Pennsylvania Press, 1983.

Lasch, Christopher. *The Culture of Narcissism*. New York: W. W. Norton & Co., 1978.

Levine, Faye. *The Culture Barons*. New York: Thomas Y. Crowell, 1976.

Lowry, W. McNeil. *The Arts and Public Policy in the United States*. Englewood Cliffs, NJ: Prentice-Hall, 1984.

———, ed. *The Performing Arts in American Society*. Englewood Cliffs, NJ: Prentice-Hall, 1978.

McDonald, William. *Federal Relief Administration and the Arts*. Ohio State University Press (Congressional Research Services copy, n.d.).

McLuhan, Marshall. *Understanding Media*. New York: New American Library, 1964.

McWilliams, Wilson Carey. "The Arts and the American Political Tradition," *Art, Ideology, and Politics*, Wyszomirski and Balfe, ed. New York: Praeger, 1985.

Mahlmann, John J. "Politics, the Federal Government and Arts Education," *NASSP Bulletin* 63, November 1979, pp. 72–78.

Mankin, Lawrence David. "The National Government and the Arts: A Policy Pastiche," paper prepared for 1979 Annual Meeting of American Political Science Association.

Marling, Karal Ann. *Wall-to-Wall America: A Cultural History of Post Office Murals in the Great Depression*. Minneapolis: University of Minnesota Press, 1982.

Mayer, Robert. "The Local Arts Council Movement," background paper for National Partnership Meeting, National Endowment for the Arts, 1980.

Mitchell, Arnold. *The Professional Performing Arts: Attendance Patterns, Preferences and Motives*. Madison, WI: Association of College, University, and Community Arts Administrators, 1984.

Morison, Bradley G., and Dalgleish, Julie Gordon. *Waiting in the Wings*. New York: American Council for the Arts, 1987.

Mooney, Michael M. *The Ministry of Culture*. New York: Wyndham Books, 1980.

Morison, Bradley G., and Fliehr, Kay. *In Search of an Audience*. New York: Pitman Publishing Corp., 1968.

Mulcahy, Kevin, and Swaim, C. Richard, ed. *Public Policy and the Arts*. Boulder, CO: Westview Press, 1982.

Music and Music Education: Data and Information. Vienna, VA: Music Educators National Conference, 1984.

Navasky, Victor S. *Naming Names*. New York: Viking Press, 1980.

A Nation at Risk. Washington, DC: National Committee on Excellence in Education, 1983.

Netzer, Dick. *The Subsidized Muse*. New York: Cambridge University Press, 1978.

Newman, Danny. *Subscribe Now!* New York: Theatre Communications Group, 1977.

Newman, Edwin. "Art vs. Arts," *ARTS Review*, Summer 1984, p. 32.

Nielson, Waldemar A. "Needy Arts: Where Have All the Patrons Gone," *New York Times*, October 26, 1980.

Novak, Michael. *The Spirit of Democratic Capitalism*. New York: Simon & Schuster, 1982.

O'Connell, Brian, President, Independent Sector. Testimony before Subcommittee on Intergovernmental Relations, United States Senate, October 20, 1980.

O'Connor, Francis. "Elitism," *American Artist*, August 1978.

———. *Federal Art Patronage 1933 to 1943*. College Park, MD: University of Maryland, 1966.

———. *Federal Support for the Visual Arts: The New Deal and Now*. Greenwich, Conn.: New York Graphic Society, 1969.

"Opinions of Ohio Citizens About Education for the Arts," Ohio Alliance for Arts Education, 1988.

Ornstein, Norman, and Elder, Shirley. *Interest Groups, Lobbying and Policymaking*. Washington, DC: Congressional Quarterly Press, 1978.

Oversight Hearing on Arts Education, Subcommittee on Elementary, Secondary, and Vocational Education, Committee on Education and Labor, U.S. House of Representatives, February 28, 1984.

Pomper, Gerald M. *Elections in America*, 2nd ed. New York: Longman, 1980.

Porter, Kirk H., and Johnson, Donald Bruce, ed. *National Party Platforms 1840–1960*. Urbana, IL: University of Illinois Press, 1961.

Quinn, Thomas, and Hanks, Cheryl, ed. *Coming to Our Senses: The Significance of the Arts for American Education*. New York: McGraw-Hill, 1977.

Radich, Anthony J. *The Politics and Administration of State Arts Agencies: Four Views*. Denver: National Conference of State Legislatures, 1985.

Read, Herbert. *To Hell With Culture*. New York: Schocken Books, 1964.

Reagan, Ronald. "The Candidates Respond," *American Arts*, May 1980.

Reeves, Richard. *American Journey*. New York: Simon and Schuster, 1982.

Refkind, Carole. "Tourism, the Arts, and the City: Design Strategy," *The Arts and Tourism: A Profitable Partnership*. New York: American Council for the Arts, 1981.

Report to the President. Washington, DC: Presidential Task Force on the Arts and Humanities, 1981.

Republican and Democratic Platforms, 1980, 1984, 1988.

Robertson, James Oliver. *American Myth, American Reality*. New York: Hill & Wang, 1980.

Rockefeller Panel Report. *The Performing Arts: Problems and Prospects*. New York: McGraw-Hill, 1965.

Sanson, Marleen. "The Arts and Power: A Study of the Relationship Between Leaders in the Arts and Political Leaders in Connecticut, 1979–1980," M.A. thesis, Goddard College, Vermont, cited by Joseph Wesley Zeigler, "The Advocacy Personality," American Arts, November 1983.

Schwartz, Tony. *Media: The Second God*. Garden City, NY: Anchor Books, 1983.

Schuster, J. Mark Davidson. *Supporting the Arts: An International Comparative Study*. Washington, DC: National Endowment for the Arts, 1985.

Steele, Richard. "Populism vs. Elitism," *Newsweek*, October 31, 1977.

Steiner, George. *Real Presences*. Chicago: University of Chicago Press, 1989.

Straight, Michael. "Government's Contributions to Creative Expression," *New Republic*, November 16, 1974.

———. "Patterns of Funding: The NEA 1965–1985," paper prepared for the American Enterprise Institute Public Policy Week, 1985.

———. "President Reagan and the Arts," *Government and the Arts*, Vol. I, No. 12, November 1981.

———. *Twigs for an Eagle's Nest: Government and the Arts 1965–1978*. New York: Devon Press, 1979.

Survey of the Public's Recollections of 1978 Charitable Donations. New York: The Gallup Organization, Inc., July 1979.

Taussig, Michael K. "Economic Aspects of the Personal Income Tax Treatment of Charitable Contributions," *National Tax Journal*, March 1967, pp. 1–19.

Taylor, Fannie, and Barresi, Anthony L. *The Arts at a New Frontier: The National Endowment for the Arts*. New York: Plenum Press, 1984.

A Trend Study of High School Offerings and Enrollments: 1972–73 and 1981–82. Washington, DC: National Center for Educational Statistics, December 1984.

Toward Civilization. Washington, DC: National Endowment for the Arts, 1988.

Urice, John K. and Hofferbert, Richard. *State Legislative Funding of, and National Endowment for the Arts Grants to, State Arts Agencies: An Assessment of Relative Impact, Interrelationships, and Effects of and upon Other Variables*. Binghamton, NY: Center for Social Analysis, 1982.

Van den Haag, Ernest. "Should the Government Subsidize the Arts?" *Policy Review*, Fall 1980.

Walker, Scott, ed. *Buying Time: An Anthology Celebrating 20 Years of the Literature Program of the National Endowment for the Arts*. Saint Paul, MN: Graywolf Press, 1985.

Warren, Robert Penn. *Democracy and Poetry*. Cambridge, MA: Harvard University Press, 1975.

Weaver, Warren, Jr. "C-Span on the Hill: 10 Years of Gavel to Gavel," *New York Times*, March 28, 1989, p. 10.

Weiss, Ted, U.S. Representative. *Congressional Record*, November 17, 1980, p. H10898.

Wyszomirski, Margaret Jane. "Philanthropy, the Arts, and Public Policy," *Journal of Arts Management and Law*, Vol. 16, No. 4, Winter 1987.

———, and Balfe, Judith H., ed. *Art, Ideology, and Politics*. New York: Praeger, 1985.

Zeigler, Joseph Wesley. "The Advocacy Personality," *American Arts*, November 1983.

———. "Friendly Persuasion: The Arts Arrive on Capitol Hill," *American Arts*, July 1983.

———. "Mending Wall," *American Arts*, September 1983.

———. "Passionate Citizenship," *American Arts*, May 1983.

Index

About the Author

TERRI LYNN CORNWELL is Director of Communications and Development for Cleveland State University's Levin College of Urban Affairs and an adjunct assistant professor in the Department of Urban Studies.

Dr. Cornwell has served as a consultant researching quality of life and economic development for The Cleveland Foundation and Cleveland Tomorrow, the leadership organization of CEOs from the city's major corporations. She was Legislative Director for the Congressional Arts Caucus in Washington, DC, one of the largest caucuses of U.S. Representatives and Senators; taught speech and theater at the University of Maryland; and was a mathematics teacher in Newark, Delaware, where she also directed children's theater.

Dr. Cornwell received her bachelor's degree in mathematics from the University of Delaware, an M.A. in music from West Chester University in Pennsylvania, and an M.A. in theater and Ph.D. in public communication from the University of Maryland.